HOW TO PAY
LITTLE OR NO TAXES
ON YOUR REAL
ESTATE INVESTMENTS

WHAT SMART INVESTORS NEED
TO KNOW — EXPLAINED SIMPLY

BY BRIAN KLINE

HOW TO PAY LITTLE OR NO TAXES ON YOUR REAL ESTATE INVESTMENT
WHAT SMART INVESTORS NEED TO KNOW—EXPLAINED SIMPLY

Copyright © 2007 by Atlantic Publishing Group, Inc.
1405 SW 6th Ave. • Ocala, Florida 34471 • 800-814-1132 • 352-622-1875–Fax
Web site: www.atlantic-pub.com • E-mail: sales@atlantic-pub.com
SAN Number: 268-1250

ISBN-13: 978-1-60138-040-1   ISBN-10: 1-60138-040-2

Library of Congress Cataloging-in-Publication Data

Kline, Brian
How to pay little or no taxes on your real estate investments : what smart investors need to know--explained simply.
      p. cm.
Includes bibliographical references and index.
ISBN-13: 978-1-60138-040-1 (alk. paper)
ISBN-10: 1-60138-040-2 (alk. paper)
1. Real estate investment--Taxation--United States.

HD255.H655 2007
343.7305'46--dc22
                        2007025068

EDITOR: Tracie Kendziora • tkendziora@atlantic-pub.com

Printed in the United States

Printed on Recycled Paper

CONTENTS

PREFACE

This book is intended to be a guide for the accumulation of wealth through a variety of real estate investments that depend on the careful and effective use of existing tax codes to accelerate the growth of wealth and preserve wealth once acquired. The methods described here are not intended to dupe the U.S. government out of taxes fairly owed. Rather, these methods follow well-established Internal Revenue Code.

This book cannot anticipate all the possible investment scenarios available. Each investment is unique and requires prudent review and planning by the investor. Hopefully, the book will provide the investor with insight that improves the review and planning process. Each real estate investor should obtain expert advice addressing specific circumstances whenever needed.

Real estate investing can be one of the surest and most dependable methods of systematically acquiring wealth. Historically, real estate outperforms the stock markets, and there are multiple benefits to ownership. An important benefit is that you, as the owner, are in a much better position to make decisions affecting future value appreciation of the real estate. You are not likely to wake one day to a news headline informing you that a dishonest chief executive of the company whose stock you own has been cooking the books and pocketing money. Rather, you can predictably increase your overall wealth through careful planning and investing.

Flexibility is another advantage of real estate investing. First is the high-level choice of investing in raw land, residential residences, commercial property, or purchasing property to open your own business. Real estate investment is open to the duplex owner who invests sweat equity to improve the property and move into a better place. It is open to the deep-pocket investor who owns multimillion-dollar office space in the heart of a prestigious metropolitan city. They may not have similar business addresses, but in the United States, the same tax laws apply to both. This book levels the playing field by providing valuable uses of the tax law that the wealthy pay large sums to learn from experts.

Just as important, this book includes information on how to develop a plan effectively using the tax code at different points in an investor's career to maximize the effect. As with knowledge of any tool, just having it in the toolbox is not enough. Knowing when to use it and obtaining the intended result is just as important. The early part of an investor's career should focus on acquiring property and gaining a foothold. Later the investor has several choices; maybe maximizing the income derived from the property, or owning multiple properties providing multiple streams of income, or focusing wealth in only a few high value properties. Pursuing one of these strategies without paying capital gain and other taxes should be part of the successful investor's career plan. Once wealth is ensured, it is time to create dependable, tax-minimized income streams to provide a reliable retirement income.

Properly done, a well-planned wealth accumulation strategy delivers amazing results through compounding interest and use of other people's money to invest in the most dependable appreciating asset — real estate.

FOREWORD

Many investors today are making huge profits on real estate investments, traditionally a surer alternative to a volatile stock market and low bond earnings. However, the key in investing in land is not the profit, but what you actually get to keep after taxes. This new book will provide a road map with hundreds of methods and insider tax secrets to help you keep more of what you earn.

Unlike stocks or other investments, owning investment property can be a very time intensive venture. The buyer must make a multitude of decisions, each one of which could lead to financial losses or gains. The day of reckoning for any real estate investor comes when he or she sells a property. What many investors do not know is that decisions made during the sale of a property can drastically affect their return on investment.

To alleviate daily demands of being aware of tax pitfalls, home owners and real estate investors need a good reference for timing their transactions to keep more of their profits. Using this book, you find out in plain English how to minimize your current income taxes and eliminate your future estate taxes while maximizing your returns on investments when buying, owning and selling real property assets. Therefore, not only do you minimize your current tax bill but you will be able to plan aggressively to reduce future estate taxes.

The author has extensive experience and has developed in-depth knowledge of issues concerning real estate taxation, providing the reader with the most financially beneficial solutions to complicated taxation issues. He also includes case studies that provide pointed examples for achieving your goal of making money without incurring undue tax losses.

You will discover how exit strategies can substantially decrease tax liability. These tactics, along with other options, including installment sales and capital gains bypass trusts, can turn a poorly performing property into a profitable sale. As a Real Estate agent in an area where investors are a primary target group of buyers, I am often asked about how to avoid capital gains tax and what type of property qualifies for capital gains tax deferment. After reading this book I feel that I can answer these questions more knowledgably.

Donna Cunningham, Realtor
Prudential Shimmering Sands Realty
148 N Tyndall Pkwy
Panama City, Florida 32404
www.donnasellsflorida.com
850-258-7435

INTRODUCTION

Entrepreneurship is alive and well in America. The dynamic forces of technology, better access to higher education, ease of obtaining credit, and the desire for financial independence enable people to profit handsomely from their entrepreneurial efforts. The real estate industry has grown consistently throughout the history of the United States. The U.S. Department of Labor data shows 484,600 people with careers related to real estate activities in 2004. Forecasts call for another 155,800 to enter real estate careers by 2014, an increase of 32 percent. Many will become rich just by investing and holding property that appreciates. Making a few good real estate transactions is one of the surest ways of joining the millionaire club. However, experts know the key to becoming a multimillionaire is to be familiar with IRS tax codes that encourage accumulation of wealth by deferring, minimizing, and avoiding capital gain taxes.

Capitalism is about acquiring, preserving, and investing wealth. Tax laws are structured to do exactly this, while also including checks and balances to protect against abuse. This book will provide the knowledge that you need to profit from real estate investments and to grow your wealth much faster simply by keeping more profit for yourself.

BUILDING WEALTH — PROFITS ARE ONLY HALF OF IT

Several profit-enhancing techniques are available to anyone owning real estate. The principle is to eliminate or defer paying capital gains taxes and depreciation recapture taxes on the profit of a real estate sale, while leveraging these enhanced profits with additional financing to increase your property holdings dramatically.

Today, the federal long-term capital gains tax is at 15 percent, the lowest rate since the 1940s. Capital gains taxes have gone through many changes that make direct comparison difficult, but the fact is that preferential treatment is now being granted to capital gains. This preferential treatment makes real estate appreciation a dependable, appealing wealth-generating strategy. Capital gains taxes have always been lower than income tax rates.

Long-term capital gains are the increase in value of an investment held for more than one year. Short-term capital gains rates are higher and result when investments are held for less than one year.

When you sell property at a profit and avoid paying capital gains taxes entirely, the strategy becomes irresistible. Essentially, the profit increases 15 percent and increases the funds available for reinvestment. Financing options abound that can be added to the sale proceeds to purchase a much higher valued property. Purchasing new investment property with the sale proceeds plus the 15 percent deferred tax as a down payment and financing 70 percent of the new purchase generates real income.

Another element, known as depreciation recapture tax, can be deferred indefinitely and can add significantly to the money available to purchase replacement investment property. All this money is now in a new property, where you own all the future appreciation that will become your wealth. As you read this book, it will become clear that using other people's money (OPM) is a great engine for generating your wealth.

Not paying capital gains seems quite simple, and something that it appears more people should take advantage of. However, it is not that simple because capital gains are included in the IRS code. This is a deferred tax because the government intends to collect the tax on the fully appreciated value at some point in time. The government is fine if you keep the wealth your entire life. Without proper retirement and estate tax planning, the government will get its share of your accumulated wealth in the end. This book includes IRS-approved strategies to eliminate or minimize these retirement and estate taxes.

EXHIBIT 0 .1 1031 EXCHANGES

TITLE 26 - INTERNAL REVENUE CODE
  Subtitle A - Income Taxes
  CHAPTER 1 - NORMAL TAXES AND SURTAXES
  Subchapter O - Gain or Loss on Disposition of Property
  PART III - COMMON NONTAXABLE EXCHANGES

-HEAD-
  Sec. 1031. Exchange of property held for productive use or
  investment

-STATUTE-
  (a) Nonrecognition of gain or loss from exchanges solely in kind
  (1) In general
  No gain or loss shall be recognized on the exchange of property held for productive use in a trade or business or for investment if such property is exchanged solely for property of like kind which is to be held either for productive use in a trade or business or for investment.
  (2) Exception
  This subsection shall not apply to any exchange of -
    (A) stock in trade or other property held primarily for sale,
    (B) stocks, bonds, or notes,
    (C) other securities or evidences of indebtedness or interest,
    (D) interests in a partnership,
    (E) certificates of trust or beneficial interests, or
    (F) chooses in action.

Exhibit 0.1 is an excerpt taken directly from the U.S. House of Representatives Code for the Internal Revenue Service. 1031 Exchanges are also called Starker Exchanges, Like-kind Exchanges, and Delayed Exchanges. The fact is that capital gains taxes do not have to be paid when §1031 provisions are met.

1031 exchanges are a tax deferment allowing individuals to retain business profits and reinvest them to continue doing business or continue investing. That is the purpose of the language about the property being held for productive use or investment and sounds like capitalism at work.

The use of the term "property" is not specific to real estate property. It refers to all property — personal and real estate. Wealthy people use section 1031 to trade up in aircraft, expensive automobiles, jewelry, oil rights, and anything held for productive use or investment that increases in value over time.

Real estate owned as part of a business, such as a retail store, certainly qualifies for a 1031 exchange, as does investment property like raw land or a rental house. Section 1031 describes what does not qualify, leaving everything else included. Stocks, bonds, and other securities are specifically excluded. The exclusion of stocks and bonds is the reason financial advisers specializing in corporate stocks and bonds are unlikely to bring this tax strategy to your attention or even have a working knowledge of it.

Keep in mind that Exhibit 0.1 is only an excerpt highlighting the intent of this part of the tax code. The full section of the code is several pages, with cross references to other portions of the code. Illegal tax avoidance has been around as long as taxes have. The rest of the code goes into what must be done for the exchange to be a recognized, legal exchange. Normal for tax code, legality brings complexity into the picture. There are timing requirements, disqualified individuals, accounting requirements, and other requirements that must be followed. Working with experts in this field greatly simplifies the process and ensures the requirements are met.

Complexity is another reason that some people choose to pay capital gains tax rather than defer into a new real estate purchase. However, section 1031 is too good a tax deferral opportunity to go unused by savvy businesspeople. Professionals have grouped together their expertise to understand fully the intricacies of section 1031. These professionals will take you through the process for reasonable fees that are much less than the tax savings you will realize.

CREATING AN INCOME STREAM WHILE DEFERRING TAXES

Holding a sales contract from real estate you sell has both income-generating and tax advantages. Since you do not receive all the capital gains at the time of the sale, the taxes are not due until you receive payment. Collecting 7 percent interest on the installment sale includes 7 percent interest on the deferred taxes — going into your bank account. Your money compounds much more when it includes your original investment plus the profit on the sale and deferred taxes.

EXHIBIT 0.2 INSTALLMENT SALE -V- NORMAL SALE		
	Normal Sale	**Installment Sale (Interest Only)**
Sale Amount	$200,000	$200,000
Original Purchase Price	$75,000	$75,000
Capital Gain	$125,000	$125,000
Proceeds at Time of Sale	$200,000	$20,000
Federal and State Taxes @ 25%	$31,250	$3,125
Net to Seller at Closing	$168,750	$16,875
7% Interest over 5 years	$59,063	$69,344
Capital + Interest after 5 years	$227,813	$276,127
Payment of Deferred Taxes	$0	$29,375
Total on Sale	**$227,813**	**$246,752**

Exhibit 0.2 shows the sale of a $200,000 rental property to demonstrate an installment sale. With an original investment of $75,000, the capital gains tax is calculated on the profit of $125,000. In a normal sale, the seller receives the full $200,000 at closing. It includes the entire $125,000 in capital gains. Combined federal (15 percent) and state (10 percent) capital gains tax rates can be around 25 percent. The seller pays $31,250 (25 percent of $125,000) in capital gains taxes for that tax year.

Over the next five years, the normal sale proceeds of $168,750 ($200,000 2 $31,350) are invested at 7 percent and earn $59,063 in interest. When included with the $168,750 principal, the seller now has $227,813 at the end of five years, good for a beginning investment of $75,000.

In the installment sale, a seller accepts a $20,000 down payment and carries a $180,000 loan with interest-only payments. This loan creates a tax deferral advantage. At the time of the sale, only a portion of the $20,000 down payment is subject to capital gains tax (similar to the way $125,000 was only a portion of the $200,000 in the normal sale).

The $20,000 has several components (explained later). Only $12,500 is taxable at the capital gains rate of 25 percent. The installment sale results with only $3,125 of capital gains tax due the year of the sale — a tax deferral of $28,125 ($31,250 – $3,125).

The installment seller invests the net at closing ($16,875) at 7 percent while also earning 7 percent on the $180,000 contract with the buyer. The compounded interest on the $16,875 and $180,000 totals $79,252 in five years. In an interest-only sale, a balloon payment of the $180,000 principal is repaid at the end of five years. Adding up the $79,252 of interest, $16,875 net at closing, and $180,000 due from the loan shows the installment sale total $276,127 in five years. The seller pays the $29,375 in deferred taxes, as they come due, keeping $246,752, which is an improvement over the normal sale of $18,939 ($246,752 – $227,813).

Installment sales provide a stream of income and defer payment of the capital gains taxes. The calculation intentionally excluded recaptured depreciation tax for clarification. It will be discussed later.

IRS ACCEPTED TAX PRACTICES

One frequent problem for beginning investors is coming up with the original investment funds. Few people know that retirement accounts can be a source for real estate investing. Individual Retirement Arrangements (IRA) are commonly established with banks or other financial institutions that have products they wish to sell to the IRA owner. These might include certificates of deposit, stock accounts, or corporate bonds they underwrite. For this reason, most IRAs are invested and managed within traditional financial markets. However, IRAs can be invested in almost anything the owner believes will bring a good return on investment.

This new knowledge opens investment opportunities to those who have qualified retirement accounts and need funds to begin growing wealth through real estate investing. IRAs, Roth IRAs, Individual Retirement Annuity, a Simplified Employee Pension (SEP), 401(k), or a Savings Incentive Match Plan (SIMPLE) can all provide funds for this purpose. Even if you are covered by an employer's retirement plan, you may qualify for an IRA, depending on your Adjusted Gross Income (AGI).

As mentioned, most IRAs are held with financial institutions that limit investing to products they sell. This book will explain how to roll over or transfer an IRA to a self-directed IRA account where you take control and begin investing in real estate, opening a door where you can dramatically outperform conventional financial institutions.

TAXPAYERS RELIEF ACT OF 1997

The Taxpayers Relief Act of 1997 brought substantial changes to the tax codes. Relevant changes to this subject include:

- Increase IRA phase-out range and modify active participant rule.

- Creation of the Roth IRA.

- Exclusion of capital gains on the sale of a principal residence.

- Increase in estate and gift tax exclusions.

- Removal of IRA 10 percent penalty for first-time home buyers.

- Lower tax rates on capital gain.

Although there have been several changes to the IRS tax code since 1997, it was the Taxpayers Relief Act of 1997 that put into motion many of the opportunities revealed in this book. Exhibit 0.3 shows just a few changes in 2006, and more became active in 2007.

EXHIBIT 0.3 EXCERPT FROM IRS PUBLICATION 590 (2006)

Traditional IRA contribution and deduction limit. The contribution limit to your traditional IRA for 2006 will be the smaller of the following amounts:

- $4,000, or
- Your taxable compensation for the year

If you were age 50 or older before 2007, the most that could be contributed to your traditional IRA for 2005 is the smaller of the following amounts:

- $5,000, or
- Your taxable compensation for the year.

Modified AGI limit for traditional IRA contributions increased. For 2006, if you are covered by a retirement plan at work, your deduction for contributions to a traditional IRA is reduced (phased out) if your modified adjusted gross income (AGI) is:

- More than $75,000 but less than $85,000 for a married couple filing a joint return or a qualifying widow(er),
- More than $50,000 but less than $60,000 for a single individual or head of household, or
- Less than $10,000 for a married individual filing a separate return.

The increased IRA phase-out range allows people with larger incomes to contribute to IRAs in 2007. Married couples filing jointly can make full contributions to an IRA if their adjusted gross income is less than $80,000. Adjusted gross incomes falling between $80,000 and $100,000 can make less than full contributions. In 2007, each spouse can contribute up to $4,000 to a traditional IRA, for a combined total of $8,000. Taxpayers over the age of 50 can contribute an additional $1,000 beginning in 2007 as part of the "catch-up" incentive. For individual taxpayers the tax-free contribution phases out between $50,000 and $60,000.

Contributions to a traditional IRA are tax deductible, and earnings grow tax-free. You deduct traditional IRA contributions dollar for dollar from your AGI. Taxes are paid in the year distributions are made to the IRA account owner, usually after retirement when the owner is in a lower tax bracket. A 10 percent penalty is applied, in addition to income tax, if funds are removed before age 59 ½. Distributions from a traditional IRA become mandatory on April 1 of the year following age 70 ½. This book goes into detail about using IRAs for real estate investing.

The Taxpayers Relief Act of 1997 gave taxpayers the Roth IRA. Contributions to a Roth IRA are not tax deductible, but the earnings from a Roth IRA are tax-free. This is a twist compared to other retirement accounts that defer taxes on contributions. In this version you invest with money that has already been taxed, but the entire capital gains tax is eliminated on your earnings. Tax-free compounded earnings make this appealing. The Roth IRA is highly suitable for real estate investing. Another advantage of the Roth IRA is a higher phase-out range than for a traditional IRA. The range is between $150,000 and $160,000 for married couples filing jointly and between $95,000 and $110,000 for individuals.

New in 2006 is the Roth 401(k). It provides the same favorable tax treatment, along with higher contribution limits and no income limitations.

Another real estate tax advantage from the 1997 tax relief act is exclusion of the 10 percent early withdrawal penalty for first-time home buyers. You are a first-time home buyer if you have no vested interest in a main home for two years. Up to $10,000 can be withdrawn from your IRA to pay for buying, building, or rebuilding a home. Covered costs include down payments, reasonable settlement costs, financing, and other closing costs. A spouse must also meet the two-year vested interest rule.

EXHIBIT 04 LONG-TERM CAPITAL GAIN RATES TAX YEAR 2006			
Filing Status	AGI	Income Tax Rate	Long-Term Capital Gain Rate
Married	$15,100–$61,300	15%	5%
	Above $61,300	25%–35%	15%
Single	$7,550–$30,650	15%	5%
	Above $30,650	25%–35%	15%
Head of	$10,750–$41,050	15%	5%
Household	Above $41,050	25%–35%	15%

The maximum tax rate on long-term capital gains was reduced from 28 percent to 20 percent in 1997. It is now at 15 percent. Examples in this book use the 15 percent rate that is typical for many investors. However, investors will fall into the lower 5 percent capital gains tax rate if their adjusted gross income is below $61,300 (in 2006). Long-term capital gains tax is paid on almost anything you own for more than one year and sell for more than you have invested in it. Your vested interest is known as "basis" and discussed in detail later. The tax is paid on the amount of profit gained. Exhibit 0.4 shows the AGI levels triggering either the 5 percent or 15 percent capital gains rates.

Prior to 1997, capital gains on the sale of a principal residence was not taxed if you bought a replacement house of higher value within two years of selling your home. Before the 1997 Taxpayers Relief Act, there was a one-time provision for avoiding capital gains on up to $125,000 profit of a main home. The owner had to be over 55 years old and have lived in the house for at least three of the past five years. Married couples were allowed up to $250,000 in tax-free profit under the same restrictions. This has changed significantly. Today, anyone can retain up to $250,000 in capital gains from the sale of their main house if they meet certain conditions. The house must be owned for at least two of the last five years and have been lived in at least two of the last five years. The allowable capital gains rises to $500,000 for most married people filing a joint return. There is no longer a one-time use limit for this tax exclusion. It can be used repeatedly as long as the requirements are met.

Increases have been made to estate and gift tax exclusion levels. In 1997 the estate tax was on the value of an estate that exceeded $600,000. In 1998 it began incrementally rising and stands at $2,000,000 in 2007. The amount of estate property that passes tax-free to heirs is scheduled to reach $3,500,000 in 2009. Annual gift exemptions have also been increased from $10,000 in 1997 to $12,000 in 2007, after which no additional increases are scheduled. This is significant considering that amounts above the exemption are taxed up to

EXHIBIT 0.5 MAXIMUM ESTATE & GIFT TAX RATES	
Year	Maximum Tax Rate
2003	49%
2004	48%
2005	47%
2006	46%
2007–2009	45%

45 percent in 2007. Furthermore, there is a sunset clause in the tax code that repeals the changes to estate taxes. Without Congressional action, the estate tax exemption will revert to $1,000,000 in 2011. This is a very high tax rate for which taxpayers want strategies to minimize or eliminate. There will be more on this subject later.

PRESERVING WEALTH WITH TRUSTS

A trust has an important role in estate planning. A Charitable Remainder Trust is a valuable tax strategy. In this trust, the beneficiary is a nonprofit charity of your choice. You benefit from a reliable lifetime income stream, and you also receive a charitable deduction at the time the trust is established. Because a charitable remainder trust is exempt from capital gains, no tax is due when the asset is sold or when the remainder is donated to the charity. In the end, a minimum of 10 percent of the original value must be left in the trust to benefit the selected charity.

Many people are not comfortable donating a major asset to charity at the expense of their heirs. There is a remedy to this. The charitable remainder trust can purchase a life insurance policy on the annuitant that is payable to the heirs. Effectively, the life insurance payoff becomes their inheritance.

THE IMPORTANCE OF PLANNING AND TIMING

You can never start too soon or too late. Planning the accumulation of wealth should involve setting attainable goals. The first step is becoming educated about how others have achieved financial independence. This book serves the purpose of educating to maximize profits from real estate investing and tax minimization. It should provide the foundation to either begin your planning phase or improve your plan by including current tax deferral, minimization, and elimination strategies.

A good plan needs to have short-term, intermediate, and long-term goals. You may begin with a goal of owning a duplex within the next two years. Within six or seven years the goal could be to acquire a small apartment building through a 1031 exchange. Long-term you may strive to own several large apartment complexes or a major office building.

People have started by first buying a bargain-priced duplex in need of maintenance and repair. Living in one residence of the duplex, they work to increase the property value. In a couple of short years, they leverage the equity into a small apartment building to begin the next phase of investing toward a wealthy life style.

Certainly, business acumen plays an important role in choosing when to buy property and when to sell property. Improving a fixer-upper in the wrong part of town is not going to achieve your goal. Part of the overall plan needs to be an education in real estate. Real estate experts keep tabs on many aspects of the industry. Business cycles, zoning laws, planned zoning changes, and industry trends are just a few. Gaining knowledge about federal tax strategies is important, but you must also learn the state and local regulations to become an expert in your local or regional real estate market.

By the time you have acquired higher quality real estate holdings, bigger decisions begin to loom. Do you want to own and manage several apartment complexes? Other options to consider include divesting into rental houses and investing in strip malls or office buildings. These are only a few of the options available. Some people choose to invest in raw land for speculation or because little effort is needed to manage the property. In addition to using 1031 exchanges to improve holdings, IRAs or other tax-free funding vehicles should be in place and working for you. These types of decisions and goals belong in the intermediate phase of your plan to grow wealth.

You do not want to become the target of a "deep-pockets" lawsuit. Even if you exercise prudent business practices, opportunistic people may become greedy and target you. There comes a point when good business judgment indicates a need to shelter your assets from a business mistake. In today's litigious society, it does not take much for those with wealth to become the target of lawsuits over minor mistakes or issues. Incorporating your business or creating limited liability companies can reduce your risk and. S corporations, limited liability companies, and limited liability partnerships are explained as methods to protect assets. The Charitable Remainder Trust and IRAs are also tools for protecting assets.

For the long term, retirement and estate planning become considerations. Plans should include moving into properties capable of generating income from installment sales. Gifting wealth to heirs and moving property ownership to trusts become important considerations. This book will introduce you to experts in all these respective areas that will help you plan and execute an effective wealth-building strategy.

Timing is also important when using these tax strategies. IRS regulations must be closely adhered to, or the transactions may not hold up to scrutiny and capital gains taxes would be levied. For instance, a delayed 1031 exchange has a 45-day timing requirement and a 180-day requirement. The delayed exchange is the most common type used. The 45-day rule requires that you formally identify replacement property within 45 days of selling the relinquished property. Escrow on the newly acquired property must close within 180 days of the relinquished property closing escrow. Details of these and other regulations that apply will be discussed.

Installment sales have timing requirements when the deferred capital gains taxes must be paid. There are timing considerations for funding IRAs and other retirement accounts. Gifting for wealth distribution to heirs has annual limits that make it necessary to consider carefully when to begin gifting. Many people wait until later in life when annual limits make it less effective to gift away significant portions of their wealth, leaving it susceptible to the high estate taxes. Finally, the timing to place assets into a Charitable Remainder Trust is critical to the IRS recognition of the trusts.

By now, you should begin seeing the importance of goal setting and planning. Unless you have a rich relative that has carefully planned their estate and soon plans to bestow it upon you, the combination of goal setting, strategy, and planning is your surest path to wealth.

SUMMARY

This introductory chapter touched on the main topics that others have successfully used to become wealthy. You should now understand that the road to wealth involves more than finding the right property, at the right price, at the right time. Doing so takes a bit of luck, and without a doubt plays a role in some people's success. A surer and more common method is using all the tools available. Becoming familiar with the tax codes that allow wealth accumulation is the education needed to set goals and incorporate a strategy into a long-term plan. Exhibit 0.6 illustrates the difference between using these tools and not using them.

You saw the difference an installment sale strategy can make. Exhibit 0.6 illustrates the difference a few 1031 exchanges can make in the accumulation of wealth. Deferring taxes from the first sale makes a substantial difference in the wealth retained. By the time this is compounded through four transactions, the result is a threefold increase in wealth.

Most of these strategies have long been part of the tax codes, but the Taxpayers Relief Act of 1997 made changes that amplify the benefits available. Now, ten years later, those that caught on quickest are reaping benefits. Effective use of 1031 exchanges, installment sales, retirement accounts, and trusts enables you to use deferred tax money to grow wealth much faster and in greater amounts than you can by avoiding the complexities of the tax codes.

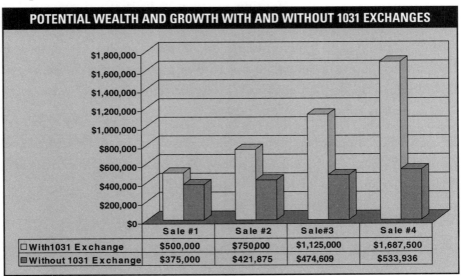

POTENTIAL WEALTH AND GROWTH WITH AND WITHOUT 1031 EXCHANGES

	Sale #1	Sale #2	Sale#3	Sale #4
☐ With 1031 Exchange	$500,000	$750,000	$1,125,000	$1,687,500
■ Without 1031 Exchange	$375,000	$421,875	$474,609	$533,936

1

WHAT TO EXPECT FROM THREE TAX STRATEGIES

Achieve and accelerate wealth building by following IRS recognized tax strategies. These well-established strategies are fully legal and acceptable to the IRS when the tax code is followed. Of course, tax code is not the easiest set of rules to understand and comprehend. The terminology has very specific meanings. Tax forms and instructions cross-reference several different sections of the code, and tax codes change frequently, although the concepts presented here have been around for almost as long as the U.S. tax code has existed.

Most of the changes involve altering tax rates, eligibility, and timing requirements. Other changes occur when taxpayers or the IRS challenge each other's interpretation of the code and its application in court. But the basic tax concepts do not have a history of changing. These are reasons that professionals specialize; tax attorneys, tax accountants, and others in the real estate profession spend a considerable amount of time and effort staying current with the tax changes.

When the time is right to apply these tax strategies, you will be wise to rely on the expertise of professionals. These are the people that the already wealthy rely on to guide them through tax-minimizing transactions. You will learn their roles and which ones to engage for specific transactions. Furthermore, case studies will give you an inside view of the industry, providing details of real circumstances and actual transactions that have benefited others.

Industry professionals, real estate investors, and businesspeople can all gain important knowledge by understanding the roles and concepts presented. Information provided here is the foundation for the strategies that follow.

HOW DEPRECIATION, BASIS, AND CAPITAL GAINS WORK

Depreciation, basis, and capital gains are interconnected in business activities and property ownership. Basis is the value of your monetary investment in the property and is heavily influenced by the purchase price. However, it does not end there. Homeowners are familiar with principal and equity that they hold in their homes — basis is neither of these.

Your basis in the property decreases as you depreciate business and investment property. The IRS recaptures depreciation when you sell it for more than its basis if a 1031 exchange or other strategy is not used. Your basis in the property increases when capital improvements are made. New capital improvements begin to depreciate after they are put into service. Capital gains result from the difference in the selling price and your investment basis. Capital gains are taxed, along with the recaptured depreciation, at the time of sale unless a tax deferral, reduction, or elimination method is used.

DEPRECIATION

Depreciation of property allows the property owner to recover the cost of the income-producing property. The assumption is that the property wears out and loses value as a result of conducting business. Depreciation is accomplished through annual tax deductions spread over a set number of years. Rental property is generally depreciated over 27 ½ years. Nonresidential rental property (commercial or business-use property) is generally depreciated over a 39-year period. Land itself is not depreciable, under the assumption that land does not wear out; the land will always be available for use. Likewise, some costs of land preparation, such as clearing and grading, are classified as part of the land. For IRS purposes, residential rental property includes buildings and structures that derive 80 percent or more of the annual income from dwelling units. Nonresidential real property is generally all other buildings and structures used to conduct business.

Buildings and structures (capital improvements) are considered permanent improvements and are depreciable. Structural components of the building include walls, windows, permanent floor coverings, doors, wiring, plumbing, heating systems, and similar apparatuses. The assumption is that these improvements will wear out and decrease in value over time.

Depreciation has two effects on your ownership of property. While you own the property and collect income from rents, leases, or other business means, the depreciation is useful for lowering profits for income tax purposes. It is not intuitive, but depreciation helps you keep more profit because it is only a paperwork transaction with no real cost associated with it.

Capital improvements are depreciated according to the IRS Modified Accelerated Cost Recovery System (MACRS). IRS Publication 946 provides percentage tables to calculate each year's depreciation.

On the other hand, you will sell the property for more than the purchased cost, and therefore it did not actually lose value. The IRS will want to "recapture depreciation" when you sell the property. This instance is where 1031 exchanges and installment sales work to your tax advantage. For cash flow reasons, you will want to depreciate property and then defer the taxes when the property is sold. The IRS makes depreciation mandatory. Even if you do not claim it on annual tax returns, they will calculate any sale transaction as if you did depreciate the property.

You can depreciate rental and business property and capital improvements that meet these conditions:

- You own the property
- You use the property for business or income-producing activity, such as a rental
- The property has a determinable useful life
- The property is expected to last more than a year
- The property does not meet an exception, such as being placed in use and sold the same year

Ownership of the property is determined by:

- The name on the title
- Obligation to pay for the property
- Responsibility for maintenance and operating expenses
- Duty to pay taxes on the property
- Risk of loss if the property is destroyed, condemned, or diminished in value

The use of the property for a business or income-producing activity is fairly straightforward; it either makes a profit or has a financial business loss during the tax year. The IRS has assigned the determinable life of the property with the 27 ½- and 39-year time periods. It is easy to say that real estate is expected to last more than one year. The final requirement that the property not be placed in business use and sold the same year assumes that the time period is too short for the property to lose value.

There are three basic factors for determining the depreciation of rental property:

1. The basis in the property (discussed shortly)
2. The depreciation recovery period
3. The depreciation method used

EXHIBIT 1.1. NONRESIDENTIAL REAL PROPERTY MID-MONTH CONVENTION STRAIGHT LINE — 39 YEARS											
Month property placed in service											
1	2	3	4	5	6	7	8	9	10	11	12
2.461%	2.247%	2.033%	1.819%	1.605%	1.391%	1.177%	0.963%	0.749%	0.535%	0.321%	0.107%
2.564	2.564	2.564	2.564	2.564	2.564	2.564	2.564	2.564	2.564	2.564	2.564
0.107	0.321	0.535	0.749	0.953	1.177	1.391	1.605	1.819	2.033	2.247	2.461

(Rows: 1, 2–39, 40)

Source: IRS Publication

There are situations in which other special accounting methods (other than MACRS) should be used for depreciation. One is for property placed in service before 1987. This property may benefit from the accelerated cost recovery system (ACRS), which can shield more income from tax. You are probably already using an accelerated depreciation method if your property is eligible, since it only applies to property acquired before 1987. If not, discuss it with a tax advisor.

Depreciation has an important effect on business activities. During profitable years, the real depreciation increases cash flow from the income by shielding it from income tax. A great thing about depreciation is that it has no cost in and of itself. The property does not need to lose actual value from wear and tear for a business owner to take the depreciation expense. In fact, most maintenance and repair costs are tax deductible as expenses. Business income or profits are taxable, and depreciation lowers the amount of income that is taxed. Because no cost is associated with depreciation, it is simply a paper transaction allowing you to keep more of your business profits.

Exhibit 1.1 is the MACRS depreciation table for property used in business (39-year depreciation). Exhibit 1.2 is the MACRS

EXHIBIT 1.2. RESIDENTIAL RENTAL PROPERTY MID-MONTH CONVENTION STRAIGHT LINE — 27.5 YEARS

Year	Month property placed in service											
	1	2	3	4	5	6	7	8	9	10	11	12
1	3.485%	3.182%	2.879%	2.576%	2.273%	1.970%	1.667%	1.364%	1.061%	0.758%	0.455%	0.152%
2–9	3.636	3.636	3.636	3.636	3.636	3.636	3.636	3.636	3.636	3.636	3.636	3.636
10	3.637	3.637	3.637	3.637	3.637	3.637	3.636	3.636	3.636	3.636	3.636	3.636
11	3.636	3.636	3.636	3.636	3.636	3.636	3.637	3.637	3.637	3.637	3.637	3.637
12	3.637	3.637	3.637	3.637	3.637	3.637	3.636	3.636	3.636	3.636	3.636	3.636
13	3.636	3.636	3.636	3.636	3.636	3.636	3.637	3.637	3.637	3.637	3.637	3.637
14	3.637	3.637	3.637	3.637	3.637	3.637	3.636	3.636	3.636	3.836	3.636	3.636
15	3.636	3.636	3.636	3.636	3.636	3.636	3.637	3.637	3.637	3.637	3.637	3.637
16	3.637	3.637	3.637	3.637	3.637	3.637	3.636	3.636	3.636	3.636	3.636	3.636
17	3.636	3.636	3.636	3.636	3.636	3.636	3.637	3.637	3.637	3.637	3.637	3.637
18	3.637	3.637	3.637	3.637	3.637	3.637	3.636	3.636	3.636	3.636	3.636	3.636
19	3.636	3.636	3.636	3.636	3.636	3.636	3.637	3.637	3.637	3.637	3.637	3.637
20	3.637	3.637	3.637	3.637	3.637	3.637	3.636	3.636	3.636	3.636	3.636	3.636
21	3.636	8.688	3.636	3.636	3.636	3.636	3.637	3.637	3.637	3.637	3.637	3.637
22	3.637	3.637	3.637	3.637	3.637	3.637	3.636	3.636	3.636	3.636	3.636	3.636

EXHIBIT 1.2 CONTINUED

Year	Month property placed in service											
	1	2	3	4	5	6	7	8	9	10	11	12
23	3.636	3.636	3.636	3.636	3.636	3.636	3.637	3.637	3.637	3.637	3.637	3.637
24	3.637	3.637	3.637	3.637	3.637	3.637	3.636	3.636	3.636	3.636	3.636	3.636
25	3.636	3.636	3.636	3.636	3.636	3.636	3.637	3.637	3.637	3.637	3.637	3.637
26	3.637	3.637	3.637	3.637	3.637	3.637	3.636	3.636	3.636	3.636	3.636	3.636
27	3.636	3.636	3.636	3.636	3.636	3.636	3.637	3.637	3.637	3.637	3.637	3.637
28	1.97	2.273	2.576	2.879	3.182	3.485	3.636	3.636	3.636	3.636	3.636	3.636
29							0.152	0.455	0.758	1.061	1.364	1.667

Source: IRS Publication 946

table used for rental property (27½-year depreciation). First, determine how many years the property has been in service, following the left side of the chart. Next, determine what month of the year the property was placed in service, across the top of the chart. The IRS assumes the property was placed in service in the middle of the month. Multiplying your basis in the property by the percentage shown determines the annual depreciation. The month the property was placed in service only affects the first year it was placed in service and the last year of depreciation.

An example will clarify how depreciation is calculated and increases income from the property. Mr. Riley bought a tenant-occupied six-unit apartment building in January of 2004 for a total cost of $600,000. The land is valued at $100,000 and not depreciable. This leaves $500,000 depreciable over 27½ years. Calculating his depreciation for tax year 2005, Mr. Riley looks up year two and month one on the residential rental property table (Exhibit 1.2). Using 3.636 percent, he determines that the year's depreciation is $18,180.

Mr. Riley's 2005 Depreciation	
Property Value	$600,000
Land Value	– $100,000
Apartment Building Value	$500,000
Year 2 Depreciation is 3.636% of $500,000 = $18,180	
Rental Income	$50,000
Depreciation	– $18,180
Other Expenses	– $ 2,000
Net Profit (or loss)	$29,820

The rental income for 2005 was $50,000, from which the depreciation and other expenses are subtracted. Mr. Riley will only report $29,820 of the $50,000 as income for 2005. This is a 36.6 percent reduction in reportable income directly attributed to depreciation. The owner is able to keep the $18,180 in cash flow without doing anything except taking the depreciation. For this reason, you will want to maximize the depreciation on the property.

For the purpose of providing a clear example of depreciation, some significant business expenses, such as loan interest, have intentionally been excluded from the example.

The $600,000 value of the entire property is known as unadjusted basis. The $500,000 value of the apartment building is the unadjusted basis for depreciation. The adjusted basis for the entire property is used to calculate capital gain when the property is sold. Several events during ownership can change the adjusted basis before the property is sold.

BASIS

Basis is the amount invested in the building when all appropriate costs are taken into account. Two versions of basis are adjusted and unadjusted. The unadjusted version is used for determining depreciation, while the adjusted version is used when the property is sold for the purpose of recovering depreciation and determining capital gains.

The basis begins with the amount it cost to acquire the property. Each year the property is depreciated, the adjusted basis decreases the amount of value you have remaining in the property. The depreciated portion has been used up in the course of business. However, depreciation is always calculated using the unadjusted basis. The basis is increased by improvements made to the property that increase the property value. The basis is decreased by events such as uninsured damage.

IRS Publication 551 provides instructions for determining the basis of business and rental property. Beginning with the purchase price, include the value of any loans used to acquire the property. Settlement fees are added to the purchase cost to increase the basis. Some of these fees include surveys, legal fees, recording fees, abstract fees, title insurance, and any taxes owed by the previous owner that you paid. Fees associated with purchase loans are deducted as business expenses and are not included in the basis.

In Mr. Riley's case, he made an $180,000 down payment, taking out a $415,000 loan and spending $5,000 in settlement fees to create a $600,000 basis in the property.

Down Payment	$ 180,000
Loan	+ $ 415,000
Settlement Costs	+ $ 5,000
Unadjusted Basis	$ 600,000

From the initial point of ownership, changes can occur that affect the basis, ultimately affecting yearly depreciation and capital gains when the property is sold. Increases in basis occur when capital improvements are made to the property. Exhibit 1.3 shows examples of capital improvements that increase your basis in the property. Accurate records for these improvements must be kept, and each improvement is depreciated according to IRS regulations.

Additions	Heating & Air	Plumbing	Interior	Grounds	Insulation	Misc.
Garage	Central Air	Septic Treatment	Kitchen Modernization	Swimming Pool	Attic	Wiring Upgrade
Bedroom	Furnace	Conservation System	Flooring	Fence	Walls	Security System
Porch	Filtration System	Filtration System	Central Vacuum	Retaining Wall	Pipes	Fiber Optics

EXHIBIT 1.3 CAPITAL IMPROVEMENTS THAT ADJUST BASIS

Some public assessments that you are charged for add to the basis of the property. These might be improvements to utilities or changes to the road in front of the business to improve access. Also, some legal fees, such as those associated with obtaining a reduced property tax assessment, can be capitalized and increase the basis in the property.

Mr. Riley believes that he can increase rent if he installs a swimming pool at the apartment building in time for the 2006 summer. He calculates how this will affect cash flow. The swimming pool will cost $15,000 and depreciate over 27 ½ years. Referring back to Exhibit 1.2, the third-year depreciation on

MR. RILEY'S 2006 PROFIT CALCULATION

Year 3 Building Depreciation is:
3.636% of $500,000 = $18,180

Year 1, Month 4 Swimming Pool is:
2.576% of $15,000 = $386

Rent Increased 10%	$53,333
Building Depreciation	− $18,180
Pool Depreciation	− $ 386
Other Expenses	− $ 2,000
Net Profit (or loss)	$32,767

Profit with Swimming Pool:
25% income tax on $32,767 = $8,192
2006 profit after tax will be $24,575

Profit without Swimming Pool:
25% income tax on $29,820 = $7,455
2006 profit after tax will be = $22,365

Swimming Pool increases 2006 Profit by:
$24,575 − $22,365 = $2,210 or 9.9%

Return on $15,000 Investment
$2,210 / $15,000 = 14.7%

the building remains constant at $18,180. Depreciation on the swimming pool must be calculated separately because 2006 is the first year of the 27 ½ years it can be depreciated. Mr. Riley plans to have the pool ready in May, which means that it will not be available the entire year, which changes the depreciation rate for the first year. Mr. Riley will be able to depreciate the pool $386 in 2006.

If Mr. Riley increases the rent 10 percent in May when the pool is ready, his rent income for 2006 will be $53,333. After subtracting the building depreciation, the pool depreciation, and other expenses, Mr. Riley will have a before-taxes net profit of $32,767. Mr. Riley is in the 25 percent tax bracket and will have to pay an $8,192 tax on this income. His profit remaining after he pays taxes will be $24,575 ($32,767 – $8,192).

If Mr. Riley does not install the swimming pool, his depreciation and profits for 2006 will be the same $29,820 as they were in 2005. The 25 percent income tax on $29,820 will be $7,455, leaving an after-tax profit of $22,365.

Accounting for both the increased rent and depreciation from the swimming pool shows after-tax profit increases by $2,210 ($24,575 – $22,365) or 9.9 percent for the year 2006. The $2,210 increase in profit is a 14.7 percent return on the $15,000 Mr. Riley invested for the swimming pool. The calculations show this will be a wise investment.

The rent increase and depreciation

FULL BENEFITS OF SWIMMING POOL IN 2007

Full Depreciation & Rent Increase in 2007 Year 2 Swimming Pool is:
3.636% of $15,000 = $545

Rent Increased 10%	$55,000
Building Depreciation	– $18,185
Pool Depreciation	– $ 545
Other Expenses	– $ 2,000
Net Profit (or loss)	$34,270

Profit with Swimming Pool:
25% income tax on $34,270 = $8,568
2007 profit after tax will be $25,702

Swimming Pool increases Profit by:

After tax profit w/Pool	$25,702
After tax profit w/o Pool	$22,365
Pool increases Net Profit	$ 3,337 or 15%

Return on $15,000 Investment
$3,337 / $15,000 = 22.2%

are only effective from May through December of 2006, so Mr. Riley next calculates the full benefits he will receive in 2007. At the end of 2007, Mr. Riley will be able to take a full year's depreciation of $545 on the swimming pool. He also collects a full year of increased rents that total $55,000. This is the third year the building has been depreciated at the constant rate of $18,185. Mr. Riley's before tax profit for 2007 will be $34,270. After paying $8,568 in income tax in 2007, the profit will be $25,702 ($34,270 – $8,568), an increase of $3,337, or 15 percent, compared to not adding the swimming pool. The $3,337 is also a 22.2 percent return on his $15,000 investment for 2007.

After calculating the increased profits obtained from depreciation and increased rents, Mr. Riley confidently decides to install the swimming pool. When he eventually sells the apartment building, his unadjusted basis in it will now be $615,000. The adjusted basis will subtract all the depreciation he takes before selling the property.

Decreases to the basis also occur. Casualty or theft loss to improved property can decrease the basis. Granting easements can result in a decreased basis. If, for some reason, the improved property is condemned, it can result in a reduced basis. A reduction in basis usually happens through an involuntary action.

Clearly, depreciation plays a major role in real estate investing. Maximizing depreciation allows you to increase profits by reducing the taxes on income produced from the property. The other important aspect of depreciation is that it is taxable when the property is sold. The IRS refers to this as recaptured depreciation.

RECAPTURED DEPRECIATION AND CAPITAL GAINS TAXES

While depreciation works well to shield income from rental and business properties, it has a negative tax consequence when the time comes to sell the properties. Although it does happen, not many people sell their investment property for less than their adjusted basis in the property. Recall, the adjusted basis is:

Original Investment + Capitalized Improvements – Depreciation = Adjusted Basis

Selling below the adjusted basis is the one situation that does not result in the potential for depreciation to be recovered and taxed at the current 25 percent rate, which is the federal rate and does not include any applicable state tax.

When rental and business property are sold for more than the adjusted basis, a capital gain occurs. The depreciation taken over the years assumed the property was being used up (consumed) in the course of business. The increased value at the time of sale (capital gain) triggers the need to recover depreciation because the value of the property did not decrease. The 25 percent depreciation recapture tax is applied to the smaller of these two amounts:

- Total depreciation allowed on the property (whether the depreciation was taken or not)

- The total gain from the property sale if it is less than the depreciation taken

Once the depreciation is recaptured and taxed at 25 percent, all remaining capital gain is subject to a 15 percent tax (5 percent for those falling into income tax brackets below 25 percent). These tax rules apply to long-term gains held for more than a year.

The example of Mr. Riley's apartment building with the capitalized swimming pool improvement shows the possible tax consequence. Mr. Riley decides to sell the apartment building for $750,000 after ten years. During the ten years, he will have depreciated the basis by $182,528. Disregarding

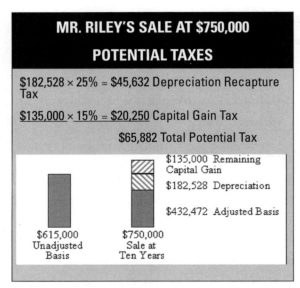

MR. RILEY'S SALE AT $750,000

POTENTIAL TAXES

$182,528 × 25% = $45,632 Depreciation Recapture Tax

$135,000 × 15% = $20,250 Capital Gain Tax

$65,882 Total Potential Tax

$135,000 Remaining Capital Gain

$182,528 Depreciation

$432,472 Adjusted Basis

$615,000 Unadjusted Basis

$750,000 Sale at Ten Years

selling expenses for simplicity, at the time of the sale the adjusted basis is $432,472 ($615,000 − $182,528), and the capital gain is $135,000 ($750,000 − $615,000). Mr. Riley potentially owes $45,632 in depreciation recapture tax and another $20,250 in capital gains tax, totaling $65,882. Mr. Riley's profit just dropped from $135,000 to $69,118 ($135,000 − $65,882). Mr. Riley had intended to reinvest the equity and profit into a larger, higher-quality apartment complex, but after paying the taxes, he is not going to be able to buy the apartment complex he intended.

Recognizing that taxes have this amount of impact may not occur until the sale is completed and the taxes are withheld or even until the taxpayer files the next year's tax return. For rental property, depreciation is exhausted at the conclusion of 27 ½ years. Recapture of all the depreciation could be taxed at 25 percent plus any capital gain. It is entirely possible to sell appreciated property but come away from the sale with less money than you originally paid for the investment. These potential tax consequences are the reasons it is important to have a tax strategy.

It is difficult to argue this tax is unreasonable when recalling that income is shielded from taxes by taking the depreciation deduction while the property is owned. However, the 1031 exchange and other strategies can defer payment of both recaptured depreciation and capital gains tax. Smart investors come away with their investment intact and are able to upgrade to a better property.

HOW 1031 EXCHANGES WORK

The premise of a 1031 exchange is that the taxpayer does not owe taxes as long as the funds remain in a like-kind investment or business. Several versions of the 1031 exchange will be covered later. All versions have one common advantage — complete deferral of capital gains and depreciation recapture taxes. There is no limit to the number of times that property can be exchanged. Through 1031 exchanges, you can continuously step up the quality of your real estate holdings without paying capital gains taxes during your lifetime.

There is no set amount of time that a property must be owned to qualify for a 1031 exchange. However, dealer status becomes an issue when it appears as though the property is inventory for sale rather than held for investment or business purposes. Property held as inventory for sale does not qualify for a 1031 exchange. Take, for example, a property acquired in an exchange and turned over for another property a year later. This property can be characterized as inventory if there is not an adequate underlying reason for the second exchange. A good reason for the short-term exchange would be that the investor transferred unexpectedly to a job in another state and wants to have the investment property near enough for hands-on management and maintenance.

Most real estate professionals are aware of and have participated in exchanges. The profession of Qualified Accommodators developed exclusively to support delayed 1031 exchanges after the Starker court case determined exchanges did not have to occur simultaneously. Today, many more people outside the real estate industry are becoming familiar with 1031 exchanges.

A LITTLE HISTORY

The number 1031 refers to Section 1031 of the U.S. tax code, which controls these transactions. The word "exchange" represents the concept that a taxpayer is not selling the initial investment but rather exchanging it for a like-kind investment. Until the Starker court case was settled in 1979, the exchange of one investment property for another had to occur simultaneously to be tax-free. This required that two parties willing to exchange properties needed to find each other; it rarely happened. In 1984, section 1031 was revised to allow time-delayed exchanges. The delayed exchange enabled a person to first sell a property and then find replacement property. The introduction of the delayed exchange made 1031 exchanges a much more manageable process, resulting in a rapid increase in its use for deferring taxes.

DECLARING TO EXCHANGE

In the delayed 1031 exchange, the businessperson or investor formally declares the intention to exchange. A qualified accommodator plays a critical role at the center of the exchange. This critical role is to ensure that the taxpayer does not gain constructive use of the money or other benefits from the sale. All financial benefits must transfer to the new property if taxes are going to be completely deferred.

The sale agreements for the relinquished property and acquired property need to include clauses that a 1031 exchange will be conducted. The purchaser and the seller do not have to be conducting an exchange themselves. However, they need to agree to cooperate with your exchange.

TIMING REQUIREMENTS

Within 45 days of escrow closing on the sold property, the replacement property must be formally identified. More than one possible replacement property can be identified. There are three methods of identifying replacement property. One is directly identifying any three potential replacement properties without regard to the price of the properties.

Another method is the 200 percent rule. This rule allows identification of an unlimited number of properties as long as the total of all the prices is not more than twice the price of the property sold. This method makes sense if you are exchanging for multiple properties instead of a single replacement property. For instance, you sell an urban office building worth a few million dollars and intend to reinvest the money into several residential houses. The 200 percent rule would allow you to identify a larger number of possible replacement properties. However, the 200 percent rule does not work well if you are exchanging a single property for another single property. In such a situation, the 200 percent limit allows identification of only two properties at best. Most likely, only one property can be identified if the purchase price exceeds what you received for the relinquished property.

The third method is identification of an unlimited number of properties regardless of their fair market value. At least 95 percent of the fair market value of these properties must be acquired (the 95 percent rule).

Once the replacement property is identified (within 45 days), you must close escrow on the replacement property within 180 days of the date escrow closed on the relinquished property. If these timing requirements are violated, the IRS is likely to disqualify the exchange and require the taxes to be paid. Weekends and holidays all count within the 45-day and 180-day rules. If the 180th day falls on a Saturday, make sure the escrow closes no later than the preceding Friday.

Another timing issue to be aware of is that the 1031 exchange must close before the taxpayer's next date to file a tax return with the IRS. Filing extensions are allowed so that the full 180 days can run. Most people file taxes on April 15. For exchanges in which the 180 days run from the middle of October through April 15 of the next year, you need to be particularly aware of this requirement. There is no reason not to begin an exchange during this time, but be sure to file for an extension on your tax return.

FINANCIAL ASPECTS OF THE EXCHANGE

Funds from selling the relinquished property remain in a trust with the qualified intermediary to prevent the taxpayer from having constructive use of the funds. These funds are released to escrow by the qualified accommodator when the replacement property is ready to close. The exchange has been completed, and the taxpayer avoids paying the capital gains and depreciation recapture taxes on the property exchange.

A 1031 exchange has an effect on the depreciable value of the replacement property. The adjusted depreciation carries forward from the relinquished property to the replacement property. The result is that only the depreciation that remained from the relinquished property, plus any additional capital (loans or the owner's money), are available for the depreciation write-off on the replacement property.

Another aspect of the 1031 exchange to be familiar with is "boot." Boot is the term used to describe any taxable money or other benefits in an exchange. As mentioned, there are many variations to an exchange. A person may elect to take part of the capital gain out of the exchange instead of reinvesting it. These funds would be taxable boot. Another example of taxable boot would be if a person received jewelry, cars, boats, or any property not classified as like-kind. The tax would be limited to the value of the not like-kind property.

Fortunately, the definition of like-kind property is generous for real estate. Raw land can be exchanged for office buildings or residential houses. Apartment buildings are exchangeable for strip malls. Active ownership of a busy manufacturing facility can be exchanged for passive, less demanding rental property. As long as the property is a business or investment real estate, it can be exchanged. One exception occurs if real estate is held as inventory rather than as an investment.

1031 EXCHANGES AND THE IRS

IRS Publication 544 — "Sales and Other Dispositions of Assets" — provides a glimpse of the IRS interpretation of distinguishing sales of property versus exchanges of like-kind property. Exhibit 1.4 provides an explanation of the difference. The point is that exchanges are fully recognized by the IRS, which has a code to define how they can legally be conducted.

EXHIBIT 1.4 EXCERPT FROM IRS PUBLICATION 544

Sales and Exchanges

The following discussions describe the kinds of transactions that are treated as sales or exchanges and explain how to figure gain or loss. A sale is a transfer of property for money or a mortgage, note, or other promise to pay money. An exchange is a transfer of property for other property or services.

Nontaxable Exchanges

Certain exchanges of property are not taxable. This means any gain from the exchange is not recognized and any loss cannot be deducted. Your gain or loss will not be recognized until you sell or otherwise dispose of the property you receive.

Like-Kind Exchanges

The exchange of property for the same kind of property is the most common type of nontaxable exchange. To be a like-kind exchange, the property traded and the property received must be both of the following.:

- Qualifying property.

- Like-kind property.

Additional requirements apply to exchanges in which the property received is not received immediately upon the transfer of the property given up. See *Deferred Exchange*, later.

If the like-kind exchange involves the receipt of money or unlike property or the assumption of your liabilities, you may have to recognize gain.

You should now begin seeing that true wealth is acquired through good business practices and opportunistic acquisition of investment property. Using the existing tax laws leaves you with more money to buy a better property — a property that generates more income or appreciates more quickly. This method is available to the beginning investor as well as the seasoned professional.

CASE STUDY —1031 TAX DEFERRAL
FROM EQUITY TRUST COMPANY

Equity Trust Company

P.O. Box 1319

Elyria, OH 44036

Web Address: **www.trustetc.com**

Telephone: 888-ETC-IRAS

E-mail: help@trustetc.com

With more than 33 years' experience and management of $2 billion in IRA assets, Equity Trust Company is a leading custodial provider of self-directed IRAs and small business retirement plans, allowing clients to increase financial wealth by investing in a variety of opportunities, from real estate and private placements to stocks and bonds.

Clients benefit from Equity Trust's extensive expertise and exceptional service, including: a personalized account management team for every client, including their own 800 number; fast and accurate processing (99.2 percent of transactions reviewed in 24 hours); and access to accounts and online bill-pay with the industry's first online account management tool, eVANTAGE.

The staff at Equity Trust Company is comprised of professionals who have considerable knowledge and experience in administering IRAs and other retirement plans and are proud of their reputation as a truly client-oriented company.

Equity Trust Company and its affiliated companies remain committed to the same core values that have helped their clients for more than 33 years. These core values consist of:

- Enabling clients to choose self-directed investments in areas where they believe they have sufficient knowledge and expertise.

- Providing education that will allow clients to better prepare for their future.

- Providing outstanding client service at a reasonable price.

Using Self-Directed IRAs Creatively

Self-directed IRAs are a powerful investment tool offering great flexibility applicable

CASE STUDY —1031 TAX DEFERRAL FROM EQUITY TRUST COMPANY

to creative investing. This capsulated story is from an Equity Trust client who found a way to profit from a bad situation by turning it into a win-win solution for all involved.

Investor's Equity Trust Self-Directed IRA Profits While Benefiting Homeowner

Leon Humphrey, an Equity Trust Company client from Gastonia, North Carolina, helped a neighbor avoid foreclosure while benefiting his self-directed IRA.

A homeowner in Humphrey's area recently closed bankruptcy and the house he owned, valued at $160,000, was headed to foreclosure due to outstanding mortgages equaling $210,000. Humphrey learned of the situation, and he saw it as an opportunity. He used his investment knowledge to help the homeowner avoid foreclosure while creating profit for his self-directed IRA. The house had three mortgages: the first for $125,000, the second for $30,000, and a third for $50,000.

Humphrey secured authorization to negotiate on the homeowner's behalf and listed the home for sale at $160,000. He then negotiated with the lenders of the second and third mortgages and purchased the second (originally $30,000) for $8,000, and the third (originally $50,000) for $3,000. Humphrey paid the mortgages from his self-directed IRA.

The house ended up selling for $160,000. After payment of the fees and the first mortgage of $125,000, Humphrey received a check for $17,440.22, which was payable to his self-directed IRA. He not only saved the owner from foreclosure, but turned a profit of more than $6,000. And all of it is tax-free. Humphrey's investment illustrates how being aware of all types of opportunities can profit an investor's self-directed IRA.

INSTALLMENT SALES FOR TAX DEFERRAL

Real estate investors and business property owners can defer payment of capital gains taxes and depreciation recapture taxes by making installment sales. This is not the indefinite deferral of taxes in the same way as a 1031 exchange. Taxes do have to be paid in the tax year that installment payments are received. This includes paying taxes on any down payment received at the time of the sale.

✓ The IRS defines installment sales in Publication 527 as: "A sale of property where you receive at least one payment after the tax year of the sale."

In many instances, an installment sale is not appropriate for beginning investors who need the liquidity of funds that an outright sale or 1031 exchange produces. When all the funds are received at the time of sale, they can quickly be reinvested into a better-quality property.

Circumstances appropriate for an installment sale can include:

- When an income stream is desirable for retirement or other income

- When property is not income producing, such as raw land, and other income-producing opportunities are not appealing

- When the interest rate earned exceeds other investment opportunities

- When an exit strategy when paying deferred taxes with inflated dollars is the best alternative

Most people are familiar with installment sales. Negotiation of the contract is between the seller and buyer as part of the sale agreement, which provides considerable leeway in the terms and conditions included in the contract. The high value of a real estate transaction makes it important for an attorney to review the contract before finalizing the sales agreement.

An installment seller needs certain tax concerns addressed in the contract terms:

- Adequate down payment for security, but low enough to minimize taxes due

- Enough down payment that net funds to the seller are enough to pay taxes due

- A clause protecting against paying the loan off early that would trigger taxes

- A clause allowing a qualified buyer to assume the mortgage; if the original buyer sells the property, you want an opportunity to avoid the entire loan being paid in full

Naturally, there are many other considerations that need to be included in the installment sales contract. Others include insurance protection, due on sale or transfer, and minimum maintenance standards. Consider consulting an attorney when drafting an installment sale contract.

CALCULATING THE PERCENTAGE FOR INSTALLMENT SALE COMPONENTS

Installment sales defer taxes. Each year installment payments are made, the taxes become reportable on your income tax return.

COMPONENTS OF INSTALLMENT PAYMENTS	
Loan Interest	Reported as Income
+ Principal	20% is Capital Gain*, 80% is Returned Basis*
Total Payment	
*percentages vary depending specifics of the installment sale	

Taxes on installment sales are divided into:

- Interest income

- Return of your adjusted basis on the property

- Gain on the sale

The down payment and installment payments contain each of these components as a percentage specific to your sale. In a simple transaction the original purchase price, five years ago, of a strip mall might have been $500,000. Today it is sold for $625,000 on an installment contract. The sales price minus the original purchase cost is the gross profit of $125,000. Dividing $125,000 by $625,000 gives you 20 percent, which is the portion of each dollar in principal payment that represents capital gain on the sale. The remaining 80 percent is your returned basis in the property. The returned basis is not taxed.

The strip mall sale for $625,000 on installment has a 15 percent down payment and is amortized over 30 years. The down payment is $93,750, creating a loan of $531,250 at 6 percent interest. The first year's monthly payments add up to $31,698

YEAR 1 INSTALLMENT PAYMENTS	
(excludes down payment)	
$ 31,698	Reported as Income
$ 1,305	20% of Principal taxed as gain
$ 5,219	80% of Principal is untaxed basis
$ 38,222	Total Installment Payments

in interest and $6,524 in principal. The entire $31,698 will be reported as interest income. The $6,524 in principal is separated into 20 percent capital gain, and the remaining 80 percent is your returned basis. No tax is owed on the returned basis because this is your original investment. Twenty percent of $6,524 equals $1,305. The 15 percent capital gains tax equals $196. Most of the capital gains tax remains deferred to future years when installment payments are made.

THE DOWN PAYMENT

The down payment at the time of sale follows much the same formula as the yearly installment payments, except there is no interest in the down payment and all the recaptured depreciation is taxed. We will use a different example that includes selling expenses of $33,000. Selling expenses include real estate commissions and other closing costs.

GROSS PROFIT	
$ 475,000	Selling Price
- $ 400,000	Original Cost
- $ 33,000	Sales Expenses
$ 42,000	Gross Profit

An office building originally costing $400,000 is sold for $475,000 after being owned for five years and writing off $72,720 in depreciation. The gross profit is the selling price of $475,000, less $400,000 original cost, less $33,000 expenses. Recall that gross profit divided by selling price determines the percentage of each payment that is capital gain. In this case, $42,000 divided by $475,000 equals 8.84 percent. Because there is no interest in a down payment, this is the percentage of the down payment that is taxable capital gain.

NET TO SELLER	
$ 75,000	Down Payment
–$ 33,000	Selling Expenses
–$ 18,930	Recaptured Depreciation Tax
–$ 995	Capital Gain Tax
$ 22,075	Net to Seller at Closing

The numbers necessary to estimate taxes owed at closing are:

- Down payment of $75,000

- $72,720 recaptured depreciation that is fully taxable at 25 percent. Recaptured depreciation tax owed is $18, 930

- 8.84 percent of down payment is capital gain, meaning $75,000 × 8.84 percent = $6,630 taxable. Taxed at 15 percent equals $995

- Costs of sale totaling $33,000

After paying selling expenses and taxes, the seller walks away from the closing with $22,075 remaining from the $75,000 down payment. The seller also has an income stream for the future.

A few changes in these numbers and the seller could owe taxes from the sale that exceed the down payment. The $75,000 down payment is 15.8 percent of the $475,000 selling price. This is not an unreasonable percentage for an installment sale intended to defer taxes. The example uses a short holding period of only five years. In a longer holding period, both the recaptured depreciation and capital gain tax could be higher. Without interest in a down payment, the capital gain and your basis are the only components. This leaves a larger amount of the down payment as capital gain. For these reasons, it is important to estimate taxes to ensure the down payment will cover the taxes due for an installment sale.

Other factors affect installment sales. Mortgages the buyer assumes on behalf of the seller are included as capital gain because the seller is no longer obligated to make the payments. Any type of indebtedness transferred from seller to buyer also applies. Installment sales are effective at deferring taxes. Like any transaction, it is best to perform calculations estimating what taxes will be due and when they will be due.

THE SELF-DIRECTED IRA

The introduction discussed the ability to invest Individual Retirement Arrangement (often known as individual retirement accounts) funds into real estate and other investments not usually available from banks and other financial institutions. IRAs are accounts for making investments that later provide income, usually after age 59 ½. No IRS code says what type of investment you must make.

Investment opportunities include:

- Residential real estate producing rental income

- Commercial real estate with rental or lease income

- Undeveloped land for appreciation

- Mortgages

- Deeds of Trust

- Limited liability companies

- Limited partnerships

The tax code explains what cannot be an IRA investment. This is in line with the IRS practice of defining what cannot be done tax-wise rather than explaining what can be done. This practice leaves many more creative options available to investors.

Specifically excluded from IRA investment are:

- Collectibles (gems, antiques, rare wines, most coins, etc.)
- Life insurance contracts

The IRS does regulate where an IRA can be held. Publication 590 lists:

- Banks
- Federally insured financial institutions
- Savings and loan associations
- Mutual fund company
- Life insurance company
- An entity approved by the IRS as a custodian or trustee

Self-directed IRAs generally are administered by IRS-approved custodians or trustees, who are passive administrators of your IRA account. This means they do not provide investment advice. The role of the custodian is to hold your investments, conduct transactions as instructed by you, and provide tax-reporting documentation. They do not sell mutual funds or other investment products. This eliminates the conflict of interest that can exist with IRAs held at more traditional financial institutions. The traditional financial institutions prefer selling their products rather than conducting transactions in other investments like real estate.

Opening an IRA with a passive custodian fully empowers you to manage your assets in the manner you think best. With that comes the full responsibility of understanding the risks involved with your chosen investments. Independent financial advisors, tax accountants, and specialized attorneys can help you manage this responsibility.

UBIT

The unrelated business taxable income (UBIT) is explained in section 512 of the internal revenue code and IRS Publication 598. Some IRA investments may have to pay UBIT taxes; investments in limited liability companies and limited partnerships are most likely to fall into this category. The first $1,000 of UBIT earned by the IRA is excluded from taxes. Amounts above $1,000 are generally taxable. Other sources of UBIT could be if the IRA operates a sales, service, or manufacturing company. The income from these businesses is unrelated to the non-taxable status of the IRA. After the business pays tax, the profits paid into the IRA are tax-free or deferred. This regulation also applies to nonprofit organizations. The intent is to avoid tax-free status for business activities that would normally be taxable.

Usually, rents for real estate property are not UBIT.

Unrelated debt financing income is a form of UBIT that results when an IRA borrows money to generate income from investments. The taxable income for unrelated debt financing is equal to the percentage of debt as a part of the total cost for the income-producing property. In other words, if your IRA purchases a $200,000 property with a $100,000 down payment and obtains financing for the other $100,000, the unrelated debt financing income is 50 percent ($100,000 debt 4 $200,000 cost). As the loan is paid off, the percentage of UBIT becomes lower. The average debt each year is used to determine taxable income.

Just because taxes must be paid on unrelated income business income is not necessarily a reason to avoid the investment. The amount paid compared to the return provided might make it a good investment. Each situation must be analyzed on its own merits.

PROHIBITED TRANSACTIONS

The self-directed IRA provides considerable flexibility in conducting tax deferred and tax-free transactions with the possibility of increasing wealth quickly and in significant amounts. With flexibility comes the responsibility to work within the tax codes. There are prohibited transactions that you must avoid; a prohibited transaction is any improper use of an IRA by you, a beneficiary of the IRA, or any disqualified person. Engaging in these prohibited transactions will result in the voiding of the IRA. If voided, the IRA is considered to have been distributed as of the first day of the year the prohibited transaction occurred and loses its tax-free or tax deferral status. Taxes will become due and a 10 percent penalty is likely to be applied, if you are under age 59 ½. Other tax penalties may also apply.

Disqualified people include your fiduciary (fund administrators and fund advisors) and members of your family. Family members are your spouse, your parents, grandparents, children, and children's spouses.

Prohibited transactions include:

- Borrowing money from your IRA
- Selling property to your IRA
- Receiving unreasonable compensation for managing it
- Using the IRA as security for a loan
- Buying property for personal use (present or future) with IRA funds

Several issues are raised when an IRA and the IRA owner invest in the same business. It is a prohibited transaction if the IRA, IRA owner, and family members own 50 percent or more of a business. Ownership below 50 percent is a gray area without adequate guidance from the IRS. Keep in mind that the term "family members" does not include the IRA owner's brothers and sisters. Siblings are not disqualified from conducting transactions with the IRA.

These rules are not specific to self-directed IRAs; they apply to all IRAs. Taking full charge of your IRA and investing in real estate can greatly increase the growth rate. It simply becomes more important to know the rules so your investment continues growing tax-free or tax deferred.

SUMMARY

This chapter was an overview of information needed to build a foundation that will be helpful to you as different variations of these and other tax strategies are explained in detail. The first part of the chapter explained the importance depreciation plays in shielding income from taxes on your investment properties. The depreciation is then recaptured when the property is sold. Or you can continue to defer the recapture through a 1031 exchange. Depreciation, capital expenses, and the original purchase price are used to calculate your basis in the property. Your basis in the property is important for determining the capital gain realized when the property is sold. These concepts will be referred to in other examples and exhibits. These terms occur frequently in real estate and tax discussions.

Three tax deferral strategies that are fully recognized by the IRS also were explained with examples of when they are best used. The case studies of these strategies help you understand how other people have successfully used them to increase wealth by investing deferred tax money. The 1031 exchange is a powerful tool that can fully defer taxes indefinitely and provide a way to consistently step up to higher quality properties. The installment sale has a definite usefulness, and using the collateralized installment sale defers taxes for longer lengths of time, if not indefinitely. Finally, we learned how the self-directed IRA has two valuable functions: The first is being a source of funds to make your investments, and the second is the IRA's ability to hold title of your properties to avoid paying taxes as you buy and sell to step up in value. Knowledge of the intricacies and the ability to apply these tools effectively will move you further down the road of wealth.

2

ELIMINATING OR REDUCING TAXES

While there are ways to completely eliminate capital gains taxes, doing so is not always in the best interest of the investor or businessperson. There are four general tax strategies: paying the tax, reducing it, deferring it, and eliminating it. You can choose any of these options but need to consider closely your current and future investment objectives.

The internal revenue code allows you to grow wealth, but is effectively structured to prevent cashing out of wealth-generating assets without paying taxes. You can grow wealth in an IRA or a business while deferring the taxes. It is not inevitable that you will have to pay income tax on traditional IRAs and capital gains tax on the sale of a business or investment property. There are methods for further deferring taxes when business or investment property is sold and even ways of fully eliminating taxes.

✓ Charitable Remainder Trusts eliminate capital gain and estate taxes altogether, but no less than 10 percent of the asset value will go to a charitable foundation.

Do not underestimate the power of a Roth IRA to create tax-free wealth. ✓ While income tax must be paid on the funds contributed to a Roth IRA, the gains and appreciation are not taxed.

REDUCING TAXES

IRAs, installment sales inside 1031 exchanges, and partial 1031 exchanges are methods of reducing taxes at the time real estate is sold.

TRADITIONAL IRAS

The first tax benefit you will receive is making a contribution to an IRA. When you and your spouse make the full $8,000 contribution (or any lesser amount depending on your income circumstances), no income tax is paid on that portion of your annual income. In some situations, your adjusted gross income may drop to an amount that puts you into a lower tax bracket. Tuck these tax savings away, and watch how compounding interest contributes to growing your wealth.

Let us consider the effect of compounded interest. When you and your spouse begin contributing to a traditional IRA early in life, the compounded interest effect is dramatic. The contribution level increases to $5,000 per individual in 2008, raising a married couple's possible contribution to $10,000. After 2008, IRA contribution increases are indexed to inflation, which makes it difficult to calculate increases beyond that. If you begin making full $8,000 contributions in 2007, step up the amount to $10,000 in 2008, and continue contributing that amount each year, the effect of compounded interest and tax savings will be substantial.

Using the 25 percent tax bracket, the income tax savings for 2007 is $2,000. Also, consider that your adjusted gross income could move you into a lower income tax bracket if your adjusted income is less than $69,300.

TRADITIONAL IRA 30 YEAR TAX SAVINGS			
	IRA Contribution	Tax Bracket	Annual Tax Savings
2007	$8,000	25%	$2,000
2008 and Beyond	$10,000	25%	$2,500
30 Year Totals	$298,000	25%	$74,500

Increasing the annual contribution to $10,000 gives you an annual tax savings of $2,500. The effect over 30 years is a total tax savings of $74,500.

Simply compounding the interest in your traditional IRA at a modest rate of 6 percent over 30 years produces a before-tax total of $883,965. Assuming your tax rate after retirement is 15 percent, you can expect to pay $132,595 in taxes. The tax rate reduction from 25 percent to 15 percent results in $88,397 saved in taxes. Including the

IRA COMPOUNDED AT 6%	
2007 Contribution	$8,000
Annual Contribution	$10,000
Years of Compounding	30 years
Interest Rate	6%
Total Interest Earnings:	$575,965
Total Projected Value:	$883,965

$74,500 unpaid income tax over the 30 years, the full tax savings from the IRA comes to $162,897.

If you contributed the same amount to a self-directed IRA that you manage and invest in real estate, the value has the potential to grow much larger. There are several variables that affect the final value. Key to the calculation is the amount the real estate appreciates each year, which is not likely to be constant. Nor is the rate constant in different regions of the country or even parts of the same city. Exhibit 2.1 shows the average increases in real estate value by national region, with the overall national average listed last. These values represent residential homes sold between 1980 and mid-2006. The aggregate increase in real estate sales prices across the country for the past 27 years was 298.85 percent. The annual average increase is slightly more than 11 percent. Keep in mind this is only residential homes; it does not include apartment buildings or commercial properties. Another major variable involved is unrelated business taxable income (UBIT), which will be applicable if your IRA makes a down payment on a real estate holding and borrows the balance of the purchase price.

EXHIBIT 2.1 PERCENT CHANGE IN CENSUS DIVISION HOUSE PRICES THROUGH Q2 2006					
Division	Rank*	1-Yr.	1-Qtr.	5-Yr.	Since 1980
Pacific	1	14.08	1.45	94.08	484.64
Mountain	2	14.06	1.71	55.52	268.58
South Atlantic	3	13.74	1.41	69.03	313.90
Middle Atlantic	4	11.02	1.40	70.45	427.84
West South Central	5	7.95	1.93	27.31	117.58
East South Central	6	7.77	1.84	27.80	177.89
New England	7	5.68	0.17	61.97	528.85
West North Central	8	4.72	0.57	34.73	199.13
East North Central	9	4.00	0.21	27.03	217.21
United States**	0	10.06	1.17	56.49	298.85

*Note: Rankings based on annual percentage change.

**Note: United states figures based on weighted division average.

Source of federal Housing Enterprise Oversight

Assume, for this example, that the IRA compounds at 6 percent for 11 years, when it reaches a value of $194,919. In year 12, the IRA purchases a modest duplex for $190,000, without a loan (avoiding UBIT). The remaining $4,919 ($194,919 − $190,000) continues compounding at 6 percent, and you continue making full contributions of $10,000. The annual net rental income from the duplex is $9,600, which compounds annually at 6 percent in the IRA. The property

DUPLEX PURCHASED BY AN IRA	Value in 5 Years	Value in 19 Years
Duplex Appreciates 11%	$320,161	$1,380,035
Annual Rental Income of $9,600 compounding @ 6%	$70,210	$372,587
Compounding IRA @6%	$66,336	$372,739
Total Value	**$456,707**	**$2,125,361**

has no mortgage, so expenses are minimal. They are likely to include property taxes and some maintenance. The rent is paid directly to the IRA, and taxes are deferred. The entire property appreciates at 11 percent per year. In five years there is $456,707 in the IRA.

Without doing anything different, the IRA has accumulated $2,125,361 in another 19 years, which is the end of the 30-year investment period the example started with. Recall that the IRA compounding at 6 percent over the same 30 years only grew to $883,965 — a difference of more than $1.2 million and a 140 percent increase for the IRA.

After owning the duplex for five years, the IRA has a value of $456,707, enough to sell the duplex and step up to a higher-quality property providing more rental income. In year 16 (11 + 5) the duplex is sold and a six-unit building is purchased for $400,000.

The balance in the IRA of $56,707 continues to compound at 6 percent,

SIX UNIT APARTMENT PURCHASED BY AN IRA	
	Value in 14 Years
Real Estate Appreciates 11%	$1,724,176
Annual Rental Income of $28,000 Compounded @6%	$687,032
Compounding IRA @6%	$350,969
Total Value	$ 2,762,177

along with your annual contributions of $10,000. You now have $28,000 of annual rental income going into the IRA, tax deferred and compounding at 6 percent. In 14 years, at the end of the same 30-year period, the value of the IRA is an impressive $2,762,177, a full 212.5 percent increase over the original IRA that spent 30 years compounding at 6 percent and another 29.9 percent improvement over what the duplex would have added to your wealth in the same amount of time.

The road to $2.7 million began with an annual income tax reduction of $2,000 that you obtained by investing $8,000 into a traditional IRA in 2007. By making a maximum IRA contribution over 30 years, the tax reduction accumulated to $74,500. Spread out over 30 years you paid a total of $298,000 into your IRA. There was another $88,397 of taxes to be saved if your retirement income moved you into the 15 percent tax bracket. With $2.7 million, you might have to forego that tax rate reduction. Through the power of tax reductions, tax deferrals, compounded interest, and two real estate purchases, the $298,000 became real wealth in the form of more than $2.7 million.

PARTIAL 1031 EXCHANGES

People invest to earn a return on the investment. It follows that they want to enjoy the earnings. The reality is, some taxes will likely be due when you withdraw money from your investment. However, there is no need to have the entire tax bill come due just to obtain some extra cash. People's circumstances vary greatly. Maybe you have a full-time career and have little need for your real estate investment money. Maybe you work full-time managing your real estate, making a good living from the profit. Many people eventually want to spend some of the investment money on a lavish vacation or need funds for a child's college education or another real-life situation. When planned for, a partial 1031 exchange can make this possible.

The partial exchange allows you to reinvest part of the funds while retaining part for personal or other business reasons. Recall the term "boot" used to describe any taxable money or other benefits in an exchange. Taxable boot can come from several sources. Cash money that you obtain from the sale of one property and the purchase of a replacement property can be a source of boot. Personal property (jewelry, artwork, etc.) you accept as partial payment in a real estate 1031 exchange is not like-kind property and is subject to tax based on fair market value. Accepting real estate that you plan to use as your residence is not like-kind property (it has to be for investment or business) and therefore is taxable boot. One to watch closely is the effect that indebtedness (mortgages and related debts) has on boot.

In addition to obtaining cash in an exchange, trading down in property value is a possibility. One reason to trade down might be to reduce the debt on the property. Remember that reduced debt counts as a capital gain because you are no longer obligated to pay the debt.

An example of how debt relief becomes taxable is if you trade a $600,000 property for a $500,000 property. The value of the relinquished property is $600,000 today, but you bought it several years ago for $450,000 with a 30 percent down payment and a $315,000 mortgage. You still owe $250,000 on the mortgage. After paying off the mortgage ($600,000 - $250,000), you have $350,000 as a down payment on the $500,000 replacement property and take out a $150,000 mortgage ($500,000 - $350,000). The $100,000 reduction in debt ($250,000 previous mortgage - $150,000 new mortgage) is taxable. If you walked away with $100,000 in cash ($600,000 selling price - $500,000 purchase price) that amount is taxable boot. You would pay 15 percent capital gains tax on a total of $200,000.

There are solutions that can reduce the potential taxes. If your intention is to both receive cash and reduce the outstanding debt, you will likely be obligated to pay the $30,000 tax on the $200,000. However, if the objective was only to obtain cash, the tax obligation can be reduced or eliminated. Three examples are:

1. Purchase an equally valued property for $600,000. Increase the mortgage to $350,000. Use $250,000 cash to pay the balance of the purchase price ($600,000 - $350,000). There is $100,000 remaining when you increased the mortgage from $250,000 to $350,000. You can take this $100,000 away as cash and pay the taxes. You will have obtained cash from your growing investment through a partial 1031 exchange that continues to defer taxes on the remaining $50,000 capital gain. The remaining $50,000 deferred gain is the $600,000 sales price less the original $450,000 purchase price less the $100,000 taken from the exchange as boot.

2. Take a loan out against the currently owned property. The drawback is repaying the loan. On the other hand, no taxes will be due if the property is not sold.

3. Upgrade your investment to a $700,000 property. Use the $350,000 cash available from selling the first property ($600,000 sales price - $250,000 mortgage) for a 50 percent down payment, substantially more than the 30 percent most commercial lenders require. After the 1031 exchange closes, you can borrow up to $140,000 against new property and still meet the 30 percent equity required by a commercial lender. This results in a higher-valued property with the potential ability to repay the loan with additional income. You do not have any tax obligation from the 1031 exchange.

The dollar values in each of these examples can be altered in several ways that might best benefit you. In Example 1 you have a capital gain of $150,000 ($600,000 selling price - $450,000 purchase price). You may choose to continue deferring taxes on $100,000 and walk away from the exchange with $50,000 of taxable boot. It is important to note that reducing debt during a 1031 exchange is a taxable event.

Example 1 is the only one leaving you with cash available for personal purposes without having to repay a loan. Example 2 has no taxes but provides cash, resulting in a loan to be repaid without an increased income source to make the payments. Example 3 has no tax consequence from the 1031 exchange and provides cash from a loan against the newly acquired property. The better real estate may provide additional income to repay the loan.

INSTALLMENT SALES IN 1031 EXCHANGES

Combining an installment sale with a 1031 exchange can be a way to accomplish important financial goals. The installment sale will create a dependable income stream, and the down payment from the buyer of the relinquished property can be used to exchange into a replacement property. This is another method of reducing tax obligations while preserving wealth.

As with most of these strategies, there can be a number of variations, limited only by people's imagination and needs. Combining two tax deferral strategies is not an uncommon practice. When combining installment sales inside a 1031 exchange, the IRS rules for installment sales are applied (IRS Publication 537), as well as the rules for 1031 exchanges (IRS Publication 544). Publication 537 has an additional set of rules that specifically apply when combining installment sales and 1031 exchanges. The specific rules governing a combined installment sale and 1031 exchange appear at the bottom of Exhibit 2.2.

EXHIBIT 2.2 EXCERPT FROM IRS PUBLICATION 537

Like-Kind Exchange

If you trade business or investment property solely for the same kind of property to be held as business or investment property, you can postpone reporting the gain. These trades are known as like-kind exchanges. The property you receive in a like-kind exchange is treated as if it were a continuation of the property you gave up.

You do not have to report any part of your gain if you receive only like-kind property. However, if you also receive money or other property (boot) in the exchange, you must report your gain to the extent of the money and the FMV of the other property received.

For more information on like-kind exchanges, see *Like-Kind Exchanges* in chapter 1 of Publication 544.

Installment payments. If, in addition to like-kind property, you receive an installment obligation in the exchange, the following rules apply:

- The contract price is reduced by the FMV of the like-kind property received in the trade.

- The gross profit is reduced by any gain on the trade that can be postponed.

- Like-kind property received in the trade is not considered payment on the installment obligation.

The first rule involves adjusting the entire transaction by removing the like-kind property from the fair market value of the entire transaction. With the like-kind property removed, everything else is taxable. In the case of an installment sale, the taxes are deferred until the year the payments are made.

The second rule is straightforward, shifting any capital gain into the replacement property, where it will continue to be deferred indefinitely.

The third rule restates the intention of a 1031 exchange, that like-kind property received in an exchange is not taxable. Therefore, capital gains tax and depreciation recapture tax do not become due on that portion of the transaction.

One thing that does occur is that the proportions of interest payment, capital gain, and recapture depreciation tax can be altered in the installment payment.

Consider a property with a fair market value of $800,000 and a basis of $500,000. In a combination exchange and installment sale, a $160,000 down payment (20 percent) is received and $640,000 is amortized over 30 years at 6 percent interest. Payments do not begin until next year. The $160,000 is used to purchase replacement property with a fair market value of $700,000. The contract price ($800,000) is reduced by the like-kind property ($700,000). The contract price becomes $100,000.

The gross profit is $300,000 ($800,000 selling price - $500,000 basis). The gross profit percentage that will be applied to the installment payments is gross profit divided by sales price ($300,000 ÷ $800,000 = 37.5 percent).

No tax is due in the first year because the down payment was exchanged for like-kind property and installment payments begin January of the next year. Next year, $38,186 of interest is paid on the installment and reported as income. The principal paid is $7,859. Of that, 37.5 percent is capital gains ($7,859 × 37.5 percent = $2,947 × 15 percent = $442 capital gains tax). The principal will continue to increase each year of the 30-year amortization period, resulting in more capital gains tax becoming due each year. Still, a monthly income stream of $3,837 has been established for 30 years. Interest is being earned on the deferred taxes, and the replacement property (with a mortgage) has indefinitely deferred the rest of the capital gain.

Consult a tax advisor regarding your particular circumstances. Different circumstances can dramatically alter the results.

CASE STUDY #2: COLLATERALIZED INSTALLMENT SALE
THE CLIENT'S PERSPECTIVE FROM S. CROW COLLATERAL CORP.

S. Crow Collateral Corp.
P.O. Box 972
Boise, Idaho 83701
Phone: 208-345-7661
Fax: 208-342-1638
E-mail: scrowcollateral@aol.com
www.scrowcollateral.com

Stanley D. Crow, J.D. is the president of S.Crow Collateral Corp. and sister company S.Crow Consulting Inc. Crow specializes in real estate and tax law. Crow has a Harvard law degree supplemented with a bachelor's degree in business and economics.

His law practice has emphasized real estate and business transactions since 1967. He is a member of the Idaho State Bar, the fourth and ninth circuits of the U.S. Court of Appeals, and is allowed to practice before the U.S. Supreme Court. Crow is an author on economic subjects and a presenter of perceptive position papers at professional conferences. Through S.Crow Collateral Corp., he provides unique services seldom found elsewhere in the real estate profession.

With insightful and dynamic use of §453 of the tax code, a collateralized installment sale offers:

- Deferment of capital gains tax

- No risk of default on the sale

- No risk of prematurely triggering capital gains tax

- An answer when the buyer wants clear title to the property

- The ability to structure payments without being dependent on the buyer's ability to pay

- The ability to save a failing 1031 exchange

- An alternative to the extinct private annuity trust

CASE STUDY #2: COLLATERALIZED INSTALLMENT SALE
THE CLIENT'S PERSPECTIVE FROM S. CROW COLLATERAL CORP.

As an installment sale accommodator, S.Crow Collateral Corp. purchases the client's appreciated real estate on an installment contract. Next, a willing buyer purchases the property from S.Crow Collateral Corp. for the fully negotiated price. Collateralization occurs by placing the sale proceeds with a third party chosen by the client. The client directs the third party to invest the untaxed funds as desired. The third party makes the installment payment to the client for S.Crow Collateral Corp. As with any installment sale, deferral of capital gains tax continues until the year's payment is received by the taxpayer. Over time, the investment grows until eventually the taxes are paid with inflated dollars.

With the original property removed from the equation, concerns common with a traditional installment sale go away. There is no risk of a loan default or the buyer paying off the contract early and triggering taxes. Pledging the funds as collateral makes the investment secure from any of your creditors and any creditors of S.Crow Collateral Corp.

Stanley Crow summarizes accommodating clients' unique needs this way:

"When it appears that there is no way to do the deal you want to do without incurring a prohibitive or excessive tax cost to do so, and everyone says, 'It can't be done,' they may be right — or maybe they just haven't dug deeply enough or thought creatively enough. Or, maybe what is needed is to look afresh at the assumptions we make without question and at the conventional wisdom we accept too easily. Maybe there *isn't* a way—but then again, maybe there is. I *really* don't like to accept 'it can't be done' as the answer. If your matter is difficult or seemingly intractable, let's see what we can do together."

One client of S.Crow Collateral Corp. is a public official who needed to reduce real estate holdings that exceeded a ceiling placed on his high public office. He entered into an installment contract with S.Crow Collateral Corp. He also worked with a 1031 intermediary to defer depreciation recapture taxes. S.Crow Collateral Corp. purchased the property on an installment contract from the 1031 exchange and resold the property to the ultimate buyer in a full cash purchase. The public official used a small down payment from the installment sale to purchase another property that did not exceed the limit imposed by holding public office, completing the 1031 exchange. As part of the final closing, the balance of funds was sent directly to the third party for investing based on the official's instructions.

He now has a smaller real estate property and receives interest-only payments

CASE STUDY #2: COLLATERALIZED INSTALLMENT SALE
THE CLIENT'S PERSPECTIVE FROM S. CROW COLLATERAL CORP.

on installment, secured by the investment held with a third party. He will receive a balloon payment for the principal at the end of 30 years.

Another S.Crow Collateral Corp. client was part of a limited partnership owning an apartment complex. His value in the arrangement was $1.9 million. When the time came to sell the apartment complex and dissolve the partnership, he was facing a $700,000 tax bill. S.Crow Collateral Corp. entered into a contract to purchase the client's share of the partnership on installments. Upon dissolving the partnership, the partner's previous share was deposited with a third party that he instructed to invest partially in mortgage funds and partly in mutual funds. He began looking for an acceptable real estate property that he intends to instruct the third party to purchase.

He has choices when the balloon payment comes due in five years. He can use the balloon payment to purchase the real estate that will be in the name of the third party. Or he can directly purchase replacement real estate with new financing and use the installment income stream to make the new payments. If this proves the best option, S.Crow Collateral Corp. can offer to amend the collateralized installment sale contract to extend the length of time that interest-only payments are available to make the debt payments.

The partner did receive a small down payment he used to pay the depreciation recapture taxes. His decision makes newly acquired real estate fully depreciable, an option he chose over a 1031 exchange, where replacement property is limited to depreciation remaining in the relinquished property, plus any new funds added to the purchase.

✓ ELIMINATING TAXES

There are ways to completely eliminate taxes in some conditions. The Roth IRA is relatively new to the tax code and gains are tax-free. The Charitable Remainder Trust provides a charitable write-off on your income tax, provides an income stream, and passes to the charity of your choice without tax consequences at the time of your death or your spouse's death. The Home Sale Exclusion will eliminate up to $500,000 in capital gain when your personal residence is sold. Annual gifting is effective in eliminating very high estate taxes.

The top estate tax in 2007 is 45 percent. Up to $2 million can be excluded from estate taxes in 2007, 2008, and 2009. Future estate tax rates are uncertain after 2009. Current tax law repeals the higher exclusion amounts and the lower estate tax rates in 2010. In 2011, the exclusion amount may revert to $1 million, and the top estate tax rate return to 50 percent if Congress does not revise the tax law. Plenty of reasons remain for you to eliminate or minimize estate taxes.

A married couple (and others) can easily accumulate wealth that leads to a high estate tax. Accumulated wealth can include a personal residence worth $750,000, investment/rental property worth $1.5 million, personal property (antiques, cars, jewelry) worth $500,000, and other investments (stocks and bonds) worth another $250,000. This quickly adds up to $3 million in wealth but is not liquid enough to provide the desired income stream for retirement. The $3 million total also exceeds the estate tax exclusion amount of $2 million effective in 2007. Often, people want to create an income stream while leaving a generous inheritance for their adult children.

Retirement means getting away from managing the investment and rental properties. However, the property has been depreciated over the years and has gone up in fair market value. Paying capital gains and depreciation recapture tax will not leave enough to invest and deliver the desired income stream.

This simplified estate estimate

Estate Property	
Residence	$750,000
Investment Property	$1,500,000
Personal Property	$500,000
Other Investments	$250,000
Estate Value	$3,000,000
Estate Tax Potential (2007)	
Estate Value	$3,000,000
Estate Exemption Allowance	-$2,000,000
Taxable Estate	$1,000,000
Estimated Estate Tax	**$425,000**

excludes other real taxes, such as state estate tax and probate costs. Estate tax rates have gone through several changes recently, and rates will likely change again soon. The 2007 estate exemption allowance of $2 million leaves the taxable portion of the estate at $1 million. Using an estate tax rate that quickly reaches the 45 percent maximum results in a realistic estimated tax of $425,000. When also faced with capital gains and depreciation recapture taxes, the consequences of selling the investments is not pleasant. However, liquidating the investments to create an income stream and still leave an inheritance to heirs can be accomplished by combining a charitable remainder trust with a life insurance policy.

CHARITABLE REMAINDER TRUST

The charitable remainder trust is an irrevocable trust providing a stream of income to you with the remaining value of the trust going to the charity of your choice in the end. In addition to donating to your favorite charity, you receive a tax deduction in the year a charitable remainder trust is established and funded. The deduction can be used in future years if it cannot all be used in one year.

Advantages of charitable remainder trusts:

- Eliminates capital gains taxes on appreciated property

- Creates a stream of income without the risk of triggering taxes or default on installment sales

- Provides a charitable tax deduction in the year it is established and funded

- Removes highly appreciated property from the estate

- Can fund a life insurance policy to provide heirs with a replacement inheritance

There are two general charitable remainder trusts:

- Charitable Remainder Annuity Trust (CRAT)

- Charitable Remainder Unit Trust (CRUT)

The charitable remainder annuity trust pays a fixed income each year corresponding to a percentage of the original investment (5 percent minimum up to 50 percent maximum). Income is paid each year regardless of how much the CRAT earns from investments. If investment returns are insufficient to provide the required income, principal will be used to pay the required income.

The charitable remainder unit trust does not require that principal be used to sustain the income stream. However, the option to use principal to pay income is available. The CRUT provides more flexibility in how income streams are paid. While the CRAT pays a fixed amount, the CRUT may increase with inflation or may not pay the desired amount in some years. Variations of how the CRUT can make payments include:

- As a set percentage of the annual value of the trust (may include paying out principal)

- Income only that does not pay anything if the trust does not obtain an income from investments. Principal is not used to make annual income payments. Provisions can be made to have missed income made up in future years

The income payment structure must ensure that at least 10 percent of the original value of the trust goes to the charity after all payments have been made.

Many people are reluctant to donate to charity without leaving an inheritance to their family; a life insurance policy can be purchased by the trust for the benefit of heirs. Because the life insurance policy is held by the charitable remainder trust, it does not count as part of the estate, thus providing an inheritance without the potential of being part of estate taxes.

A $2 million property placed in a charitable remainder trust by a couple in their mid-70s can be expected to receive an annual income of $140,000 for the rest of their lives. This assumes they receive 7 percent of the original trust's value each year with payments made at the end of each quarter. The calculation assumes the trust earns 5.8 percent annually. In addition to not paying capital gains when the property is sold, they are able to take a $538,438 charitable tax deduction. Their probability of outliving the income stream is only 3.77 percent.

CHARITABLE REMAINDER TRUST CALCULATION	
Date of transfer	Jan. 01, 2007
Fair market value of property transferred	$2,000,000
Annual annuity rate	7%
Payment frequency	Quarterly
Return on Investment	5.80%
Age of husband on the gift date	77
Age of Wife on the gift date	77
Annual Income Payment	$140,000
Value applied to tax deduction	$538,438
10% remainder to charity	Yes
Probability of surviving after income stops	3.77%

The example does not include purchasing a life insurance policy for the benefit of heirs. This decision is often based on two factors. First, is there sufficient wealth to provide an inheritance? Second, age and health can be determining factors if life insurance can be purchased. A couple at age 77 is likely to have difficulty obtaining life insurance. If your strategy includes replacing wealth donated to charity with a life insurance policy, it is best to do it at a younger age and in good health.

ROTH IRA

Contribution limits to Roth IRAs are generally the same as for traditional IRAs, the biggest difference being that contributions are taxed as income before being contributed to the Roth IRA. Distributions, on the other hand, are tax-free from a Roth IRA. The result is capital gain tax-free investments in real estate.

Qualified distributions for Roth IRAs differ from traditional IRAs. Qualified Roth IRA distributions must meet the following:

- Since you have already paid taxes on Roth contributions the original contributions can be withdrawn tax-free at any time.

- Qualified distributions cannot begin until five years after a Roth IRA has been set up for you and contributions have been made.

- You must be at least 59 ½ to receive qualified distributions unless:

  ◊ The distribution is for a first-time home purchase.

  ◊ The distribution is due to a disability.

  ◊ Distribution is made to a beneficiary of your estate after you die.

- Unlike traditional IRAs, forced distributions from a Roth IRA are not required beginning at 70 ½.

- Beneficiaries of your Roth IRA also receive distributions tax-free.

Examples in the traditional IRA discussion are also applicable to Roth IRA investments. There are no tax savings each year a contribution is made. The benefit is elimination of capital gains tax when you begin receiving distributions on the wealth that has been created.

HOME SALE TAX EXCLUSION

A personal residence may be subject to capital gains tax when it is sold. Capital gain up to $250,000 per individual ($500,000 for married couples) is fully excludable when certain conditions are met. Your primary home does not have to be on a traditional foundation to qualify. Examples of qualifying homes include:

- Houses

- Mobile homes

- Houseboats

- Condominiums

- Cooperative apartments

- Sale of land adjacent to home (in some cases)

Determining if a gain has occurred is accomplished by

Selling Price
- Selling Expenses
Amount Realized

Amount Realized
- Adjusted Basis
Gain (or Loss)

Selling expenses include commissions, advertising fees, legal fees, and loan points paid by the seller. The adjusted basis is usually the original purchase cost plus any capital improvements that have been made. An adjustment would be made for business activities, like a home office that has been depreciated.

The $250,000 will be tax-free if it passes these three tests:

- Owned the home for at least two of the last five years

- Lived in the house as a primary residence at least two of the last five years

- Have not excluded gain from another home within the last two years

Married couples must meet the following conditions to qualify to exclude $500,000:

- Married and filing a joint return for the tax year

- Either you or your spouse meets the ownership test

- Both you and your spouse meet the test for living there two of the last five years

- Neither of you has excluded gains from another home within the last two years

For many people these conditions are easily met without needing to give it much thought. Others have events occur in their lives that make it necessary to make sure the three qualification rules are met.

1. A couple purchasing a house and living in it for two years may move to another state for a better job opportunity. The house is rented for two years, and the couple has now owned it for four years. The couple realizes they should sell the house before the end of the fifth year.

2. A newly married couple has each owned separate homes for more than five years. They move into her house after the marriage and rent his house out. After two years, he sells his house while he can still take the full $250,000 capital gain exclusion. One year later, they want to sell her house and move into a larger home. Although they are married, only $250,000 gain can be excluded on her house because he took the $250,000 exclusion on his house within the last two years.

3. A man buys a house and eight months later accepts a great job offer in another part of the country. He continues to own and rent the house out for four years before selling it but never lives in it again. He meets the ownership test but fails the use test. He does not qualify for the $250,000 exclusion.

4. The ownership and use tests are treated as completely separate. A man buys the apartment he has lived in for eight years when the apartments are sold as condominiums. Only months after the purchase he moves to care for a sick relative. He does not move

back into the condominium but sells it within five years. He meets both the ownership and use test.

Exceptions to the use and ownership rules are made for:

- Uniformed and foreign service members on extended duty

- People that become physically or mentally unable to care for themselves

- Death of a spouse and the surviving spouse does not remarry before the sale of the house

A reduced exemption (qualifying for less than the $250,000) may occur due to:

- A change in employment

- Health

- Unforeseen circumstances

IRS Publication 523 explains how to apply for and calculate the exclusion. Vacation homes, second homes, and rental properties are not eligible for the primary residence capital gains tax exclusion. However, it is certainly possible to re-characterize these properties so that they can qualify. Essentially, the same tests must be met — the most significant being to live in the house for two out of five years, since presumably you already own the property. Consider the depreciation recapture tax on these properties before deciding to re-characterize them as a primary residence. The 25 percent depreciation recapture tax will apply.

In addition to charitable remainder trusts and primary home exclusion, there is one more way to eliminate taxes.

GIFTING

Gifting away a portion of your wealth eliminates the estate tax on the value that is gifted. The gift can be in the form of money, personal property, or real estate. The biggest limitation to gifting is the annual limit. In 2007 it is $12,000 per recipient; you can give to as many people as you wish but no more than $12,000 to each.

Generally, the following gifts are not taxable gifts:

- Gifts that are not more than the annual exclusion for the calendar year

- Tuition or medical expenses you pay directly to a medical or educational institution for someone

- Gifts to your spouse

- Gifts to a political organization for its use

- Gifts to charities

Gifts following these rules are not taxable to the person making the gift or the person receiving the gift. Gifts are not deductible except qualified charitable donations.

You and your spouse are allowed to combine gifts to an individual that total $24,000 tax-free in any single year. Combining this can be a powerful tool to transfer wealth to your children (or anyone you choose). Giving a child and spouse the maximum each year totals $48,000 per year. If you have three married children, you might gift the maximum of $144,000 annually.

52,000

Exceeding the annual tax-free gift brings into play the Unified Transfer Tax. Any gifts to an individual exceeding the annual limit accumulate over your lifetime and will be subtracted from your estate exemption allowance. For 2007, the Gift Tax Unified Credit is $345,000. This is a lifetime limit, and the limit in effect the year of your death applies.

The unified credit against taxable gifts will remain at $345,800 (exempting $1 million from tax) through 2009, while the unified credit against estate tax increases during the same period. The following table shows the unified credit and applicable exclusion amount for the calendar years in which a gift is made or a decedent dies after 2001.

	For Gift Tax Purposes		For Estate Tax Purpose	
Year	Unified Credit	Applicable Exclusion Amount	Unified Credit	Applicable Exclusion Amount
2002 and 2003	345,800	1,000,000	345,800	1,000,000
2004 and 2005	345,800	1,000,000	555,800	1,500,000
2006, 2007, and 2008	345,800	1,000,000	780,800	2,000,000
2009	345,800	1,000,000	1,455,800	3,500,000

One way of using the unified credit to your advantage is if you have property likely to appreciate significantly that you want to gift to someone.

An example is a small apartment building worth $369,800 ($345,800 unified credit + $24,000 annual tax-free gift for a married couple) located in an area expecting rapid property value increases. Gifting the property now would remove it and, more importantly, the future appreciation from your estate. As long as the value is below the $345,800 gift tax unified credit (after subtracting the annual tax-free gift), no gift tax would be due the year the gift is made.

If the property has appreciated in value to $600,000 by the time of your death, the net effect on your estate remains at the $345,800 level rather than the appreciated level.

Once you have accumulated sufficient wealth to be financially independent and assured of living the life style of your choice, it becomes time to consider how you will pass additional wealth on to your heirs.

Beginning early with tax-free annual gifts is an effective way of avoiding the very high estate tax rates. These tax rates have been fluctuating and are unpredictable in the future. In 2010, the current estate tax rates will be repealed, and the estate tax exclusion will return to $1 million in 2011, a dramatic change from the $3.5 million in effect during 2009. Annual gifting should be part of your long-term tax strategy.

SUMMARY

By now, you should realize that there are indeed many sections of the internal revenue code that allow individuals to acquire and hold wealth. These include ways to pass significant amounts of wealth from one generation to the next. As you begin planning the steps to your wealth, consider closely where each of these methods can be best applied.

The previous chapter discussed methods to acquire and shield wealth with 1031 exchanges, installment sales, and self-directed IRAs. This chapter moved from strategies for acquiring wealth to strategies for preserving wealth. The partial 1031 exchange is effective to reap partial benefits of your wealth while continuing to defer taxes on most of your property as you trade up. The installment sale inside a 1031 exchange demonstrates a method of extracting profits at a slower rate while earning interest on deferred taxes and indefinitely deferring taxes on the like-kind property that is exchanged.

Charitable remainder trusts eliminate capital gains, create a charitable tax deduction, and remove highly appreciated property from an estate subject to high tax rates. The Roth IRA eliminates capital gains tax by investing with money on which income tax was previously paid. The sale of a primary residence can exclude capital gains up to $500,000 for a married couple. Certainly, giving your money away is a tax-free way to transfer it to the next generation and help them on their way to growing wealth.

3

QUALIFIED RETIREMENT ACCOUNTS

A qualified retirement plan is one that follows the requirements of Section 401 of the tax code. Meeting the provisions of Section 401 bestows favorable tax treatment on the plan. Employers establish 401 plans for the benefit of employees.

The first advantage of a tax-deferred retirement account is that income tax is not paid on contributions. For those in the 25 percent tax bracket, contributing $4,000 in a year, the advantage is $1,000 (25 percent of $4,000). If your income had not been tax-deferred, you would have paid $1,000 in tax on the $4,000. Essentially, it only cost you $3,000 ($4,000 2 $1,000) to gain the benefit of $4,000. Even without an employer matching the contribution, it gains 25 percent immediately.

If, at the time of retirement, your tax bracket lowers to 15 percent based on less income, it is an additional tax savings. Retirement accounts (other than Roth accounts) are taxed on distributions paid during retirement. A general premise of these accounts is that the tax on distributed funds will be lower when the taxpayer qualifies for a lower income tax rate in retirement.

Several variables control the amount of annual contributions made to an account. Different account types have different contribution ceilings. Decisions made by the employer can affect the amount contributed. The amount of income received by individuals also affects the amount contributed.

DIFFERENT ACCOUNT TYPES

A variety of account types exist, creating optional ways to save for retirement and increase wealth tax-free. Most have been around for decades, although the Roth 401(k) only became available in 2006.

401(K)

The 401(k) is possibly the best-known retirement account, imaginatively named for the subsection of the IRS code governing it. An employer must establish the plan for employees. All employees must be eligible to participate, but rules allow exclusion of unionized employees in some situations.

The employer may choose to contribute to the plan or not.

The 2006 limit to contributions was $15,000. Future contribution limits are indexed to the cost of living. An employer's plan may set a lower allowable contribution limit. IRS code allows people over 50 years old to contribute an additional $5,000 (also indexed to the cost of living) as a catch-up contribution. The first 6 percent of funds an employer contributes to the 401(k) is above and beyond the contribution limit. Your $15,000 contribution, plus an employer's matching 6 percent on a $40,000 salary, would total $17,400.

Distributions from 401(k) accounts can only be made upon:

- Attaining age 59 ½
- Termination of employment

- Hardship

- Disability

- Death

If you have a 401(k) from a previous employer, it can be rolled over into an IRA or other portable retirement account.

ROTH 401(K)

The Roth 401(k) was first offered in 2006. Similar to the Roth IRA, there is no income tax deduction allowed for contributions. The tax advantage is taken when distributions are made tax-free on the earnings.

You can contribute to both a traditional 401(k) and a Roth 401(k) in the same year. However, the $15,000 (in 2006) ceiling defined by the traditional 401(k) cannot be exceeded by the combined contributions. The $5,000 catch-up clause for those over age 50 does raise the ceiling.

Because this plan is new, not all regulations have been codified. Current proposals for distributions removed before the account has been established for five years would include earnings as part of gross income for the year. The portion of the distribution that has already had income tax paid would not be included as gross income. The tax-free earnings would be taxed on this disqualified distribution. Other penalties may also be applied. Consider a $5,000 withdrawal from a Roth 401(k) account with a $10,000 balance made up of $9,400 in contributions and $600 in earnings. The first $4,700 of the $5,000 would not be subject to income tax. The $300 distributed as earning would be subject to income tax in the year withdrawn.

These were still proposed regulations at the time this book was written. The proposed regulations were 50 pages long and subject to change. The proposed regulations were unclear about the beginning of the five-year period if a Roth 401(k) account is rolled over into a Roth IRA. One proposal counted the five years as beginning when the contribution was originally made to the Roth 401(k), and in another proposal the five-year period begin again when the rollover occurred.

One regulation does appear to be clear: Roth 401(k) accounts can be rolled over to another Roth 401(k) or to a Roth IRA but not to any other types of accounts.

Exhibit 3.1 provides a comparison between the new Roth 401(k), the Roth IRA, and a traditional 401(k) account. Advantages of the Roth 401(k) over the Roth IRA are the lack of an income limit and the ability to fund up to $15,000 ($20,000 for those over 50).

EXHIBIT 3.1 SOURCE IRS PUBLICATION 4530 (2006)		
Feature Comparisons of Roth 401(k), Roth IRA, and Traditional 401(k) Retirement Accounts		
Feature	**Designated Roth 401(k) Account**	**Roth IRA**	**Traditional, Pre-Tax 401(k) Account**
Contributions	Designated Roth employee elective contributions are made with after-tax dollars.	Roth IRA contributions are made with after-tax dollars.	Traditional, pre-tax employee elective contributions are made with before-tax dollars.
Income Limits	No income limitation to participate.	Income limits: • Married $160,000 • Single $110,000 (modified AGI)	Same as designated Roth 401(k) account. No income limitation to participate.
Maximum Elective Limits	Combined* employee elective contributions limited to: $15,000 in 2006 ($20,000 for employees 50 or over)	Contribution limited to: $4,000 in 2006 ($5,000 for employees 50 or over)	Same combined* limit as designated Roth 401(k) account.

EXHIBIT 3.1 SOURCE IRS PUBLICATION 4530 (2006)			
Taxation of Withdrawals	Withdrawals of contributions and earnings are not taxed provided they are a qualified distribution — the account is held for at least five years and made: because of disability, after death, or after attainment of age 59 ½	Same as designated Roth 401(k) account, and can have a qualified distribution for a first-time home purchase.	Withdrawals of contributions and earnings are subject to federal and most state income taxes.
Required Distributions	Distributions must begin no later than age 70 ½, unless still working and not a 5 percent owner.	Same as designated Roth 401(k) account; and can have a qualified distribution for a first-time home purchase.	Same as designated Roth 401(k) account.
* This limitation is by individual, rather than by plan. Although it is permissible to split the annual employee elective contribution between designated Roth contributions and traditional pre-tax contributions, the combination cannot exceed the deferral limit — $15,000 ($20,000 if age 50 or over).			

Because 401(k) accounts are entrusted with employers, they have not been available to purchase real estate in the way a self-directed Roth IRA can. At a time when people transition from one career to another often, the Roth 401(k) can be converted to a Roth IRA when a person changes jobs. The significance is that a much larger amount can be contributed to a Roth 401(k) and then converted to a self-directed Roth IRA. The increased contribution level has the ability to obtain an account balance capable of purchasing real estate much sooner.

DECIDING BETWEEN ROTH AND TRADITIONAL IRAS

Some serious thought should be given to what you think your income tax rate will be when the time comes to begin taking distributions from a traditional IRA. The concept behind the traditional IRA is that you defer taxes in the beginning and pay them when they are distributed, along with income tax on the earnings. If your adjusted gross income after retirement remains in one of the upper tax brackets, the Roth IRA may be a better choice because the earnings are tax-free.

This brings up compounded interest again. Let us look at the tax difference between a regular IRA and a Roth IRA when the retirement tax rate applied to a traditional IRA reduces to 15 percent or remains at 25 percent. Both IRAs have an $8,000 contribution made annually. A 6 percent return is obtained for the first 11 years until the balance reaches $142,146 and is sufficient to make a real estate purchase. The real estate appreciates annually at 11 percent and produces an income profit of $1,200 (a modest amount considering the effect depreciation has on profits). The $1,200 coupled with the annual $8,000 contribution increases the annual contribution to $9,200 in year 12. After 19 years (30 years including the first 11) the IRA is worth $1,613,921. This is the same for either a regular or Roth IRA.

The same contributions, totaling $240,000, have been made to both accounts over the 30 years. However, $2,000 of income tax had to be paid each year before the Roth IRA could be funded. Compounding the $2,000 in the same manner as the IRAs shows the income tax portion of the Roth IRA, if invested, would have a value of $384,516

IRA Growth Prior to Real Estate Purchase	
Annual Contribution	$8,000
Compounded @ 6%	
Total in 11 years	$142,146
IRA Growth After Real Estate Purchase	
Annual Contribution	$9,200
Compounded @ 11%	
Total in 19 years (end of 30 years)	$1,613,921

after 30 years. This is the compounded cost of paying the annual Roth IRA $2,000 tax.

Here is where it gets interesting. The regular IRA pays taxes on the entire IRA account (contributions and earnings are both taxable when distributed). When the retirement tax rate is 15 percent, the total tax bill comes to $242,088 on the $1,613,921 account balance. The regular IRA performed $142,428 better than the Roth IRA, resulting in a $242,088 cost for the traditional IRA versus a $384,516 cost for the Roth IRA.

Total IRA Contributions - $8,000 x 30 Years	$240,000
Annual Income Tax Paid by Roth IRA @ 25%	$2,000
Investment Value of Roth Income Tax Paid Compounded Annually @ 6% for 11 Years	$35,536
Investment Value of Roth Income Tax Paid Compounded Annually @ 11% for 19 Years (Value at end of 30 years)	$384,516
Entire $1,613,921 in Regular IRA Taxed at 15%	$242,088
Entire $1,613,921 in Regular IRA Taxed at 25%	$403,480

If wealth has accumulated and retirement income keeps the taxpayer in the 25 percent bracket, the story changes. The regular IRA requires a total of $403,480 to be paid in income tax. In this scenario, the Roth IRA does $18,964 better than the regular IRA because the tax cost was lower at $384,516.

Many variables have been excluded to simplify this example. Neither the future value of money nor present value of money has been accounted for. Other tax reduction or elimination strategies may be added to the scenario. The purpose is to demonstrate that choosing between a regular or Roth IRA can have long-term consequences. One reliable study found that 44 percent of households would benefit more from the Roth IRA than the regular IRA. It depends on independent circumstances and answers to questions that cannot be known for many years.

GENERAL INFORMATION ABOUT SEP, SIMPLE, AND KEOGH PLANS

- Businesses (including sole proprietors) can deduct contributions made to these retirement plans

- Earnings are tax-free until qualified distributions are taken

- Contributions to the plans are tax deductible by either the employer or employee, depending on who makes the contribution

- Expenses of administering the plans are tax deductible by the business if the retirement plan does not charge administration fees of participants

SEP-IRA

Simplified Employee Pension (SEP) allows an employer to contribute to employees' IRAs. The SEP has relaxed IRS reporting rules, making it easier for small businesses to establish a retirement plan. The employee owns and controls the IRA, while the employer is able to contribute to it. If the SEP follows the IRS model, prior approval of the retirement plan is not required. It can also relieve the small business owner of having to file annual retirement plan information returns.

Annual contribution limits by the employer are 25 percent of employees' gross income, up to a maximum of $44,000 in 2006 and indexed to the cost of living after that.

Employers may vary the annual contribution amount or skip contributions some years.

SIMPLE

The Savings Incentive Match Plan for Employees (SIMPLE) can be created as either a SIMPLE IRA or a SIMPLE 401(k). Employers with less than 100 employees can set up SIMPLE plans.

Both the employer and employee can contribute to a SIMPLE IRA. The employee can elect to have a percentage of his or her income tax deferred into the account. The employer has to make at least a 3 percent matching contribution to participating employees, or the employer can make non-elective contributions of 2 percent to all employees, including those who do not have contributions withheld from their salary. The employer deducts contributions. Combined employer and employee contributions cannot exceed $10,000 in 2006. For those over age 50 the catch-up amount raises to $12,500. The amount is indexed to the cost of living in $500 increments beginning in 2007.

Either a SIMPLE IRA can have all employee accounts directed to a single financial institution or each employee can specify the institution of their choice. If the employer chooses the financial institution, the employee can choose to have the funds transferred to the institution of their choice.

Although a SIMPLE IRA cannot be designated as a Roth IRA, the contributions made to a SIMPLE IRA do not subtract from contributions an employee can make to a Roth IRA. A SIMPLE IRA can be rolled over to another SIMPLE IRA at any time or it can be rolled over to any other IRA after two years of participation in the SIMPLE IRA.

Early withdrawal of funds will generally be faced with a 10 percent penalty, plus inclusion of the distribution as income for the tax year. However, the penalty is increased to 25 percent if the funds are withdrawn within two years of beginning the plan.

A SIMPLE 401(k) generally follows the rules of the Simple IRA except the funds are set up in a trust rather than an IRA. Rules for managing the trust are similar to those for other qualified plans.

COMPARISON OF INDIVIDUAL CONTRIBUTION LIMITS						
Year	Traditional/ Roth	Traditional/ Roth Catch Up	SIMPLE	SIMPLE Catch Up	401(k)	401(k) Catch Up
2006	$4,000	$5,000	$10,000	$12,500	$15,000	$20,000
2007	$4,000	$5,000	Indexed to Cost of Living in $500 Increments after 2006			
2008	$5,000	$6,000				
2009	$5,000	$6,000				

KEOGH OR QUALIFIED PLAN

A qualified plan may be called a Keogh plan or an H.R. 10 plan. It can be established by most business entities, including sole proprietors. Contributions made by the employer are generally tax deductible, and contributions made by employees (including earnings and gains) are tax deferred until distributed.

These plans are fully funded and tax deductible by the employer. There are several different ways these plans can be set up. Depending on the method selected by the employer, contributions made by employees may or may not be tax deferrable. Similarly, there are several ways these plans may be distributed or rolled over. In some cases, the benefits are not transferable. Instead, retirement payments begin when the participant meets the retirement requirements of the plan. The ability to roll over these accounts must be determined on a case-by-case basis.

OTHER TAX FAVORABLE SAVINGS ACCOUNTS

Contributions to a Coverdell Education Savings Account (ESA) are not tax deductible, but qualified distributions are (including gains), similar to a Roth IRA. Up to $2,000 can be contributed per year, per child, until they reach the age of 18. Individuals can make a full contribution if they have an adjusted gross income under $95,000 ($190,000 for married couples filing jointly). Contribution limits phase out for individuals with adjusted gross income between $95,0000 and $110,000 ($190,000 and $220,000 for married couples filing jointly).

These accounts can be held at any U.S. bank or other IRS-approved entity that covers Coverdell Education Savings accounts. Financial companies that provide self-directed IRAs often offer these education accounts, opening up self-directed investment opportunities.

Expenses qualifying for tax-free distributions of earnings include:

- Elementary, secondary, and higher learning institution expenses

- Tuition, fees, books, supplies, and tutoring

- Room and board, uniforms, transportation, and computer equipment

Health Savings Accounts (HSA) are another type of tax-favorable account to consider. These became legal in 2003. Intended to help offset health care expenses for individuals, contributions are income tax deductible even if you do not itemize deductions. Qualified distributions are not taxed either. The HSA provides two tax breaks to help with your health care expenses.

The HSA works similar to the education savings account and can be established with some financial institutions providing self-directed IRAs. Most medical expenses are covered, including preventative care, vision, and hearing health care. Individuals can contribute the lesser of their health plan deductible or $2,650. Families can contribute the lesser of a health plan deductible or $5,250.

SELF-DIRECTED IRA ACCOUNTS

The reason for the discussion of the previous account types is that most are portable and capable of being converted into self-directed IRA accounts, either traditional self-directed IRAs or self-directed Roth IRAs. While SIMPLE Plans, SEP Plans, and 401(k) plans can be invested in real estate (and other investments), if your employer set up the account, it is unlikely to be self-directed. Under certain conditions (usually time requirements, such as two years after beginning participation in a SIMPLE), you can convert these accounts to self-directed IRAs.

If you are a sole proprietor (or business owner), you can establish a self-directed 401(k) or a retirement account other than an IRA. The increased contribution amounts for these accounts may make them preferable to an IRA. Depending on your circumstances, the combination of your contribution and the business matching contribution can be as high as $44,000 in 2006 and $49,000 if the catch-up clause applies.

QUALIFYING AND OPENING AN ACCOUNT

After you select the type of self-directed account that best suits your needs (it is fine if your needs change later), you will need to determine if an account transfer or a rollover is most suitable. A transfer occurs when the funds move directly from one financial institution to another without you obtaining access to the funds at any time. There are no restrictions on the number of transfers conducted each year. A transfer also minimizes the possibility that a disqualified transaction can occur that incurs a penalty or even disqualifies the IRA.

A rollover occurs when your current financial institution (or employer) sends the check directly to you rather than into a new account established for your benefit. You have 60 days to complete the rollover. Funds can be rolled over only once every 12 months. There are reasons you may prefer a rollover rather than a transfer, but the risks of a disqualified transaction increase. One reason might be that you have a short-term (less than 60 days) use for the funds, possibly as the middle person for a profitable real estate transaction. With careful timing, you might purchase a property and sell it again within the 60 days. The gain that you make would be reportable to the IRS in that tax year. However, the IRA funds would be rolled into the new account with all the tax advantages still intact.

WRITING THE PLAN DOCUMENT

Custodians of self-directed retirement accounts usually already have plan documents approved by the IRS. The IRS requires three easy steps be followed to establish SIMPLE IRA plans for yourself and your employees:

1. Execute a written agreement to provide benefits to all eligible employees.

2. Give employees certain information about the agreement.

3. Set up an IRA account for each employee.

The custodian will provide you with a form that becomes the plan document after it is completed. Although the plan document does not have to be filed with the IRS, it is a legal document, and the provisions must be followed. Accomplishing Step 1 (execute a written agreement) and Step 2 (give employees certain information) only requires completing IRS form 5305-SIMPLE and providing a completed copy to the employees. Completing the form requires selecting certain options and setting a few limitations, such as not allowing employees making less than $5,000 to participate. The major sections of form 5305-SIMPLE follow:

EMPLOYEE ELIGIBILITY REQUIREMENTS

1. General Eligibility

a. Full Eligibility. All employees are eligible.

b. Limited Eligibility. Eligibility is limited to employees who are described in both (i) and (ii) below:

(i) Current compensation. Employees who are reasonably expected to receive at least $_____ in compensation (not to exceed $5,000) for calendar year.

(ii) Prior compensation. Employees who have received at least $ _____ in compensation (not to exceed $5,000) during any calendar year(s) (insert 0, 1, or 2) preceding the calendar year.

2. Excludable Employees

The Employer elects to exclude employees covered under a collective bargaining agreement for which retirement benefits were the subject of good faith bargaining.

SALARY REDUCTION AGREEMENTS

1. Salary Reduction Election.

An eligible employee may make an election to have his or her compensation for each pay period reduced. The total amount of the reduction in the employee's compensation for a calendar year cannot exceed the applicable amount for that year.

2. Timing of Salary Reduction Elections

a. For a calendar year, an eligible employee may make or modify a salary reduction election during the 60-day period immediately preceding January 1 of that year. However, for the year in which the employee becomes eligible to make salary reduction contributions, the period during which the employee may make or modify the election is a 60-day period that includes either the date the employee becomes eligible or the day before.

b. In addition to the election periods in 2a, eligible employees may make salary reduction elections or modify prior elections _____. If the Employer chooses this option, insert a period or periods (e.g., semi-annually, quarterly, monthly, or daily) that will apply uniformly to all eligible employees.

c. An employee may terminate a salary reduction election at any time during the calendar year. ☐ If this box is checked, an employee who terminates a salary reduction election not in accordance with 2b may not resume salary reduction contributions during the calendar year.

CONTRIBUTIONS

1. Salary Reduction Contributions.

The amount by which the employee agrees to reduce his or her compensation will be contributed by the Employer to the employee's SIMPLE IRA.

2. Contributions.

a. Matching Contributions

(i) For each calendar year, the Employer will contribute a matching contribution to each eligible employee's SIMPLE IRA equal to the employee's salary reduction contributions up to a limit of 3 percent of the employee's compensation for the calendar year.

(ii) The Employer may reduce the 3 percent limit for the calendar year in (i) only if: (1) The limit is not reduced below 1 percent; (2) The limit is not reduced for more than two calendar years during the five-year period ending with the calendar year the reduction is effective; and (3) Each employee is notified of the reduced limit within a reasonable period of time before the employees' 60-day election period for the calendar year.

b. Non-elective Contributions

(i) For any calendar year, instead of making matching contributions, the Employer may make non-elective contributions equal to 2 percent of compensation for the calendar year to the SIMPLE IRA of each eligible employee who has at least $_____ (not more than $5,000) in compensation for the calendar year.

(ii) For any calendar year, the Employer may make 2 percent non-elective contributions instead of matching contributions only if:

1. Each eligible employee is notified that a 2 percent non-elective contribution will be made instead of a matching contribution; and

2. This notification is provided within a reasonable period of time before the employees' 60-day election period for the calendar year.

Establishing employee eligibility, defining salary reduction agreements (the amount the employee contributes), and defining how the employer will contribute is all that is required to establish a SIMPLE IRA retirement plan. Including the employer's contribution, an individual can have up to $10,000 contributed annually.

If an employer chooses to allow the employees to decide the financial institution receiving the contribution, use IRS form 5304-SIMPLE rather than 5305-SIMPLE.

SETTING UP SEP-IRA ACCOUNTS

Establishing SEP-IRA accounts is even easier. Doing so is accomplished by completing IRS form 5305-SEP. Decisions and information required are:

Eligibility Requirements (check applicable boxes)

The employer agrees to provide discretionary contributions in each calendar year to the individual retirement account or individual retirement annuity (IRA) of all employees who are at least ____ years old (not to exceed 21 years old) and have performed services for the employer in at least ____ years (not to exceed three years) of the immediately preceding five years.

This simplified employee pension (SEP) ☐ includes ☐ does not include employees covered under a collective bargaining agreement, ☐ includes ☐ does not include certain nonresident aliens, and ☐ includes ☐ does not include employees whose total compensation during the year is less than $450 (for 2005).

SEP Requirements

The employer agrees that contributions made on behalf of each eligible employee will be:

A. Based only on the first $205,000 of compensation.

B. The same percentage of compensation for every employee.

C. Limited annually to the smaller of $44,000 or 25 percent of compensation.

D. Paid to the employee's IRA trustee, custodian, or insurance company (for an annuity contract).

Completing this short form enables the employer to contribute up to $44,000 to employees' SEP-IRAs, making it an attractive option for a sole proprietor wanting the benefits of both taking the business expense and contributing substantially more to their retirement account.

LETTERS OF INSTRUCTION TO THE CUSTODIAN

Once the self-directed account is funded, the funds need to be invested. Most custodians of self-directed accounts provide a form specific to real estate transactions to ensure the required information is provided. Completing the instructions typically includes:

- Identifying the account involved

- Making sure real estate titles accurately show the IRA account as owner

- Identifying documents the custodian must sign to complete the transaction on behalf of your IRA

- Identifying to whom, where, and how much in funds will be provided for the purchase

- Identifying the real estate being purchased, including information about any rental income that will be deposited to the IRA

- Providing information about other financing that may be subject to unrelated business tax income (UBTI)

- Identifying information about the escrow agent handling the closing

Two important items to remember about the self-directed IRA: The custodian only follows the directions you provide, and they do not provide investment advice. You or your representatives will need to gather all the necessary information for the transaction. The one area to which you want to pay careful attention is how the property is titled. Usually, the title will be some version of "Self-direct IRA Company Custodial for the Benefit of 'Account Owner's Name' IRA." All the legal paperwork must use the correct name to ensure proper ownership by the IRA account and integrity of tax-favorable treatment.

PARTNERING UNTAXED AND AFTER-TAX FUNDS

In some situations, you may decide to personally purchase property along with your IRA. You will need to be careful not to violate the prohibited transactions, but it is not difficult. The prohibited transaction you should be wary of is using your IRA as a guarantee for loans. This is avoided by keeping all purchase costs, business expenses, and income clearly prorated between IRA funds and personal funds. Exhibit 3.2 and the example that follows explain how to keep both the IRA and your personal accounts correctly balanced.

EXHIBIT 3.2 PURCHASE $350,000 APARTMENT WITH COMBINED IRA AND PERSONAL MONIES			
Purchase Costs	Total	IRA 40%	Personal 60%
Earnest Deposit	$3,500		$3,500
Purchase Price	$350,000	$140,000	$210,000
Closing Costs	$3,200	$1,280	$1,920
Earnest Deposit Adjustment		$1,400	($1,400)
Purchase Totals	$356,700	$142,680	$214,020
Rent and Deposit Income	$57,600	$23,040	$34,560
Expenses			
Utilities	$850	$340	$510
Grounds Keeping	$600	$240	$360
Apartment Maintenance	$1,200	$480	$720
Insurance	$4,700	$1,880	$2,820
Taxes	$5,100	$2,040	$3,060
Expenses Total	$12,450	$4,980	$7,470
Mortgage Payment (annual)	$15,960	N/A	$15,960
Annual Cash Flow	$29,190	$18,060	$11,130

A small apartment house costing $350,000 is purchased 40 percent by your IRA and 60 percent by you personally. The IRA will contribute $140,000 toward the purchase, and you personally contribute $210,000. Even if you do not have the $210,000 available in cash, there are ways to complete the deal without the IRA taking out a loan that will cause it to pay UBTI tax. You cannot take out a loan directly against the property being purchased.

You can, however, borrow the money from another source. A loan against your primary residence or another property will work.

Essential to this arrangement is maintaining full segregation of your funds and the IRA funds. Making the earnest money deposit with only your personal funds would not be a problem because escrow has not closed and IRA funds are not yet involved with the transaction. Exhibit 3.2 shows just this – your personal funds being used for the earnest deposit. Once a purchase agreement is signed, the next step is sending a letter of instruction to the custodian of your IRA directing them to issue a check for escrow. All closing costs and the purchase price must be divided by the 60 percent proportion owned by you and the 40 percent proposition owned by the bank. A $1,400 adjustment for the earnest deposit must be made from the IRA to you when escrow closes.

The undivided interest of 60 percent personal and 40 percent IRA continues during the ownership of the apartment complex. The IRA receives 40 percent of the rental and security deposit income and pays 40 percent of expenses. You personally receive 60 percent of the rental and security deposit income and pay 60 percent of the expenses. Additionally, you have to pay the mortgage taken out on your primary residence or other property. Technically, the mortgage is a completely separate transaction from the apartment building, but it does affect your cash flow, so it has been included. Over the course of a year, your IRA receives $29,190 in positive cash flow, and you receive $11,130. You and the IRA enjoy the benefit of the property's appreciation in value. No UBTI is due because the IRA did not take out a loan.

The partnering of money for investment just discussed involves untaxed funds from a traditional IRA

2006 UBTI RATES APPLIED TO REAL ESTATE PURCHASED WITH DEBT FINANCING

- $0 - $1,000 = Exempt
- $1,000 - $2,050 = 15%
- $2,050 - $4,850 = 25%
- $4,850 - $7,400 = 28%
- $7,400 - $10,050 = 33%
- Over $10,050 = 35%

(or other retirement account) and after-tax money that you provide. There are several other versions available to you. Some involve only combinations of pretax dollars and others combine the pretax and after-tax dollars. You and your spouse can each own part of a real estate property through individual IRAs. You can partner with other relatives' or friends' IRAs. You can partner with relatives' and friends' after-tax funds. Many imaginative methods are available to partner money to purchase real estate that includes your self-directed IRA.

LEVERAGING AND UNRELATED BUSINESS TAX INCOME

As self-directed IRAs become better known, banks are becoming more willing to lend money to self-directed IRAs. This certainly opens more investment possibilities, but, at the same time, they likely will cost the IRA unrelated business tax income (UBTI).

An Internal Revenue Service requirement allowing an IRA to obtain a loan is that the loan must be non-recourse toward the IRA and the IRA owner. This means only the property purchased by the IRA with the loan proceeds can be used to secure the loan. No other repayment guarantees are allowed. The loaning institution cannot have rights to other IRA assets or to your personal assets. For this reason, you can assume that a loan-to-value ratio between 70 and 80 percent will be required by most banks. Your IRA will need to make a 20 to 30 percent down payment on the property.

UBTI rates are very high and are constructed to ramp up to 35 percent very quickly. Many states apply an additional UBTI rate as well. The UBTI is collected on income attributed to the loan. Income proportionate to the property cost financed by the loan is the portion that must pay UBTI. Funds provided directly by the IRA do not pay UBTI on the income received. As the loan is repaid, the amount of UBTI decreases.

Paying UBTI requires the IRA to file a federal income tax return that it would not otherwise file. Some of the more conservative tax professionals believe that an IRA filing a federal tax return invites more scrutiny by the IRS.

However, there are ways to leverage an IRA purchase. A $500,000 rental property providing $110,000 of rental income is an example to consider. The IRA directly purchases $300,000 of the property and borrows the remaining $200,000. Assume principal has been paid on the loan during the year, and the average amount of ownership attributed to the loan during the year is 39 percent; this is the amount of the income subjected to UBTI after accounting for other business expenses and deductions.

Depreciation and other expenses lower the net income to $81,000 ($110,000 income − $29,000 expenses). Of the $81,000 in net income, 39 percent ($31,590) must pay UBTI tax, less the $1,000 exemption. After applying the increasing tax rates, a total UBTI tax of $9,785 is estimated.

$81,000 less the $9,785 UBTI tax leaves $71,215 of income generated for the IRA. This is a 14.2 percent return on the $500,000 investment. To determine if this is an adequate return you can compare it to other investment opportunities that do not encounter a UBTI tax. Also, recall that in future years, as the loan amount is paid down, less of the income will be subject to UBTI.

UBTI ESTIMATED ON $110,000 RENTAL INCOME WITH 39% LOAN AVERAGE	
Rental Income	$110,000
Depreciation	$17,000
Other Expenses	$12,000
Net Income	$81,000
UBTI Rent ($81,000 3 39%)	$31,590
Less Exemption	$1,000
Rent Subject to UBTI	$30,590
$2,050 @ 15%	$308
$2,050 2 $4,850 @ 25%	$700
$4,850 2 $7,400 @ 28%	$714
$7,400 2 $10,050 @ 33%	$875
Over $10,050 @ 35%	$7,189
Estimated UBTI Tax	$9,785

Another similar tax is the Unrelated Debt Finance Income (UDFI). In this scenario, you pay a tax similar to UBTI, but it is applied to the profit when you sell an IRA-owned property that still has debt financing. If you purchased a $100,000 property with 50 percent financing and later sell it for $200,000, the UDFI tax would be applied to $50,000 of the $100,000 gain on the sale. This assumes that it was an interest-only loan, and the 50 percent debt financing did not decrease while you owned the property. Otherwise, the tax would be applied to the highest percent of debt that occurred during the tax year the property was sold. If the IRA pays off the loan in full at least 12 months prior to the sale, no UDFI will be due.

The UBIT and UDFI are two of the more complex tax laws. As always, consult a qualified tax professional before making important decisions.

USING THE 60-DAY RULE

An opportunity exists to use IRA money to generate money outside the IRA on a short-term basis. Every 12 months an IRA can be rolled over from one account to another. Sixty days are allowed between the time the money is withdrawn from the old account and the time it is deposited into the new account. During this time, you have access to the funds (you cannot access transferred IRA accounts). The amount going into the new account must be exactly the same amount removed from the previous account unless you have not made your annual contribution. Granted, there are risks to short-term investments if you do not have other money available to roll over into the new IRA if the short-term investment has a

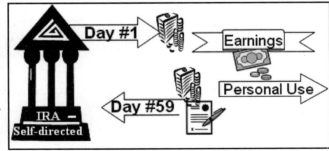

loss or exceeds 60 days. When the risks can acceptably be managed, you can benefit from the investment return during that tax year.

The concept is simple: Develop a plan for the short-term investment.

Withdraw the funds for a rollover into a new IRA. Invest the funds for 59 days. The earnings are separate from the IRA and can be used personally. Have the documentation prepared, and on day 59, open the new IRA by funding at the same level as the account closed 59 days earlier. Maintain documents showing that the new IRA was funded at the exact amount as the previous IRA and within the allotted 60 days.

A short-term investment of $50,000 can earn $500 for personal use. This amount will be included with your income tax for the year. Other alternatives earning a larger return are possible, depending on your creativity. Consideration needs to be given to the fact that your IRA will not be earning for itself during this time.

SUMMARY

Details about qualified retirement accounts may have been enlightening for you. Most people associate these plans as being available only through employers, not realizing these opportunities are available to individuals. There are many tax advantages for retirement accounts and are structured to accommodate creative people. Options range from those needing to fund small amounts with the SIMPLE to establishing traditional IRAs up to the self-employed (or small business owner) desiring to contribute tens of thousands of dollars annually.

You may choose between SEP, SIMPLE, 401(k), and traditional IRAs, all of which have contributions made from pretax income. These provide an immediate tax advantage because the contribution amount is not taxed in that tax year. Theoretically, the tax on the contribution and earnings will be lower when distributions occur during retirement when you are in a lower tax bracket. Applying a few of the principles presented here should create enough retirement income.

Another option available is the Roth IRA and Roth 401(k). Contributions are made after income tax has been paid. The benefit received is that all earnings are tax-free from distributions during retirement. There is no concern about which tax bracket you will be in or what the prevailing income tax rates will be in the future. Also, the Roth 401(k) offers, for the first time, a retirement account without an annual income ceiling.

Establishing retirement accounts with passive custodians for self-directed investments opens up many possibilities. Setting up one of these accounts is simple through either a transfer or a rollover. Once opened and funded, real estate transactions are easily made. The custodians provide standardized forms and sale agreement terminology that ensure property is correctly titled to the IRA to preserve the tax-favored standing.

Real estate investing of retirement accounts is becoming more common. You have several options for how to fund a purchase even if your IRA does not currently have enough money. You may use other personal funds in a partnership arrangement. A similar partnership arrangement is optional by joining with a spouse's IRA, the IRA of any other person, or the personal funds of another person. It is also becoming more common for banks to make non-recourse loans to IRAs for the purpose of purchasing real estate. The option to leverage a purchase and pay the UBTI tax should be carefully calculated before being entered into. As with most major financial decisions, it is wise to obtain the advice of a qualified tax consultant to assess your individual circumstances. Nonetheless, you now have the basic tools and knowledge to begin building your own road to wealth and riches.

CASE STUDY #3: EQUITY TRUST COMPANY

Equity Trust Company
P.O. Box 1319
Elyria, OH 44036
Web Address: www.trustetc.com
Telephone: 888-ETC-IRAS (382-4727)
E-mail: help@trustetc.com

With more than 33 years' experience and management of $2 billion in IRA assets, Equity Trust Company is a leading custodial provider of self-directed IRAs and small business retirement plans, allowing clients to increase financial wealth by investing in a variety of opportunities from real estate and private placements to stocks and bonds.

The stated mission of Equity Trust is to help investors make tax-free profits through education, innovation, and a commitment to understanding their individual needs. While all companies rely on profitability to survive, the truly successful ones do so through a dedication to quality service. Equity Trust's ultimate goal is to provide complete client satisfaction.

Equity Trust has two affiliate companies that increase value for clients, Mid Ohio Securities (an in-house brokerage service for traditional investment assets) and Retirement Education Group (provides programs and products to educate investors on the power of self-directed IRAs).

Vice president Jeffrey A. Desich leads Equity Trust's efforts to help clients create tax-free wealth. He has been involved with self-directed investing all his adult life and with Equity Trust for ten years. Desich is client-centered and a nationally sought professional speaker, providing education and insights about real estate investing with self-directed IRAs and other investment subjects. CBS Market Watch and Investor's Business Daily are among the publications to which he has provided expert quotes and information. Desich holds Series 7 and 27 licenses with the National Association of Security Dealers, as well as a Life and Health Insurance License with the state of Ohio.

One of the things Desich and Equity Trust often cite as the most important benefit to investing in self-directed IRAs is compounding interest.

CASE STUDY #3: EQUITY TRUST COMPANY

Self-Directed IRAs and the Power of Compounding Interest

Albert Einstein called it "the most powerful force on earth," and more than 200 years ago, Benjamin Franklin defined the concept of compounding interest as "the stone that turns all your lead into gold."

How does it work? The power of compounding interest comes from the fact that the original investment, as well as the income derived from that investment, is re-invested.

Compounding interest can be especially dramatic when the effect of taxes is removed from the equation. Do you know how much money you would have in 30 years if you invested just one penny today and doubled it every year? The answer will astound you: It is $10,737,418! Now, suppose you had to pay taxes of 31 percent on your investment? Over the same 30 years, you would have only $68,644. Obviously, no one can expect to double an investment every year for 30 years. Nonetheless, this example certainly illustrates the combined effects of compound interest and taxation.

Using a self-directed IRA as an investment vehicle allows investors to benefit from the full power of compounding interest. This is due to the fact that investments made within a self-directed IRA are tax-deferred or, in the case of the Roth IRA, tax-free.

With the power of compound interest on their side, Equity Trust clients can take advantage of the many plans and services offered by Equity Trust.

Desich comments about some of Equity Trust Company's most popular offerings:

"Our most popular plans include the traditional and Roth IRA, Simplified Employee Pension (SEP) plan, Savings Incentive Match Plan for Employees (SIMPLE), Individual(k), Roth Individual(k), Health Savings Accounts (HSAs), and Coverdell Education Savings Accounts (CESA). Equity Trust clients benefit from the tax advantages, including tax-free and tax-deferred profits of those plans with the ability to invest in anything not prohibited by the IRS including real estate, private placements, tax liens, stocks, mutual funds, bonds, etc."

The traditional and Roth IRAs provide clients tax-advantaged government savings accounts. The traditional IRA allows for yearly tax deductions based on contributions. The investment inside the traditional IRA grows tax-free until distribution, when it will be subject to income tax. The Roth IRA does not offer yearly tax deductions, but there are no taxes due upon distribution, unlike the traditional IRA.

CASE STUDY #3: EQUITY TRUST COMPANY

Equity Trust has quickly enabled clients to take advantage of the new Roth 401(k) retirement plan that the U.S. Congress enacted beginning in 2006. Equity Trust recommends the Roth 401(k) to clients wanting Roth tax advantages (i.e., tax-free distributions) with a substantial contribution limit ($15,000). Also, Equity Trust encourages clients interested in a Roth IRA, but who do not qualify because of income limits, to consider the Roth Individual(k).

Among the large selection of plans available at Equity Trust is the highest allowable contribution plan, the SEP-IRA. For real estate investors, self-employed individuals, sole proprietors, or small business owners, the Simplified Employee Pension Plan (SEP) enables them to contribute the most toward their own and their employees' retirement and therefore allows them to receive the largest tax deductions. An employer (investor, self-employed, or sole proprietor) may contribute up to 25 percent of each eligible employee's annual compensation to a maximum of $44,000. The employer may contribute annually, but it is not required every year.

In addition, Equity Trust offers the Savings Incentive Match Plan for Employees (SIMPLE) and recommends the plan to clients that want to save more than a traditional or Roth will allow (clients can contribute up to $10,000 or $12,500 if over 50 with the SIMPLE), but make less than $40,000 a year.

Equity Trust also keeps clients informed about tax-favorable accounts like the Health Savings Accounts (HSA) and Coverdell Educational Savings Accounts (CESA). The CESA is a trust or custodial account created for paying qualified education expenses of the designated beneficiary of the account. The HSA can reduce an investor's health insurance premiums by as much as 70 percent, and HSA contributions are tax-deductible (subject to limitations).

In addition to its array of services, Equity Trust allows clients to access and manage their accounts through an easy-to-use online account management tool called eVANTAGE. This all-in-one portal allows investors to review their investment activities and make transactions, such as paying property-related bills or verifying receipt of monthly rental payments. The clients' account information is directly downloadable into Quicken, Money, or other financial software.

This case study not only touches on the agility eVANTAGE provides, but highlighted in the following capsule are the Portfolio Positions and bill payment screens. Other features include:

- Investment Detail
- Recent Activity

CASE STUDY #3: EQUITY TRUST COMPANY

- Cash Transactions
- Online Trading
- Open New Accounts
- User Profile

The Portfolio Positions view displays all your current investments in your self-directed IRA with Equity Trust. If you want to see the transaction detail for any of your investments, click your IRN number to see your investment detail.

Paying bills from your IRA has never been easier. Choose "Online Bill Pay" to pay bills from your IRA account conveniently and easily. If your bill is less than $1,000, you do not even need to sign and fax the Bill Pay DOI. We will do it all electronically, saving you time and effort — time that you can spend doing deals.

EQUITY TRUST COMPANY

Why Equity Trust is the preferred choice in self-directed IRA investing ...

- 33 years' experience assisting investors to create tax-free wealth

- Management of over $2 billion in IRA assets, to help clients secure their financial future

- More than 140 self-directed IRA specialists ready to serve clients

- Personalized account management teams for every client, including their own personal 800 number to ensure personalized attention for every call

- Low all-inclusive fee schedule — clients do not pay fees on every transaction

- Online account management 24 hours a day, seven days a week with eVANTAGE, the industry's first online account management tool — pay bills online, fill-out forms, download information into Quicken or Money financial software programs, check account status at anytime and from anywhere.

- Quick and accurate investment processing (99.2 percent of transactions reviewed in 24 hours) with the fastest turnaround times in the industry

- Online trading through our affiliate, Mid-Ohio Securities, member NASD/SPIC — only self-directed IRA custodian with online trading

- Highly regulated — clients can trust Equity Trust with their investments

4

1031 EXCHANGES

Recall that 1031 exchanges both defer capital gains tax and depreciation recapture tax, making the use of an exchange one of the most tax-favorable codes. Since the IRS acceptance of deferred exchanges became reality in 1991, people have been using exchanges to preserve and add to their wealth in ever-increasing numbers. An entire profession has developed to accommodate the growing use of this tax-deferral strategy. Certainly, a real estate agent or broker should be able to spot an opportunity for a client to benefit from an exchange.

A likely scenario is any time a client intends to sell one property and quickly acquire another. Common reasons for real estate clients to benefit from a 1031 exchange include:

- Change in investment type
- Seeking a property that provides more revenue
- Selling a single property and buying multiple properties
- Desiring to change from a difficult to manage property to an easier one
- Management-free investment into a tenant-in-common arrangement
- Relocating out of the region and not wanting to be a long-distance landlord

- The need to relocate a business to a better location

- The need to relocate for expansion

- Converting a rental property to personal residence to take advantage of the $500,000 principal home sale exclusion

The list of ways people can benefit from an exchange quickly becomes very long. One advantage often overlooked is that a person conducting an exchange may be able to sell the relinquished property without inflating the sale price because of financial pressure to recover the taxes that would be lost. In return, the lower sale price becomes motivation for the buyer of the relinquished property, who may be unfamiliar with and reluctant to transact business through an exchange.

This chapter provides the details to enable anyone to recognize an opportunity for an exchange. You will understand the mechanics of an exchange and many creative ways to benefit.

SAFE HARBOR

The IRS issued "safe-harbor" regulations in 1991. These provided approved procedures for exchanges under tax code section 1031. Before the IRS procedures, exchanges were easily challenged on a variety of tax issues. With the 1991 regulations, tax-deferred exchanges are easier, less expensive, and far less susceptible to IRS challenges. In general, the entire §1031 is the safe harbor for exchanges.

Use of the safe harbor regulations is not mandatory but does simplify the process and safeguard your financial interest in the exchange. Use of an exchange accommodator or qualified intermediary is a key provision for a safe exchange. The terms "exchange accommodator" and "qualified intermediary" are used interchangeably throughout the profession. The IRS does not license, regulate, or define qualified intermediaries. Rather, the IRS defines people that cannot be a qualified intermediary for an exchange.

Those disqualified from being an intermediary include:

- Any person who acts as the taxpayer's agent, employee, attorney, or broker

- Any brother, sister, spouse, ancestor, or lineal descendant

- Any corporation where 10 percent of the outstanding stock is owned by or for the taxpayer either directly or indirectly

- Any beneficiary of a trust where the taxpayer is the grantor

EXHIBIT 4.1 EXCERPT FROM IRS PUBLICATION 544

Like-Kind Exchanges Using Qualified Intermediaries

If you transfer property through a qualified intermediary, the transfer of the property given up and receipt of like-kind property is treated as an exchange. This rule applies even if you receive money or other property directly from a party to the transaction other than the qualified intermediary.

A qualified intermediary is a person who enters into a written exchange agreement with you to acquire and transfer the property you give up and to acquire the replacement property and transfer it to you. This agreement must expressly limit your rights to receive, pledge, borrow, or otherwise obtain the benefits of money or other property held by the qualified intermediary.

A qualified intermediary cannot be either of the following.

- Your agent at the time of the transaction. This includes a person who has been your employee, attorney, accountant, investment banker or broker, or real estate agent or broker within the 2-year period before the transfer of property you give up.

- A person who is related to you or your agent under the rules discussed in chapter 2 under Nondeductible Loss, substituting "10%" for "50%."

Exhibit 4.1 is a brief excerpt from IRS publication 544 explaining the role of a qualified intermediary in accordance with a safe harbor 1031 exchange. In reality, the profession of qualified intermediaries was developed specifically to conduct 1031 exchanges. These teams of professionals conduct 1031 exchanges on a daily basis. Important roles that a professional qualified intermediary will perform on your behalf include:

- Fully protect the client from actual or constructive receipt of money or other property prior to completion of the exchange.

- Have a total understanding of and be knowledgeable about current applicable regulations.

- Have a working knowledge of all the secondary problems and pitfalls an exchange transaction may encounter and willingly seek resolutions.

- Protect the integrity of the exchange agreement between the qualified intermediary and the taxpayer.

- Educate the client with information relevant to the exchange, including different types of exchanges.

- Prepare the necessary documents to convey both the relinquished and replacement property from the sellers to the buyers.

- Calculate tax basis of the newly acquired replacement property for depreciation purposes.

A key role of the professional qualified intermediary is to always be aware of changes in applicable tax law. For many of these professionals, 1031 exchanges are their sole business. They maintain multimillion-dollar bonds as insurance against inappropriate loss of client assets. Although not specifically licensed by the government, many are members of the Federation of Exchange Accommodators (FEA), a national trade organization dedicated to keeping members current on tax law, as well as innovative ideas of how 1031 exchanges can best serve clients. The knowledge and experience of these professionals ensures that your exchange is conducted in accordance with the safe harbor procedures.

LIKE-KIND AND DISQUALIFIED PROPERTIES

As noted before, real estate is broadly defined as like-kind as long as it is not held as inventory that is regularly and immediately available for sale. It also must be within the Untied States but does not include properties in U.S. territories.

There is a small distinction made between the categories of business property and investment property. A business property can be exchanged for an investment property, but one additional rule applies to business property: A business property must be owned for at least one year before it can qualify for a 1031 exchange.

Rental property is included in the category of investment property. Rental properties include single residences, apartments, and offices. Other investment property is raw land and vacation property held for profit.

Real Estate Properties Are All Like-Kind

Any Type Can be Exchanged for Any Other

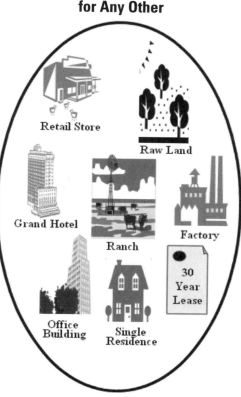

Business property can be a factory, a motel, a retail operation, or any other property used to conduct business or a trade.

It should be noted that the inventory and equipment used in a business may or may not qualify for a like-kind exchange with real estate. Business equipment can be exchanged for other like-kind business equipment. It can be included in the exchange if it meets the IRS definition of incidental property (shown in Exhibit 4.2).

EXHIBIT 4.2 EXCERPT FROM IRS PUBLICATION 544

Disregard incidental property. Do not treat property incidental to a larger item of property as separate from the larger item when you identify replacement property. Property is incidental if it meets both the following tests:

- It is typically transferred with the larger item.
- The total fair market value of all the incidental property is not more than 15% of the total fair market value of the larger item of property.

A real estate leasehold with a minimum of 30 years remaining (including extensions) is also like-kind property eligible to be exchanged for any other property.

A single real estate property does not need to be exchanged for another single property. Any quantity or combination of properties is acceptable. A ranch can be exchanged for three condominiums in the city. A high-rise office building can be exchanged for acres of timberland. Four single-family homes can be sold in an exchange, and the proceeds can be used to purchase a golf course.

Whole interests are not a prerequisite either. Two or more people can sell separately owned properties and join the proceeds together in the purchase of a replacement property in which they own an undivided interest. However, limited liability and partnership provisions can complicate this type of transaction.

Unlike the long list of properties qualifying for a 1031 exchange, the list of disqualified properties is short:

- Personal residence
- Foreign property
- Property held as inventory

Although you may purchase a rental house through an exchange and later convert it into a personal residence, once the residence is used as a personal home it no longer qualifies for an exchange, unless converted back to a rental. Foreign property cannot be used in a tax deferral exchange, although a foreign national owning property in the United States can be party to an exchange. Property held for inventory, such as subdivision lots, is classified as dealer status property and is not eligible for an exchange.

The liberal and flexible ability to exchange any type of property for any other compared to the short list of disqualified properties is a clear indication that 1031 is intended to allow individuals to grow wealth through tax deferral. Along with the freedom to defer taxes on most any business or investment property, there is no limit to the number of exchanges that can occur. It is almost intuitive that wealth can be obtained by borrowing other people's money and repeatedly trading up into real estate that produces more income and in which you own the increase in appreciation along with the income the property produces.

MORE ADVANTAGES OF 1031 EXCHANGES

Acquiring better cash-producing properties and deferring both capital gains and depreciation recapture taxes are most definitely some of the biggest advantages of exchanging business and investment property, but do not overlook other advantages.

A 2005 National Association of Realtors report states that 28 percent of home purchases were made by investors. Many of these investors were sure they would purchase a different property within two years. These investors are ideal candidates to benefit from tax-favorable 1031 exchanges. They have already discovered the power of leveraging other people's money and are fully engaged in stepping up their real estate portfolio to ever-higher values.

The 1031 exchanges provide real estate owners with a wide range of opportunities to meet personal investment objectives, including increased leverage, improved cash flow, diversification, reduction of management obligations, geographic relocation, and consolidation. There are thousands of unique ways to arrange exchanges in a way that can meet almost every investment or business need. Ultimately, the exchange process allows investors to reorganize and improve their real estate portfolios to best suit their unique interests and needs without a financial loss to taxes.

Some common reasons investors choose 1031 exchanges:

- Increase depreciation deduction
- Reposition assets financially
- Increase leverage
- Property consolidation or diversification
- Eliminate or create joint ownership
- Construct improvements on property
- Reduce management obligations
- Estate and retirement planning

ACCURATELY CALCULATING CAPITAL GAIN

Chapter 1 went through the details of calculating basis and depreciation. Details about calculating capital gains tax that were left out for clarity are covered here. Real estate professionals often lump depreciation recapture tax and capital gains together. This book has attempted to be clear about the difference. This difference is important because the tax rates vary and the application of each tax is different. This example should make the differences clear.

It has been noted that many states apply capital gains taxes and depreciation recapture taxes in addition to the federal government. The example goes through the full calculation to determine the combined taxes. You will need your state's specific tax rate to estimate taxes you might owe without conducting a 1031 exchange.

Begin by calculating the adjusted basis:	
Original Purchase Price	$200,000
plus Improvements	+ $ 50,000
minus Depreciation	- $ 25,000
equals the Adjusted Basis	= $225,000
Next, calculate the Capital Gains:	
Full Selling Price	$400,000
minus Adjusted Basis	- $225,000
minus Selling Costs	- $ 18,000
equals Capital Gain	= $157,000
Calculate Total Potential Taxes:	
Federal depreciation recapture tax is 25 percent of $25,000	$ 6,250
*Federal capital gains tax is 15 percent of $157,000	$23,550
**State capital gains tax at 7.35 percent of $157,000	$11,775
Total Potential Tax	= $41,575

*Federal capital gains tax rate is either 5 percent or 0 percent for those in lower tax brackets.
**At the time this was written, 41 states had a long-term capital gains tax that varied from 2.7 percent up to 12 percent. Some states also imposed a sales tax.

MI
4.35%

INCREASING DEPRECIATION AND DEFERRING TAXES

In the scope of wealth growth, it is necessary to increase the depreciation on property occasionally to maintain and increase cash flow and profits. The 1031 exchange is ideally suited to accomplishing this. When an exchange is successfully completed, the basis from the sold property carries forward to the new property. If the replacement property has the same fair market value (purchase price) as the relinquished property, you will have exactly the same basis in the new property, resulting in an identical annual tax write-off for depreciation, which is unlikely to be a desirable position. Increased depreciation is obtained by acquiring a higher-valued property.

As established in Chapter 1, depreciation can significantly improve the cash flow from your property. The answer to growing wealth through 1031 exchanging is to acquire a property that produces more income by including the deferred taxes to make the purchase and increasing your basis in the new property so that more depreciation can be taken annually to shield the increased cash flow from income tax.

ANNUAL EXPENSES AND INCOME	
Expenses	
Depreciation	$1,818
Mortgage Interest	$2,506
Insurance and Tax	$1,020
Other Expenses	$650
Total Expenses	$5,994
Income (Profit)	
Rental Income	$7,500
Less Expenses	($5,994)
Taxable Income	$1,506

The case of Ms. Miller exchanging a single residence for a multiplex rental will demonstrate the results that can be obtained. Ms. Miller purchased a small house as her personal residence at age 21 for $60,000. By the time she was 25, she had established her career in the business world and was able to acquire a larger personal residence. Because of low interest rates, a healthy real estate market, and a solid career, her lender was very willing to finance the larger house while allowing her to maintain the original mortgage so the smaller house could be rented.

Ms. Miller had made a $6,000 (10 percent) down payment on the small house. The monthly mortgage payments, including taxes and insurance, came to $375 ($4,500 annually). She was able to rent the house for $625 monthly ($7,500 annually). Other expenses came to about $650 each year. The land, which cannot be depreciated, was worth $10,000. She was able to depreciate the remaining $50,000, amounting to $1,818 each year. Renting the house resulted in only $1,506 of taxable income each year. However, the $1,818 in depreciation was not paid to anyone and was effectively tax-free profit. Paying 25 percent income tax on the $1,506 left her with $1,130 plus the $1,818 depreciation write-off. Total after-tax income generated annually by the rental house was $2,948 ($1,130 + $1,818).

This arrangement was satisfactory to Ms. Miller for several years. She was gaining equity by paying the principal down each year, and the property was appreciating in value. Having positive cash flow of $2,948 was icing on the cake. She lived in the house for four years and rented it for seven years, and it appreciated in value to $189,000. She began considering the purchase of a multi-unit complex that would provide additional income and have a higher value to take better advantage of the 11 percent appreciation rate that real estate averages.

Having rented the house to others for seven years, she knew that she was not eligible to

FINANCIAL POSITION IN THE 8-PLEX	
New Basis	
Single House Basis Carried Forward	$44,740
Increased Basis from Loan	$534,000
New Basis	$578,740
Expenses	
Annual Mortgage	$34,140
Annual Depreciation	$21,043
Annual Property Tax	$7,920
Annual Insurance	$3,300
Other Expenses	$7,000
Total Annual Expenses	$73,403

eliminate capital gains tax by using the principal residence exclusion of $250,000. A 1031 exchange that deferred capital gains and depreciation recapture tax allowed Ms. Miller to use all her equity to purchase an eight-unit apartment building in a better section of the city.

Ms. Miller realized that she could raise the rent on the small house to increase her income, but the depreciation write-off could not be increased to shield the increase in the rent. Moving up to a multiplex apartment via a 1031 exchange was definitely the best alternative.

Ms. Miller could only depreciate the seven years that the house was rented and made no capital improvements, leaving her with an adjusted basis of

$47,274. Her capital gain on the sale was $128,726. The total taxes deferred by using a 1031 exchange came to $23,121 on this single-family residence.

After accounting for the $13,000 in selling expenses and paying off the remaining $42,500 mortgage, Ms. Miller had $133,500 available to make a (20 percent) down payment on a $667,500 property. Based on her established record as a reliable borrower, her lender was pleased to help her become the landlord of the eight-unit apartment complex for $660,000, which completed the exchange in less than the allotted 180 days.

The new basis for depreciation includes the $44,740 carried forward

THE 1031 EXCHANGE

Selling	Depreciation	
	Purchase Cost	$60,000
	7 Years of Depreciation	($12,726)
	No Capital Improvements	$0
	Adjusted Basis	$47,274
	Capital Gain	
	Selling Price	$189,000
	Adjusted Basis	($47,274)
	Selling Costs	$13,000
	Capital Gain	$128,726
	Deferred Taxes	
	Taxes Deferred	
	Capital Gain @ 15%	$19,309
	Depreciation Recapture	$3,812
	Total Deferred	$23,121
Purchasing	Reinvestment	
	Selling Price	$189,000
	Selling Expenses	($13,000)
	Mortgage Payoff	($42,500)
	Available for Reinvestment	$133,500
	Down Payment	$133,500
	80% Loan	$534,000
	Available for Purchase	$667,500

from the house in the 1031 exchange. Adding to that is the $534,000 of financing taken out to purchase the apartment building. The new basis in the depreciable basis in the building is $578,740. Other expenses associated with the larger real estate holding also increased. The mortgage expense is $34,140. The annual depreciation of the new basis is $21,043. Total expenses now come to $73,403 each year.

Having an eight-unit apartment building in a better part of the city produces much more income, fully offsetting the expenses. The annual rental income from the new investment is $84,000 and annual depreciation of the new basis is $21,043. A full accounting of the annual expenses leaves $10,597 that Ms. Miller will pay income tax on.

INCOME FROM 8-PLEX	
Annual Income	$84,000
Depreciation	($21,043)
Annual Mortgage	($34,140)
Property Tax	($7,920)
Insurance	($3,300)
Other Expenses	($7,000)
Taxable Income	$10,597
Taxable Income	$10,597
Tax @ 25%	($2,649)
Depreciation	$21,043
Actual Income	**$28,991**

Accounting for the $2,649 paid in income tax and adding the $21,043 of depreciation back into the annual income, the actual income Ms. Miller will have free and clear each year is $28,991. By stepping up to a better property, Ms. Miller has leveraged other people's money to increase her after-tax rental income from $2,948 to $28,991 annually, almost a tenfold increase. She also has gained ownership of real estate that can be expected to continue appreciating attractively in the future.

This more complex example includes some typical expenses that a rental property owner can deduct from income as business expenses. Other typical rental property expenses include:

- Advertising
- Cleaning and maintenance
- Insurance
- Management fees
- Other loan interest
- Supplies
- Utilities
- Other costs of doing business
- Business transportation
- Commissions
- Legal and other professional fees
- Mortgage interest
- Repairs
- Taxes
- Depreciation

DISADVANTAGES

For anyone that intends to remain invested in real estate, there are not many real disadvantages to using a 1031 exchange. A few analysts consider the reduced basis carried into the replacement property to be a disadvantage because less depreciation is available. While this is certainly true, it only reflects the importance of having a real estate tax specialist review your specific circumstances. The flipside is that selling the property outright and paying the taxes results in less money being available to invest in replacement property.

The last example enabled Ms. Miller to leverage $133,500 into a $660,000 purchase. If she had paid the $23,500 in taxes that were deferred, she would have only been able to leverage $109,000. A 20 percent down payment reduces her ability to borrow up to $545,000. A $545,000 property compounding at 11 percent for five years will be worth $918,357. A property valued at $660,000 compounding at the same rate and amount of time will be worth $1,112,138. The full depreciation on $545,000 property for five years will be $98,917. The reduced depreciation on the $660,000 property is $104,315. This is not a case where the reduced basis in the property is detrimental to the investor. The fact that several variables need consideration in each potential 1031 exchange makes seeking tax advice critical.

The additional costs involved with a 1031 exchange can also be a small disadvantage. The services of a professional qualified intermediary for a typical 1031 exchange will be approximately $500. Add a few hundred dollars for tax advice and possibly extra escrow charges, and the additional cost of a 1031 exchange could be around $2,000. This is substantially below the amount gained from most exchanges.

Strict timing requirements and adherence to other rules to keep the exchange IRS-compliant may intimidate individuals or add stress to the sale and purchase processes. Helpful professionals, knowledgeable of potential pitfalls, go a long way to alleviate these issues.

COMMON PITFALLS TO AVOID IN EXCHANGES

1. Becoming categorized by the IRS as a real estate dealer rather than an investor. This is particularly true for developers that have an inventory of subdivision lots for sale or other real estate inventory. People holding both inventory property and investment property must keep the two clearly segregated in order to qualify for 1031 exchanges.

2. The partnership pitfall prevents distributing an interest in a partnership. The partnership itself can exchange partnership property.

3. Construction 1031 exchanges allow you to use sales funds to construct a new property or remodel an existing one as the replacement property. The 180 days still apply while construction projects may be out of the control of the future owner. Also, you cannot exchange property that you own and use the proceeds to improve another property that you already own.

4. Exchanging property that involves related parties (relatives and business entities) requires a two-year holding period before the property can be exchanged again.

5. If the seller carries back financing, it may be taxable on an installment sale. There are options that a tax advisor can provide.

6. Exchanging multiple properties in an exchange complicates it, both in identifying multiple replacement properties and in ensuring all escrow closings occur within the specified time.

All these are discussed in later chapters and proven solutions are provided.

IMPORTANCE OF TIMING

Another short word on the importance of timing requirements in the 1031 exchange. Recall that you have 45 days to identify replacement property once escrow closes on the relinquished property, and you are limited to 180 days to close escrow on the replacement property. These times run concurrently, not consecutively. Beginning to look for replacement property at the same time you begin looking for a buyer for the relinquished property may give you an advantage you have not considered. With a willing buyer, it might be possible to delay the closing of the relinquished property if you are having difficulty finding the replacement property. Of course, the ideal solution is to open the exchange with both properties already positioned for closing. Naturally, that is not going to happen very often.

Neither the 45-day identification period nor the 180 days until escrow takes weekends or holidays off. Be sure to close escrow the week before the deadline if either of these critical days falls on a weekend or holiday. There is no recourse once the date has passed.

The IRS requires an exchange to be completed before the filing of the exchanger's tax return for the tax year in which the exchange began. This means a taxpayer who begins an exchange after October 31 and intends to make use of the full 180 days needs to file for an extension of their tax return from April 15 to August to obtain the use of the full 180 days. The fact that you are engaged in an exchange is a valid reason to file the extension.

In the business world, 180 days is a long time, and priorities have a way of changing. Stay in touch with your professional qualified intermediary during this time and be sure both of you are fully aware of the status of all transactions.

DUE DILIGENCE

Due diligence is not an IRS requirement, but it is very important to conduct a due diligence study on the replacement property. Performing due diligence is not restricted to properties purchased in 1031 exchanges. It must be performed on any real estate being seriously considered for purchase. In the case of a 1031 exchange, performing due diligence can be affected by the 180-day time restriction. Properly planned for, adequate time is available to complete the due diligence.

Most often, the three-properties identification method is used to formally identify the potential replacement properties. Simultaneous due diligence is needed on all three properties, in the event that problems are found with the most preferred property. Also consider performing preliminary due diligence early in the 45-day identification period. This could prevent a problem property from being included on the short list of three identified potential replacements.

7 EVALUATIONS FROM DUE DILIGENCE
1. Cash flow and profitability
2. Appraisal and sales comparables
3. Rental market (for rental property)
4. Market trends
5. Engineering reports
6. Environmental
7. Financing information

Seriously consider the use of professionals in the due diligence field. In addition to providing their professional experience, they can check several properties simultaneously. This is a task that an individual or couple would find difficult to perform.

The results of performing due diligence can be applied to several important considerations. A few are:

- Correct value of the real estate.

- Profitability or financial performance.

- Unknown or undisclosed problems (structural, financial, leases, tenants, environmental).

- Insurability of the real estate.

- Lender acceptance.

An astute seller of the property will anticipate that you will conduct a thorough due diligence and will have most of the needed documents available. Regardless of if they are immediately available or must be gathered, any sale agreement must contain a list of the documents that you need the seller to provide. The agreement should also contain a clause stating how much time (30 days minimum) is available to complete the due diligence.

At a minimum, each property's due diligence report should include seven sections on the properties. Cash flow and profitability need to include a net operating income calculation.

NET OPERATING INCOME

A net operating income calculation includes all the income and expense numbers but does not include taxes, depreciation, or financing costs. This will enable you to compare, accurately and fairly different properties under consideration. The seller's financial information can be used as a beginning point, but make adjustments based on what you believe to be current rental rates and realistic expenses. The income calculation includes gross rents (allowing for a realistic vacancy rate) and any other income (such as nonrefundable deposits). The expense calculation includes all costs to manage, maintain, and repair the property, but does not include capitalized expenses. The objective is a financial picture showing whether the property is free and clear of any debt or taxes.

CALCULATING NET OPERATING INCOME WITH $625,000 SELLING PRICE	
Gross Rent	$150,000
Other Income	$ 5,000
Potential Gross Income	$155,000
Less Vacancy Rate	$ 7,000
Adjusted Gross Income	**$148,000**
Less Operating Expenses	$ (46,000)
Net Operating Income	$102,000

COMPARING 3 NET OPERATING INCOMES			
Property	**Selling Price**	**NOI**	**Ratio**
1	$625,000	$102,000	0.1632
2	$595,000	$ 89,000	0.1496
3	$675,000	$115,000	0.1704

Next, create a ratio for comparing the net operating income of one property with another. Divide the net operating income by the selling price. Dividing an expected net operating income of $102,000 by the selling price of $625,000 provides the ratio of 0.1632. Properties with higher ratios are producing more net operating income compared to the selling price. Making sure that you have an apples-to-apples comparison is important. The sources of income may be different from property to property, and the expenses will likely be different. It is not important that income and expenses come from the same source; what is important is that all the correct ones are included. One rental property might have tennis and basketball courts that require maintenance but do not provide direct income. The expense of maintaining them should be included even though another potential property does not have these amenities. If a different property receives income from a laundry facility, include the income. The net operating income method accounts for all the variables and produces a direct and straightforward comparison.

MORE DUE DILIGENCE

Comparisons of recent sales and market trends are also important to compare. Because gaining from appreciation is an investment goal, you would not want to mistakenly invest in a location with a below-average or negative appreciation trend.

Engineering reports need to provide a thorough and accurate understanding of the structure's physical condition. Each property may have unique engineering requirements, but at a minimum the following chart shows what need inspections:

NEED INSPECTION

- Age of the structure.
- Condition of the roof, include inspection for leaks, soundness, and any previous roofs still existing underneath the existing roof.
- Age and condition of appliances, furnaces, and hot water heaters.
- History of any code violations and current state of compliance.
- Wall, ceiling, and substructure insulation (check for asbestos and formaldehyde).
- Windows and doors operate correctly and are in good repair.
- Crumbling and cracking foundation.
- Settling of the foundation or shifting of the structure.
- Signs of moisture leakage or mold in the basement or elsewhere.
- Electrical is in repair and up to code; ample electrical is available for any planned remodeling.
- Plumbing is in repair and up to code; rainwater drains away from the structure.
- Condition of septic or sewer.
- Condition of any chimneys or duct work.
- Inspect any damage to determine what caused it and if permanent repairs have been made.
- Unique requirements of the property.

Environmental inspections require you to check at least the following:

- Use of asbestos.
- Lead paints.
- Underground tanks, including abandoned tanks.
- Wetlands, both part of the property and adjacent.
- Soil sampling.
- Current and future zoning compliance and any pre-existing variances.

Documents and financial information you will want available for review and calculations:

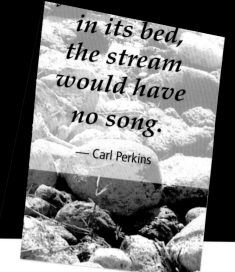

in its bed, the stream would have no song.

— Carl Perkins

- Monthly profit and loss statements going back a year or more.
- No less than three years of balance sheets.
- Copies of current loan documents, mortgages, trusts, and title.
- No less than three years of tax returns.
- History of rent payments.
- History of vacancy rates.
- Records of all security and other deposits, including verification of escrow or other accounts.
- Current leases, including addendums and riders.
- Three or more years of property tax statements.
- Current insurance policy including all addendums, riders, and disclosures.
- Any pending or past litigation history.
- All service contracts — landscaping, swimming pools, cable TV, property management, and alarm systems.
- Maintenance and repair agreements, records, and invoices.
- Two or more years of utility statements — water, electric, gas, sewer, and waste removal.
- Inspection reports for fire systems or other pertinent equipment.
- Copies of any current and prior appraisals, surveys, and legal descriptions.
- Any current or prior engineering and environmental reports.
- Employment information for management, employees, and union contracts.
- Details on anything unique about the property.

Other issues you will want information about:

- The type and life style of existing and future tenants.

- Information about the local economy, including unemployment rate, average incomes, conditions of neighborhood businesses, and roads.

- Seller's motivation for exiting the property.

As these documents, inspections, and reports become available, go through them with a fine-tooth comb. Have an attorney review existing contracts and legal papers. An accountant needs to review the books. The seller is obligated to disclose known deficiencies, but that does not relieve you of the responsibility to perform due diligence before closing the deal. The weightiness of this task varies greatly depending on the property being purchased. Due diligence for a duplex is not much more than what a first-time home buyer might face. On the other hand, due diligence for a 1,000-unit apartment complex will be more difficult and time consuming. The long list of tasks assuring everything happens implies a team effort is required. Roles of the team members you may want to put together prior to a 1031 exchange will be discussed in a later chapter.

SUMMARY

This chapter covers 1031 exchanges in more detail, beginning with the IRS guidelines that create a safe harbor for the exchange when carefully followed. Professional qualified intermediaries remain up to date on changes and are familiar with potential pitfalls and resolutions to most complications that might occur in a 1031 exchange.

Like-kind properties are broad in definition, allowing almost any real estate holding to be exchanged for another real estate holding. Disqualification of properties is mostly limited to properties outside of the United States and those held as inventory for immediate sale.

A 1031 exchange example illustrates the ability to leverage a small holding into a much better holding, while simultaneously relocating to a better section of town. The result is better cash flow and improved profits based on an increased income and increased depreciation to shield the income. This is accomplished with other people's money, but you keep the wealth from the income and the appreciation of the property.

5

THE 1031 PROCESS
STEP-BY-STEP

Every 1031 exchange is unique due to financial considerations, properties involved, the investor's goals, and many other factors. Besides each exchange transaction being distinctive, there are different types of exchanges. The deferred, delayed, or Starker exchange is the most prevalent and is discussed here. Other common types of 1031 exchanges include reverse exchanges, construction exchanges, multi-party exchanges, and tenant-in-common (TIC) exchanges, which are discussed in the next chapter.

BASIC RULES TO A FULLY TAX-DEFERRED 1031 EXCHANGE

These are the rules that must be met to qualify for a fully tax-deferred 1031 exchange. Rules one through five must be met for any 1031 exchange to qualify for tax-favorable treatment. Meeting these rules qualifies a 1031 exchange to IRS requirements. One through five are the minimum when a partial exchange is desired and boot will be taken as part of the exchange.

Rules six through eight are not IRS requirements but must be complied with to defer all the capital gain and depreciation taxes. Investors not wishing to defer taxes fully do not have to comply with rules six through eight but should clearly understand the tax consequences before entering into an exchange.

1. Properties qualifying for an exchange must be for business use or investment ("productive use," as phrased by the IRS).

2. Property must be of like-kind (which is generously interpreted by the IRS).

3. A qualified intermediary is required.

4. The investor cannot have constructive receipt of sale proceeds at any time.

5. The 45-day identification period and 180-day closing requirements must be met.

6. Price of the replacement property must be equal to or greater than the relinquished property.

7. The amount of mortgage on the replacement property must equal or exceed that on the relinquished property.

8. All the funds from the sale must be reinvested in the replacement property.

THE GENERIC PROCESS

There are four primary steps to completing a deferred exchange. Each exchange will go through this process. However, the tasks within each step may vary to accommodate the "exchanger's" (real estate investor's) needs.

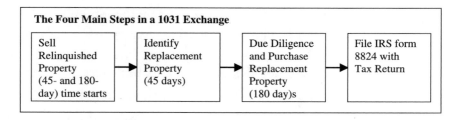

The Four Main Steps in a 1031 Exchange

Sell Relinquished Property (45- and 180-day) time starts	Identify Replacement Property (45 days)	Due Diligence and Purchase Replacement Property (180 day)s	File IRS form 8824 with Tax Return

A formal partnership and a single individual often take different steps when preparing to sell the relinquished property. A partnership may need to take complex legal steps if one partner wants to exchange a partial interest in a property and dissolve the partnership. A partnership can own property and conduct a 1031 exchange in the name of the partnership. However, the partnership may not be exchanged itself. The IRS will likely interpret the exchange of one partner's share of the real estate as being the exchange of the partnership. The IRS has ruled against this practice, and it is imperative that anyone considering this type of exchange obtain knowledgeable legal and tax advice. An individual with full ownership of the property to be relinquished does not face this obstacle.

Someone in a different situation may have a vacation home that they wish to exchange. They may need to re-characterize it for business or investment use by renting it out for a year or more to establish the business use.

Divorces are another common circumstance that can create a slightly different need in the 1031 exchange process. Clarifying proportionate ownership may be needed following a divorce if both spouses remain partial owners. Name changes following a divorce could require property title changes prior to an exchange. In most, if not all, situations the necessary accommodations must be made prior to the exchange occurring. It is wise to obtain competent advice from an experienced professional before entering an exchange if there are extenuating circumstances.

1031 EXCHANGE PROCESS

Step One — Sale Transaction

1. Review the 1031 exchange requirements, including any regulation changes.

2. Consult with your real estate and legal advisors about the planned transaction.

3. Negotiate and complete the purchase and sale agreement for the relinquished property as you would for any real estate transaction. Enter a clause in the agreement to the effect of:

1031 EXCHANGE PROCESS

"A material part of this transaction is the successful completion of an IRS Code Section 1031 deferred exchange. 'Name of buyer' agrees to cooperate with 'John Doe' in signing those documents necessary to complete the exchange, provided that 'Buyer' shall incur no additional costs or liabilities in excess of those which would have occurred had this been an outright 'purchase/sale' and not an exchange."

4. Have your real estate attorney review all pertinent documentation before it is signed.

5. Enter into a 1031 exchange agreement with your chosen qualified exchange intermediary.

6. Notify your qualified intermediary if any of these conditions apply:

  a. You intend to withdraw cash from your exchange transaction before or after you complete the transaction.

  b. You intend to request a refund of the earnest money deposit previously deposited as non-exchange funds.

  c. You intend to use a seller carry-back note (seller financing) in the transaction.

  d. Personal property will be included in the 1031 exchange.

  e. You intend to remodel or construct new improvements on the replacement property and need to consider a construction exchange.

  f. You become aware of any discrepancy in the 1031 exchange documentation, property titles, or other relative documents.

7. You or your real estate agent will forward the sales agreement to the closing agent. Notify the closing agent that this is a 1031 exchange and provide the name of your qualified intermediary.

8. Your qualified intermediary should provide you with a form requesting the information they need before contacting the closing agent.

9. The qualified intermediary notifies the buyer that you have assigned the contract to them for execution.

10. The qualified intermediary prepares all 1031 forms and forwards them to the closing agent. Once the closing agent receives the forms, you will be contacted to sign them. The closing agent should provide copies of all the documents.

11. When the sale is complete, the funds from the sale are deposited with your qualified intermediary.

1031 EXCHANGE PROCESS

12. The closing begins the 45-day period to identify replacement property. Of course, you will have already begun this process. The 180-day time period begins at the same time.

Step 2 — Identifying Replacement Property

1. You have 45 days to identify and report your potential replacement properties. Most qualified intermediaries provide a form requesting the specific information needed to correctly identify the properties. Any one of these three methods can be used to identify replacement property:

   a. Any three properties of your choosing.

   b. The 200 percent rule (identify as many as desired up to 200 percent of relinquished property).

   c. The 95 percent rule (unlimited number of properties, but you must purchase 95 percent of the value identified).

2. Written and signed notification of the specific properties identified must be given to your qualified intermediary. This is a critical requirement for complying with the IRS requirements.

3. Give careful consideration to the time that the seller is notified that a 1031 exchange is involved. Notification is required but should not occur prior to completing negotiations on the sale; otherwise, the seller gains an upper hand in the negotiation if they know you are under time constraints and are within the 45-day period. An addendum about the 1031 exchange should be added to the purchase/sale contract when negotiations are complete.

4. Perform due diligence of the potential properties and make a purchase decision.

Step 3 — The Purchase

1. Enter into the purchase/sale agreement.

2. Add an addendum notifying the seller that this is a 1031 exchange. The language should include:

   " 'Name of seller' herein acknowledges that it is the intention of 'name of buyer' to complete an IRS section 1031 tax-deferred exchange and that the Buyer's rights and obligations under this agreement may be assigned to 'name of qualified intermediary' for the purpose of completing such exchange. Seller agrees to cooperate with the Buyer and/or its assignees in a manner necessary to complete said exchange at no additional cost or liability to the seller."

1031 EXCHANGE PROCESS

3. Have your real estate attorney review all pertinent documents before signing them.

4. Notify your qualified intermediary with contact information for the closing agent and provide any instructions needed for your qualified intermediary to release the purchase funds from the escrow account.

5. The qualified intermediary notifies the seller that you have assigned the contract to them for execution.

6. The qualified intermediary prepares all 1031 forms and arranges for the escrow funds to be forwarded to the closing agent to complete the purchase. Once the closing agent receives the forms, you will be contacted to sign them. The closing agent should provide copies of all the documents.

7. The 1031 exchange is complete.

8. You will receive any boot due from the exchange if it was not a fully tax-deferred exchange.

Step 4 — Filing your Income Return

1. Prepare and file IRS form 8824 with your federal tax return. File any state-required tax forms.

2. The qualified intermediary will provide a 1099 form to you and the IRS for any interest your sales proceeds earned in escrow.

The overall process is relatively simple. However, the tax consequences that result if an IRS requirement is not met underscore the importance of involving experienced professionals in the process.

HOW THE MONEY FLOWS IN A 1031 EXCHANGE

In the past, the title or deed for the properties was transferred through the qualified intermediary. Several problems arose when the qualified intermediary temporarily became responsible for the property immediately before a sale took place. Any late disclosures occurring during escrow were potentially the responsibility of the temporary owner, such as finding contaminated groundwater just before closing. Additional costs were also incurred for the multiple title changes that no one benefited from and the necessity for the intermediary to carry extra insurance against unknown problems arising. A ruling by the IRS made it clear that direct titling between buyers and sellers is acceptable. Although it is not a requirement, almost all 1031 exchanges now involve direct deeding between buyers and sellers.

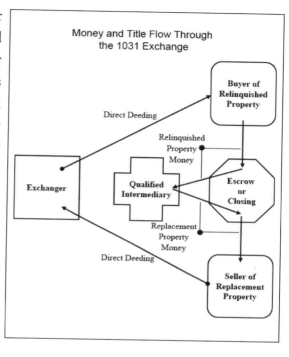

On the other hand, the IRS is very clear about the exchanger not gaining constructive receipt of the money used in the exchange. When escrow closes on the relinquished property, the funds are remitted to the qualified intermediary. The intermediary places them in a secure interest-bearing account until the money is sent to escrow to purchase the replacement property.

The amount of time the money remains in the secure interest-bearing account will vary depending on how long it takes to complete the purchase of the replacement property. However, hundreds of thousands or even millions of dollars can earn substantial interest during this time. The interest can be handled in different ways. Many intermediaries give the exchanger the option of using the interest to pay the intermediary's fee for conducting the exchange. The exchanger also has the option of paying the intermediary's fee from another source and either using the interest toward the replacement purchase or receiving the interest after the exchange is complete.

A set of quick calculations will determine which the better option for the exchanger is. A sale for $500,000 deposited for three months at 5 percent compounding monthly will earn $6,276 of interest. However, $100,000 deposited for only two months at 5 percent will only earn $835. Specific factors in your exchange will determine the intermediary's fees, but it will take a complicated exchange for the fees to approach $6,000. Take a few minutes to determine how the interest earned from the sales proceeds is best used.

CASE STUDY #4: 1031 EXCHANGES
FROM 1031 EXCHANGE ADVANTAGE, INC.

http://www.1031exchangeadvantage.com
Info@1031exchangeadvantage.com

West Coast:
681 Encinitas Blvd. Suite 403
Encinitas, CA 92024

East Coast:
190 Main Street Suite 403
Hackensack, NJ 07601

David P. Greenberger, Esq., is president of 1031 Exchange Advantage Inc., a full service, qualified exchange accommodator. Greenberger is president of the east and west coast operations. Twenty successful years as a real estate attorney gave way to inspiration and the realization that 1031 Exchange Advantage Inc. is the best way to serve his clients' real estate and tax needs.

Greenberger has written articles for real estate magazines and appeared as an expert on the television program Real Estate Roundtable. Greenberger is a frequent key speaker at 1031 seminars across the Untied States. In addition, 1031 Exchange Advantage Inc. provides educational seminars with a professional focus for real estate attorneys and real estate agents.

CASE STUDY #4: 1031 EXCHANGES FROM 1031 EXCHANGE ADVANTAGE, INC.

Greenberger and the staff at 1031 Exchange Advantage enjoy working closely with all clients but take a special pleasure introducing first-time exchangers to the process and strive to make the experience stress-free. Clients confirm individual tax savings of more than $50,000 on a single exchange. Repeat clients have returned to conduct more than ten individual 1031 exchanges.

Greenberger is so confident that people will become repeat clients that he has a simple guarantee: "Tax Free or No Fee." By that, he means that if you go through the steps for an exchange and conclude the deal is not right, there will be no exchange fee unless the deal closes with taxes deferred.

1031 Exchange Advantage Inc. accommodates all types of exchanges and thrives on creative solutions. Exchanges covered include:

- The Residence Retirement Exchange
- The Investment Retirement Exchange
- The Successful Business Exchange
- The Travel the World Exchange
- The Cross Country Exchange
- The Wedding Exchange
- The Cash Flow Exchange
- The Partial Owner Exchange
- The Partnership Interest Exchange
- The Reverse Exchange
- The Build-to-Suit Exchange
- The Home Office Exchange
- The Tenants-in-Common Exchange
- The Triple Net Lease Exchange
- The Oil and Gas Mineral Rights Exchange

An exclusive 1031 Exchange Advantage Inc. educational tool is the exchange roadmap. The roadmap includes a checklist for investors to plan and organize each transaction. By creating the roadmap, the company made it easy to accomplish the goal of educating U.S. investors about the tremendous tax-deferral opportunities and exchange offers.

Greenberger makes this statement about the roadmap:

"We designed the roadmap to help trigger creative investment scenarios that can enhance the earning power of real estate investments. The guide shows how to eliminate unnecessary complication to ensure a smooth and profitable exchange transaction."

CASE STUDY #4: 1031 EXCHANGES
FROM 1031 EXCHANGE ADVANTAGE, INC.

Summary of Roadmap Steps for Exchanging Property and Creating Wealth

1. Understand the concept of what you are trying to accomplish to fit the rules to your facts.

2. Plan and get good advice BEFORE you exchange.

3. Any sale can be turned into an exchange in minutes with the right QI prior to closing the sale — even if the buyer does not cooperate.

4. Increasingly agents, attorneys, accountants, and the like are being sued and being held accountable for not advising clients of the possibility of an exchange and its value. Make sure your professional understands 1031 exchange options.

5. Choosing the right Qualified Intermediary (required by the IRS to complete a 1031 exchange) is the best choice one can make.

6. Often people confuse section 121 and its requirements with section 1031. They are apples and oranges. But you can now use both on the same property if the property qualifies.

7. Like-kind real estate means any kind of real estate can be traded for any other kind of real estate — not just condo for condo or vacant land for vacant land, as once was required.

In addition to the west coast headquarters in Encinitas, California and east coast headquarters in Hackensack, New Jersey, 1031 Exchange Advantage Inc. offers services from branch offices in:

- Delray Beach, Florida
- Greenbelt, Maryland
- Clearfield, Pennsylvania
- Garden City, New York
- Farmingdale, New York

INVESTOR'S ROLE

The real estate investor has several roles in the 1031 exchange and may be called by several names: the real estate agent's client, the qualified intermediary's client, or the client of another service provider. The investor may also be called the taxpayer or exchanger. All these terms are commonly used regarding the real estate investor's role in a 1031 exchange.

The investor is the decision-maker for the team, is at the center of the transaction, and is by far the person with the biggest financial interest and risk. The investor should have an overall plan, not just for the 1031 exchange but a lifetime wealth-building plan. Any particular exchange should be another step down the road to wealth.

Advisors should be well informed of the investor's plan and should have their memories refreshed when discussing the major step of exchanging property. The investor should consider and discuss with advisors any extenuating circumstances that may need to be corrected before entering into an exchange. The reasons for an exchange should be clear before the decision is made. Is the investor:

- Stepping up the value of a particular investment?

- Entering into a more promising business opportunity?

- Seeking to increase income?

- Diversifying?

- Creating an income stream?

- Liquidating?

- Attempting to accomplish multiple goals concurrently?

The list of reasons for exchanging properties can go on, but whatever the objective, it should be clear to the investor and the advisors. Once the objective is established, a plan specific to the 1031 exchange can be created. Research is performed to determine if the exchange involves an acceptable level of risk. Although a professionally conducted exchange should contain little risk of failure, the consequences of a failed exchange should be considered. Each known risk should be assessed and have a mitigation plan put into place. This may all sound as if risk of a failed exchange is high, but that is not the case. The worst outcome of a failed exchange is that the investor will pay the taxes that would be owed in a normal sale of the property. If that level of risk is acceptable, there is little to fear from a failed exchange. Still, some planning can minimize any risk and is worth the effort when selling a major investment or business property.

Once advisors have been consulted and a plan is put into place, the investor begins with step one of the process and leads the team through the process, remembering to let the professionals take responsibility for their roles.

TEAM MEMBERS' ROLES

A 1031 exchange must coordinate the efforts of several professionals. The exchange timing requirements, assignment of a qualified intermediary to conduct the transactions, safekeeping of large amounts of money not directly controlled by the owner, and other details make teamwork important. Fortunately, using people experienced with 1031 exchanges means they will understand the need for teamwork and will understand their roles and the roles of others.

REAL ESTATE AGENT OR BROKER

A key role of the real estate agent or broker is early recognition that a 1031 exchange can benefit a client. The agent may need to provide the client with preliminary education and put the client in contact with a qualified intermediary willing to provide the detailed information enabling the client (exchanger) to make a final decision. While the agent cannot offer direct legal, tax, or accounting advice, questions can be asked and issues discussed that help the client think through the decision of how to best benefit from a 1031 exchange.

Once the decision to exchange is made and a buyer for the property has been found, the agent needs to know the requirements regarding disclosing to the buyer that a 1031 exchange will be used. The agent will want to explain that the seller will be assigning the sales contract to a qualified intermediary. The selling agent needs to be sure the buyer's agent is well versed in 1031 exchanges and can provide any needed education the buyer needs if they have concerns.

Timing the notification of the seller of the replacement property that a 1031 exchange will be used is very important. A disclosure too early in the process can jeopardize the buyer's negotiation position. The seller will become aware that the property is one of three the buyer has identified if the 45-day identification period has passed. Keep in mind that negotiations may begin before the property is formally identified (less than 45 days into the exchange). This enhances the buyer's negotiating position. The seller assumes a much stronger position in negotiating the final price, terms, and conditions of the sale once notified it is a 1031 exchange. The seller becomes aware that the buyer is under time constraints and will likely use this to their advantage. The real estate agent's role is to protect their client's position. It is advisable to structure the sales agreement to allow an addendum after the sales agreement has been completed.

Some standard real estate purchase/sale contracts have a clause specifically requiring the seller's permission before the buyer can assign the contract to a third party, as is the case with a qualified intermediary. The real estate agent should ensure this clause is removed.

FINANCIAL ADVISOR

The investor should use a tax advisor/accountant experienced in exchanges. If the current one is not, it would be wise to find one that is before entering the exchange. The financial advisor plays a vital role that goes beyond watching out for the tax consequences to the client. The 1031 capable financial advisor needs to be able to advise the client on the desirability of the exchange financially and on a personal goal level.

The accountant or tax advisor should be watching out for the client's overall financial wellbeing. Perhaps the investor has become too heavily invested in real estate and at this point in their life needs to consider a more diverse portfolio. The advice might be to take some boot in the form of cash or securities that will be taxed but can be reinvested elsewhere. Other considerations to discuss with the client:

- Dividing a single property into multiple properties for inheritance reasons.

- An installment sale (seller carry-back note) inside the exchange if the investor needs more liquidity.

- How to extract the investor from a partnership arrangement that does not qualify for a 1031 exchange (this requires legal advice also).

- Tenant-in-common (TIC) arrangements that often provide a more dependable income but less appreciation.

- The reverse of the TIC when small residential investments tend to appreciate quickly but often provide less income.

- The effect that carrying the depreciated basis forward into the replacement property will have on future cash flow.

- Proper IRS documentation required when deferring both the capital gains and depreciation recapture taxes. A future sale will require accounting for the deferral.

- Risks associated with overleveraging a property.

- Suggesting a client use a 1031 exchange to convert non-cash-flow raw land into a cash-producing property.

- Pointing out that raw land neither produces cash nor is depreciable; the client will gain two benefits.

- The possibility of re-characterizing an investment property into a personal residence and taking the $250,000 exclusion ($500,000 for qualified married couples) when the proper requirements are met.

A key role your financial advisor should perform is structuring the loans or mortgage used to purchase the replacement property.

A tax accountant can fill the added role of preparing the exchanger's form 8824 that will be submitted with the exchanger's federal tax return.

A QUALIFIED INTERMEDIARY

The IRS uses the word "qualified," although no individual or organization is qualified by the IRS or any other government agency. A qualified person or organization is simply one that the IRS has not deemed to be disqualified. IRS code prohibits certain representatives or advisors of the taxpayer from being qualified. Accountants, attorneys, and realtors who have served taxpayers in their professional capacities within the previous two years are disqualified from serving as a qualified intermediary in an exchange.

Qualified intermediaries may have several different but similar titles; they can also be known as facilitators or accommodators, but all play the same basic function in a 1031 exchange. Many became experts in the exchange process because they were already professional tax attorneys, financial advisors, or tax experts. Their role in the process prevents them from being direct advisors to the exchanger. They can provide education and explain the process. However, ultimately the exchanger must rely on his or her own knowledge and outside advisors regarding how the exchange rules affect their specific transaction.

The primary tasks of the intermediary:

- Acquire the relinquished property from the buyer.
- Transfer the relinquished property.
- Hold the sale proceeds to prevent the exchanger from constructive receipt.
- Acquire the replacement property from the seller.
- Transfer the replacement property to the exchanger.
- Submit a 1099 form to the exchanger and IRS for any interest earned on the sales proceeds.

All of this can be done without the intermediary acquiring title to the property.

A qualified intermediary typically provides a minimum of three different documents: the exchange agreement, an assignment, and a notice to the other party. The exchange agreement is the contract between the exchanger and the intermediary, setting the rules, conditions, and requirements of the exchange. The assignment of the sales contract to the qualified intermediary must also be in place. This is because, theoretically, the intermediary steps into the client's shoes and sells the property. The third document the intermediary provides is a notice to the other party (the buyer of relinquished property and the seller of replacement property) advising that the transaction is a 1031 exchange. The purpose of notification to the other party is to prove that the exchange was in place at the closing.

The Exchange Agreement usually provides for:

- An assignment to the intermediary of the exchanger's contract to buy and sell real estate.

- A contract for the intermediary to receive the proceeds due to the seller at closing.

- A statement that direct deeding is used.

- Laying out the requirements of the IRS code in which the taxpayer can have no rights to the funds being held by the intermediary until the exchange is completed or the exchange terminates without being completed.

- Details of the 45-day and 180-day rules.

- An assignment of the contract to purchase replacement property to the intermediary.

- A closing where the intermediary uses the exchange funds and direct deeding to acquire the replacement property for the seller.

There are hundreds of qualified intermediaries, many of them competitively priced. Some are members of the Federation of Exchange

Accommodators (FEA), a national trade association providing educational resources, ethical guidelines, and other resources to members. Consider more than only the fee schedule of a professional qualified intermediary. They should be bonded and insured to a level adequate to protect your sale proceeds. Additionally, they need to have a solid structure for conducting the transaction and well-established procedures that are consistently followed.

Other services you should expect of a professional qualified intermediary:

- Full disclosure of all financial transactions for the exchangers records.

- Expedited services if the 180-day period is threatening a deal close to closing.

- A process for reviewing documents for both potential problems and technical errors.

The qualified intermediary plays a crucial role in the exchange but should not be substituted for good financial and legal advice. The role of the intermediary is to safeguard the transaction in several ways, not the least of which is to hold the sales proceeds until you are ready for the intermediary to close on the purchase of your replacement property. Experience, attention to technical details, and financial responsibility are critical to the success of your 1031 exchange.

LEGAL COUNSEL

An attorney may play a major role or a minor role in a 1031 exchange, depending on the exchanger's preferences and needs. In a complex exchange, the exchanger might elect to have an attorney highly experienced in real estate and exchanges take a leading role. In conjunction with a financial advisor, the two may make recommendations on everything from what basic strategy the exchanger should take to putting the specific exchange structure together.

More often, the role of the attorney is to review real estate and exchange contracts for risk to the exchanger and for omissions and to counsel the exchanger on relevant legal issues. An attorney may be the first to spot an unrecognized reason to conduct an exchange when it presents the opportunity to get a client out of a legally troublesome property without incurring taxes. The exchanger may decide to have an attorney present to review closing documents for relinquished property, replacement property, or both.

The investor should make sure their attorney has experience doing 1031 exchanges or should find one that does, preferably in the state the relinquished and replacement properties are located.

HOW RELATED PEOPLE AFFECT A 1031 EXCHANGE

Related people are different from disqualified people. The distinction needs to be clear. Disqualified people cannot act as your intermediary. However, you can conduct a 1031 exchange with related people. A two-year holding period applies to exchanges between related people. This is the only holding time period specifically given by the IRS for investment property (a one-year holding period exits for business property). The related person that purchases the property must retain ownership for a minimum of two years. Failure to do so will trigger capital gains and depreciation recapture tax for the related party that relinquished the property.

EXHIBIT 5.1 – EXCERPT FROM INTERNAL REVENUE CODE

(f) Special rules for exchanges between related persons

(1) In general

If—

    (A) a taxpayer exchanges property with a related person,

    (B) there is nonrecognition of gain or loss to the taxpayer under this section with respect to the exchange of such property (determined without regard to this subsection), and

EXHIBIT 5.1 – EXCERPT FROM INTERNAL REVENUE CODE

(C) before the date 2 years after the date of the last transfer which was part of such exchange—

   (i) the related person disposes of such property, or

   (ii) the taxpayer disposes of the property received in the exchange from the related person which was of like kind to the property transferred by the taxpayer, there shall be no nonrecognition of gain or loss under this section to the taxpayer with respect to such exchange; except that any gain or loss recognized by the taxpayer by reason of this subsection shall be taken into account as of the date on which the disposition referred to in subparagraph (C) occurs.

(2) Certain dispositions not taken into account

For purposes of paragraph (1)(C), there shall not be taken into account any disposition—

(A) after the earlier of the death of the taxpayer or the death of the related person,

(B) in a compulsory or involuntary conversion (within the meaning of section 1033) if the exchange occurred before the threat or imminence of such conversion, or

(C) with respect to which it is established to the satisfaction of the Secretary that neither the exchange nor such disposition had as one of its principal purposes the avoidance of Federal income tax.

(3) Related person

For purposes of this subsection, the term "related person" means any person bearing a relationship to the taxpayer described in section 267 (b) or 707 (b)(1).

(4) Treatment of certain transactions

This section shall not apply to any exchange which is part of a transaction (or series of transactions) structured to avoid the purposes of this subsection.

   (B) in a compulsory or involuntary conversion (within the meaning of section 1033) if the exchange occurred before the threat or imminence of such conversion, or

   (C) with respect to which it is established to the satisfaction of the Secretary that neither the exchange nor such disposition had as one of its principal purposes the avoidance of Federal income tax.

(3) Related person

  For purposes of this subsection, the term "related person" means any person

EXHIBIT 5.1 – EXCERPT FROM INTERNAL REVENUE CODE

bearing a relationship to the taxpayer described in section 267 (b) or 707 (b)(1).

(4) Treatment of certain transactions

This section shall not apply to any exchange which is part of a transaction (or series of transactions) structured to avoid the purposes of this subsection.

This assumes that a third (unrelated) party is part of the replacement property transaction. If both the relinquished property and replacement property involve related parties, the two-year holding period applies to both. Exchanges with related parties are complex, and the complexity increases dramatically if boot or cash is involved.

It is especially important to obtain legal and tax advice from an experienced attorney if an exchange is being considered between related parties. The definition of related parties goes well beyond family members. Several business entities and relationships are involved.

Related parties under the rules are:

- Members of a family, including brothers, sisters, half-brothers, half-sisters, spouses, ancestors (parents, grandparents, etc.), and lineal descendants (children, grandchildren).

- An individual and a corporation of which the individual owns, directly or indirectly, more than 50 percent in value of the outstanding stock of the corporation.

- Two corporations that are members of the same controlled group as defined in §1563(a), except that "more than 50 percent" is substituted for "at least 80 percent" in that definition.

- A trust fiduciary and a corporation when the trust or the grantor of the trust owns, directly or indirectly, more than 50 percent in value of the outstanding stock of the corporation.

- A grantor and fiduciary, and the fiduciary and beneficiary, of any trust.

- Fiduciaries of two different trusts, and the fiduciary and beneficiary of two different trusts, if the same person is the grantor of both trusts.

- A tax-exempt educational or charitable organization and a person who, directly or indirectly, controls such an organization or a member of that person's family.

- A corporation and a partnership if the same person owns more than 50 percent in value of the outstanding stock of the corporation and more than 50 percent of the capital interest, or profits interest, in the partnership.

- Two S corporations if the same person owns more than 50 percent in value of the outstanding stock of each corporation.

- Two corporations, one of which is an S corporation, if the same person owns more than 50 percent in value of the outstanding stock of each corporation.

- An executor of an estate and a beneficiary of such estate, except in the case of a sale or exchange in satisfaction of a pecuniary bequest.

- Two partnerships if the same person owns directly, or indirectly, more than 50 percent of the capital interests or profits in both partnerships.

- A person and a partnership when the person owns, directly or indirectly, more than 50 percent of the capital interest or profits interest in the partnership.

The basic concept is to prevent individuals or businesses from establishing business relationships specifically for the intention of exchanging a property to themselves as owner of another business entity. If this can be accomplished, it is possible for the business entity to sell the property quickly and not owe any capital gains or depreciation recapture tax. A person owning the business that first relinquishes the property in an exchange and then immediately sells it for little or no tax through another business can indirectly accomplish a cash sale without tax consequence.

SUMMARY

This chapter brings together the tasks and mechanics to conduct a time-deferred 1031 exchange, the most commonly used exchange for deferring capital gains and depreciation recapture taxes. A well-developed plan makes what at first appears to be a complex process into a routine process performed by an experienced and knowledgeable team.

Put the team in place, share the details of your plan with them, and avail yourself of their advice before formally beginning the exchange process. An early step in the plan should be an analysis of the property you intend to sell, to ensure no surprises once it enters the exchange process. Legal ownership described on the title is of particular concern. Make sure the property title is not hampered by an unwanted partnership, name change, divorce decree, or other event that may have happened years ago and become temporarily forgotten.

Each team member has a key role and functions to perform in the exchange process. Experienced and knowledgeable team members should understand each other's roles. This works to your advantage in several ways. The team ensures adherence to timing requirements, proper sale/purchase contract language, accurate documentation preparation, accurate instructions to escrow, and strategic timing of the 1031 exchange notification to the seller of your replacement property. With planning and a solid team, the 1031 exchange should be a smooth process, moving you into ownership of a better real estate property. Compared with a traditional taxed sale, the tax-deferred 1031 exchange entitles you to greater wealth accumulation.

6

USEFUL VARIATIONS OF 1031 EXCHANGES

Although the time-delayed 1031 exchange is most frequently used, there are other types of exchanges that may better suit your needs and strategy. Besides location, location, location being critical to real estate purchases, the timing of a property's acquisition can be crucial as well. Accumulated wealth puts you in the position to quickly purchase a property when the time is right. The reverse 1031 exchange can be very beneficial to making a time-sensitive purchase.

Under other circumstances, you may want to use the sales proceeds from your relinquished property to remodel or renovate the new property. A construction 1031 exchange can be the answer to using tax-deferred funds to prepare the new property for your specific needs.

In 2002, the IRS issued guidelines for exchanging tenant-in-common real estate properties. This in turn enabled exchangers to obtain triple net leases, a desirable investment for some people. These often have low or no management requirements for the owner. They are considered very secure investments in high-end real estate that most investors could not afford to own independently. Purchasing partial ownership became possible with the recent IRS guidelines. Although anyone can make this investment, it is often suitable to those approaching or entering retirement who no longer want to actively manage property.

THE REVERSE EXCHANGE

The reverse exchange offers the same tax-deferral benefits as a delayed exchange, the major difference being that the replacement property is purchased before the relinquished property is sold. Several reasons create a need to purchase the replacement property first. One occurs when a highly desired property becomes available and is expected to sell before you can sell the relinquished property.

Be it good fortune or careful planning, you may find your replacement property ready to close in escrow before the relinquished property. The reverse exchange becomes an option if the seller will not delay the closing.

An exchanger concerned that a replacement property will be difficult to locate and close on within the allotted 180 days may elect to use a reverse exchange. Both the purchase and sale transactions must be completed within 180 days, but an exchanger may have more confidence about selling the relinquished property than finding a replacement property.

A reverse exchange is also appropriate when a well-planned exchange on your behalf begins to fall apart because the buyer of the relinquished property unexpectedly cannot complete the deal. Escrow does not close, and the 180-day clock does not begin. If there is a strong desire to acquire the replacement property, a reverse exchange can be entered into while looking for another buyer for the relinquished property.

Again, we see that unique circumstances play a role in many 1031 exchanges. Whatever the reasons, the reverse exchange may be the best way to complete a real estate deal and still defer the taxes.

The relinquished property held by the intermediary is often referred to as the "parked" property. What most in the business call reverse exchanges, the IRS refers to as "parking transactions."

EXHIBIT 6.1 EXCERPT FROM IRS BULLETIN 2004-33

Rev. Proc. 2000-37 addresses "parking" transactions. See sections 2.05 and 2.06 of Rev. Proc. 2000-37. Parking transactions typically are designed to "park" the desired replacement property with an accommodation party until such time as the taxpayer arranges for the transfer of the relinquished property to the ultimate transferee in a simultaneous or deferred exchange. Once such a transfer is arranged, the taxpayer transfers the relinquished property to the accommodation party in exchange for the replacement property, and the accommodation party transfers the relinquished property to the ultimate transferee. In other situations, an accommodation party may acquire the desired replacement property on behalf of the taxpayer and immediately exchange that property with the taxpayer for the relinquished property, thereafter holding the relinquished property until the taxpayer arranges for a transfer of the property to the ultimate transferee. Rev. Proc. 2000-37 provides procedures for qualifying parking transactions as like-kind exchanges in situations in which the taxpayer has a genuine intent to accomplish a like-kind exchange at the time that the taxpayer arranges for the acquisition of the replacement property and actually accomplishes the exchange within a short time thereafter.

In September of 2000, the IRS released Revenue Procedure 2000-37, which provided safe harbor guidelines for the reverse exchange. In August of 2004, that procedure was modified by IRS Bulletin 2004-33. Key provisions are:

- A taxpayer (exchanger) may not hold title to both the relinquished property and replacement property at the same time. Title to either the replacement or relinquished property can be moved to the intermediary.

- The taxpayer enters into an exchange agreement with a qualified intermediary that states that the taxpayer intends to meet the requirements of Section 1031 and Revenue Procedure 2000-37. The agreement needs to be entered into within five days of when the qualified intermediary purchases the replacement property.

- The party holding the parked replacement property must be a qualified intermediary, a limited liability company under the intermediary's control, or another business entity under the intermediary's control.

- There must be proof of intent for the parked property to be part of the exchange.

- Within 45 days of the purchase of the parked property, the taxpayer must complete the identification process by listing the parked property.

- The qualified intermediary must transfer the title to the parked property to the exchanger on or before the 180th day from the date of acquisition.

Keep one aspect in mind about a reverse exchange: If the already purchased replacement property is close in value to the property you will be relinquishing, selling the relinquished property for anything more than the cost of the replacement property can have tax consequences.

The IRS safe harbor guidelines also enable the exchanger to:

- Provide money to the qualified intermediary for acquiring the replacement property.

- Guarantee any loans used to acquire the replacement property.

- Manage the replacement property during the parking period.

- Lease the property from the qualified intermediary.

- Supervise construction and improvements on the replacement property.

A reverse exchange is more complex than a typical deferred exchange. A professional qualified intermediary must accomplish several, more complex tasks. Recall that direct deeding is used in a typical exchange. This is not true for the purchased property in a reverse exchange. The intermediary must take the title to the purchase property until the relinquished property is sold. If not properly handled, additional risk can arise for the exchanger and the intermediary. With property ownership comes responsibility for the property. Issues like environmental problems or liability during remodeling become a concern to the intermediary. and financial stability of the intermediary becomes a concern for the exchanger if the process is not properly structured. The exchanger does not want the problems of someone else's troubled reverse exchange, being handled by the intermediary, to affect their own exchange.

Commonly, professional intermediaries establish a separate limited liability company (or similar business entity) to hold ownership of the property in each reverse exchange. This effectively isolates the ownership of each property from other reverse exchanges and business conducted by the qualified intermediary. Establishing the limited liability company (LLC) requires additional paperwork, applications, registration, and payment of related fees. Besides risk management, this establishes the LLC as the legal owner separate from the exchanger. Separate ownership is a requirement of the IRS guidelines for a reverse exchange.

The qualified intermediary becomes involved in the financing arrangements to acquire the replacement property in a reverse exchange. Some lenders do not understand the reverse exchange well and are reluctant to make loans on this type of arrangement. Knowing the title on the property will transfer from the LLC to the exchanger in a short amount of time adds to the complexity for uninformed lenders. Nonetheless, financing can be arranged and it will need to pass through the LLC to purchase the property.

Of course, multiple title transfers add to the complexity. The LLC must also obtain commercial liability insurance on the property while it holds the title. A lease must be prepared to allow the exchanger to manage the property. Accounting records must be established for the LLC. And when the exchange closes, the LLC must be dissolved, which includes filing tax returns on behalf of the LLC.

The reverse exchange is an important tool for the real estate investor to be familiar with and quite possibly will be used at some time. The complexity and many extra steps add to the fees that professional qualified intermediaries charge.

Other variations to the reverse exchange include transferring the title to the intermediary of the property that will be relinquished. This allows the exchanger to take direct control of the replacement property by having the LLC own the soon-to-be relinquished property. Combining a construction exchange with a reverse exchange is one more variation examined later in this chapter.

The IRS safe harbor guidelines add considerable safety for these transactions. It should be noted that IRS Bulletin 2004-33 also stated an ongoing concern with transactions that combine related people, leaseholds, and construction improvements. No safe harbor exists for this situation, as the IRS continues a study.

EXHIBIT 6.2 EXCERPT FROM IRS BULLETIN 2004-33

The Service and Treasury Department are continuing to study parking transactions, including transactions in which a person related to the taxpayer transfers a leasehold in land to an accommodation party and the accommodation party makes improvements to the land and transfers the leasehold with the improvements to the taxpayer in exchange for other real estate.

WHEN OPPORTUNITY MAKES THE REVERSE EXCHANGE THE RIGHT OPTION

Mr. Fritz owned several commercial properties in a mid-sized city located in the Midwest. He had been the landlord of a well-established equipment rental business for 14 years. Being a seasoned landlord, Mr. Fritz attended local zoning department meetings and stayed well informed about local business trends and developments. He was aware the equipment rental establishment was a mature business in an older section of the city catering to the do-it-yourself type and small local contractors. The customer base was mostly homeowners who were nearing retirement and were less likely to be undertaking the type of renovation projects that the equipment rental business depended on for steady business. Mr. Fritz knew that in the next couple of years the business owner was likely to retire and not renew the lease. He had decided to sell the business before it became necessary to find a new lessee willing to remodel the building and grounds into a business appropriate for the changing neighborhood.

Because he stayed informed about proposed zoning changes, Mr. Fritz was interested in acquiring a commercial property on the other side of town where a new principal road was planned for construction and commercial development was being encouraged. Mr. Fritz was about to conclude his study when an ideal strip mall came onto the market because the owner needed to relocate to another state for health reasons. The owner offered a favorable price and terms to Mr. Fritz if he would close the sale within 45 days. Being an informed real estate owner, Mr. Fritz had been planning to use a 1031 exchange involving the equipment rental business. He also knew his planning was far enough along that he could accomplish the due diligence on the new property within the allotted 45 days. The dilemma was that he had not prepared the current property for sale. He wanted to paint the building, re-stripe the parking lot, and make a few other changes, along with organizing the documents that a prospective buyer would need for their due diligence. Fortunately, Mr. Fritz was knowledgeable about reverse 1031 exchanges and signed a sales agreement to complete the purchase of the replacement property in 45 days if the due diligence was acceptable and the needed financing could be obtained.

Mr. Fritz contacted the qualified intermediary that he had used before and signed a reverse exchange agreement. Mr. Fritz arranged the loan while the intermediary established the LLC that would hold the property until the equipment rental business was sold. A contractor began the painting and other improvements on the property that would be relinquished, while Mr. Fritz consulted with his financial and legal advisors about both transactions. Everything went according to plan, and the replacement business passed the due diligence study. Mr. Fritz instructed his lender to deposit the funds with the LLC, which used them to purchase the strip mall according to the negotiated sales agreement. Mr. Fritz followed all the 1031 exchange requirements, including formal identification of the replacement property.

Ten days after the strip mall purchase was completed, the improvements to the equipment rental business were finished and that property was placed on the real estate market. Mr. Fritz had 170 days remaining to close a sale on the equipment rental business. He was confident he could obtain the full asking price.

CONSTRUCTION EXCHANGE

A construction exchange (also called an improvement exchange or a build-to-suit exchange) allows the exchanger to use proceeds from the relinquished property to purchase the replacement property and construct improvements on it. The benefits of keeping the tax-deferred funds combined with new financing could enable the exchanger to build exactly the facility they need to maximize a business opportunity. The tax deferral may be key in accomplishing a particular goal.

A construction exchange might be conducted if a needed structure does not exist or is not for sale at the location the investor wants and can also be used for a retail establishment requiring a major remodeling before it is suitable for the new business.

Requirements unique to the construction exchange:

- Tax-deferred proceeds used for the construction must be spent within the 180-day window that begins with the sale of the relinquished property.

- The property title will be held by an LLC or other business structure established by the professional qualified intermediary.

- A lease can be established between the LLC and the exchanger if the exchanger intends to supervise the construction project.

- A lender assisting the financing must be informed and possibly educated about a construction exchange.

- The LLC or intermediary will pay the construction bills as instructed by the exchanger.

- Accounting books will be established for the LLC by the intermediary.

Naturally, other required 1031 exchange provisions apply. The replacement property must be identified within 45 days and exchange agreements must be in place. Formal identification of the replacement property is a little more complicated because the improvements either do not exist or the structure will be altered significantly. Careful attention should be used to formally identify the replacement property under construction so that the description substantially describes the final construction. For instance, changing the placement of the main entrance on a corner property can change the street address at final construction. Frequently, building plans are attached to the formal description of the replacement property.

Completing a construction exchange does not necessarily require that all the construction be completed with the 180-day window. However, any relinquished property money not used for purchase or on construction within 180 days becomes taxable boot. If all the money held by the intermediary has been spent on the project within the 180 days, additional financing can be used to complete the project. Paying contractors early for work that will be completed after the 180 days does not qualify for tax-deferral treatment. The exchanger's basis and depreciable value in the property need to be well documented if the project extends beyond the 180 days. Photographs, construction invoices, and other documents should record the project's status at the end of the 1031 exchange.

There are limits to the variations on 1031 exchanges. As Exhibit 6.3 points out, using the proceeds from a relinquished property to build on property you already own does not qualify as a construction exchange.

Given that restriction, it may be surprising that a related person can be a contractor on a construction exchange and the exchanger themselves can even be the contractor as long as they do not profit on the project. Profit would be considered a way of obtaining boot without paying the applicable taxes.

GROWING WITH A CONSTRUCTION EXCHANGE

> **EXHIBIT 6.3 EXCERPT FROM IRS BULLETIN 2004-33**
>
> An exchange of real estate owned by a taxpayer for improvements on land owned by the same taxpayer does not meet the requirements of § 1031. See DeCleene v. Commissioner, 115 T.C. 457 (2000); Bloomington Coca-Cola Bottling Co. v. Commissioner, 189 F.2d 14 (7th Cir. 1951). Moreover, Rev. Rul. 67-255, 1967-2 C.B. 270, holds that a building constructed on land owned by a taxpayer is not of a like kind to involuntarily converted land of the same taxpayer. Rev. Proc. 2000-37 does not abrogate the statutory requirement of § 1031 that the transaction be an exchange of like-kind properties.

Megalumber is a lumber wholesaler established in 1993. It distributes wholesale lumber materials to contractors and has outgrown its existing facility. Many industry developments have occurred that can improve the way lumber is handled and loaded onto trucks for delivery to work sites, but the current facility was originally a WWII warehouse that has outlived its useful life, and further improvements are impractical. There is no choice but to build a new facility.

After consulting with advisors, management understands the tax implications of building a new facility and then selling the existing facility after making the move. The conclusion is that a construction 1031 exchange is the best alternative. One of Megalumber's clients, a contractor, inquires about purchasing the existing facility for demolition and rebuilding an industrial park on the site. A deal is arranged to sell the facility and lease it back until the replacement facility can be moved into.

Building plans are drawn up and a raw parcel of land is located to build on. The estimate to build the new facility is six to nine months. The cost of the finished new facility will far exceed the sale price of the relinquished property. A study concludes that if the sale money is used to pay for the raw land and the first phase of construction, it will be fully used in about four months, and the construction 1031 exchange will fully defer capital gains and depreciation recapture taxes.

A construction agreement is entered into with a qualified intermediary that establishes an LLC to receive the money from the sale of the relinquished property. The LLC completes the sale and receives the money, and Megalumber enters into a lease with the new owner. The LLC purchases the raw land for the new facility with proceeds from the relinquished property. These same funds are used to pay invoices for constructing the new facility. Relinquished sale proceeds are exhausted in less than four months, and the title to the new facility is transferred from the LLC to Megalumber. The construction 1031 exchange closes with full deferment of taxes.

COMBINING A REVERSE AND CONSTRUCTION EXCHANGE

Using provisions of the reverse and construction 1031 exchanges may be the right solution. This arrangement allows the exchanger to purchase the replacement property and make improvements on it before selling the relinquished property. Of course, the 45-day, 180-day, and other 1031 requirements must be met to qualify as a safe harbor exchange.

An example of best applying this variation is if a business wants to transfer to another location that requires remodeling or construction before the move can occur. It is similar to the example used for the construction exchange, except the relinquished property is sold after the move instead of before the move. Because the exchanger cannot own both properties at the same time, one of them must be transferred to a qualified intermediary, using a temporary LLC to hold ownership of the property.

One small twist to the combined exchange is that the soon-to-be relinquished property is sometimes transferred to the intermediary. This often happens when lenders are not willing to provide construction financing that is not secured by the property under construction. The exchanger transfers ownership of the property to be relinquished to the intermediary and purchases the replacement property by providing funding to the intermediary. The title to the new property is passed to the exchanger, while ownership of the relinquished property remains with the LLC pending a sale. The exchanger does not have constructive receipt of both properties at the same time. Purchase and/or construction loans are secured by the new property. When construction is complete and the business moves into the new location, the intermediary sells the relinquished property.

The other version occurs if the intermediary takes the title to the replacement property, and the exchanger provides funds (via a loan or personal funds) for the construction on the new property. Again, the relinquished property is sold after the exchanger takes possession of the new property.

SNAPSHOT OF ALTERNATIVE EXCHANGE STRATEGIES		
Exchanger's Conditions	Alternative Exchange	Special Steps Followed
Replacement property will be purchased first and relinquished property sold second.	Reverse Exchange	• A qualified intermediary (QI) establishes an LLC that purchases the replacement property and holds it until the exchanger sells the relinquished property. • The exchanger leases or manages the replacement property. • When the relinquished property is sold, the QI holds the money. • The exchanger purchases the replacement property from the LLC using money from relinquished property and other funds. The reverse exchange is closed.

The exchanger wants to build to suit on the replacement property.	Construction Exchange	• QI holds the money from the sale of the relinquished property. • The QI opens an LLC to purchase and hold the replacement lot during the construction period. • The exchanger supervises the construction under a written agreement. • All funds for acquisition and construction invoices go through the QI based on review and instructions from the exchanger. • The exchanger is transferred the title when construction is complete or the exchange closes.
The exchanger builds on the replacement property first and sells the relinquished property second.	Reverse Construction Exchange	• The exchanger uses a combination of the steps from both types of exchanges. The soon-to-be relinquished property may be transferred to the LLC to obtain financing on the replacement property.

TENANTS IN COMMON

In 2002, the IRS issued Revenue Procedure 2002-22 regarding tenants-in-common (TIC) arrangements relative to 1031 exchanges. It should be noted that this procedure is intended for obtaining private letter rulings and is not specifically a safe harbor for TIC exchanges. However, the information provided about what must be included to obtain a favorable private letter ruling essentially provides guidelines for TIC exchanges.

A tenants-in-common arrangement occurs when there are multiple owners of the same property and each has an undivided interest in the property. It is unique from a partnership because each owner has the right to buy and sell partial ownership without the consent of other owners. Prior to the IRS issuing Revenue Procedure 2002-22, this was considered a gray area that the IRS might construe as a security or buying and selling of a partnership, both of which are specifically disqualified from 1031 exchange tax-favorable treatment. Recall that the IRS tends to define what cannot be done rather than what is allowable. From that perspective, the release of the procedure has been interpreted by knowledgeable professionals as a green light to exchange TICs.

EXHIBIT 6.4 EXCERPT FROM IRS PROCEDURE 2002-22

Rev. Proc. 2002–22

SECTION 1. PURPOSE

This revenue procedure specifies the conditions under which the Internal Revenue Service will consider a request for a ruling that an undivided fractional interest in rental real property (other than a mineral property as defined in section 614) is not an interest in a business entity, within the meaning of § 301.7701–2(a) of the Procedure and Administration Regulations.

The central characteristic of a tenancy in common, one of the traditional concurrent estates in land, is that each owner is deemed to own individually a physically undivided part of the entire parcel of property. Each tenant in common is entitled to share with the other tenants the possession of the whole parcel and has the associated rights to a proportionate share of rents or profits from the property, to transfer the interest, and to demand a partition of the property. These rights generally provide a tenant in common the benefits of ownership of the property within the constraint that no rights may be exercised to the detriment of the other tenants in common. 7 Richard R. Powell, Powell on Real Property §§ 50.01–50.07 (Michael Allan Wolf ed., 2000). Rev. Rul. 75–374 (1975–2 C.

A TIC is generally exchanged in the same manner as a traditional deferred 1031 exchange. The benefits that can be obtained through TIC ownership are what set it apart from other exchanges. With multiple owners the property acquired can be very expensive and normally out of the financial reach of individual investors. Individuals acquiring partial ownership of expensive office buildings in major cities are within the scope of a TIC. Destination shopping malls, large distribution centers, and industrial warehouse complexes are often owned in TIC arrangements. Premier apartment buildings in major cities, large boat marinas, and many other upscale investments are made possible through TIC exchanges. The point is that investments available to institutional investors are now available to individuals and qualify for tax-deferred treatment.

Advantages of a TIC exchange and ownership include:

- Real estate management troubles are eliminated.

- Potential increase in after-tax cash flow.

- Properties are known and due diligence performed before entering the 1031 exchange (45-day and 180-day risks are almost eliminated).

- Often packaged with non-recourse financing available.

- Investments may be spread over several different properties and geographical areas.

- Economies of scale.

What does the IRS require for TIC exchanges and ownership?

- There can be no more than 35 owners of the property.

- Each owner must have the right to sell all/ part of their share in the building without first obtaining agreement from other owners.

- Each owner must be free to mortgage their share without permission from others.

- Generally, the title is held in your name; no partnerships or other business entities are allowed.

- All profits and losses are divided according to percent of ownership.

- All owners share in any debt placed on the building as a whole.

- Investors do not operate as a business entity. No corporation or partnership tax returns are filed on behalf of the real estate or group of owners. Owners execute all contracts (or hire a professional property manager).

- Co-owners must follow passive investment rules. The property cannot be turned into a business operated by one or more of the owners.

- Major decisions must be unanimous regarding the sale of the entire building, hiring managers, refinancing, and tenant leases.

- When the property is sold, all loans or liens must be paid and remaining money distributed to owners, proportionate to ownership.

Exchanging into a tenant-in-common property is of particular interest to investors preparing for retirement, although these arrangements are available to any qualified investor. The level of investment is usually higher than the beginning investor can afford, often starting at $250,000 or more. This is necessary to ensure that 35 or fewer investors are able to pool sufficient capital to purchase a high-end property. Often TIC arrangements include triple net lease arrangements.

TRIPLE NET LEASES

These properties are managed and operated by the tenants or professional managers hired by the tenants. In a triple net lease the occupant has responsibility for all costs associated with the property. These generally include:

- Operating expenses
- Property taxes
- Utilities
- Insurance premiums
- Maintenance and repairs
- Grounds upkeep

Occupants of triple net lease properties tend to be financially stable companies and enter into long-term leases that may run 15 to 20 years or longer. The property owners are only responsible for the building structure, roof, and sometimes the parking area. The occupants in this arrangement gain the advantage of ownership-like control without the upfront expense of purchasing the property.

PARTNERSHIPS IN EXCHANGES

When property has co-owners and it is clear that a partnership does not exist, no problems arise if one or more co-owners enter into an exchange while others do not. As individuals with undivided interest in the property, they are each free to either exchange to defer taxes or outright sell the property and pay the taxes.

The IRS code specifically prohibits the interest in a partnership to have tax-favorable treatment in an exchange. There are a few distinctions that need to be understood about what this means.

An individual cannot sell their ownership share of a partnership and replace it by purchasing an ownership share in a different partnership. A partnership that owns investment or business real estate in the name of the partnership can use a 1031 exchange to defer taxes. If all the partners agree to use a 1031 exchange, there is no issue. Problems arise when one or more partners want to enter into an exchange and other partners do not; this prevents the partnership from being able to use an exchange. One partner selling a portion of the partnership's property constitutes selling a portion of the partnership itself.

Distributing the property proportionately into the partners' names and then conducting individual 1031 exchanges will likely be determined as exchanging a partnership by the IRS. Clearly, this will not be granted tax-favorable treatment.

The IRS does not depend solely on a partnership registering with a state to determine if a partnership exists. There are four methods to determine if a partnership exists.

- Property title is held in the name of the partnership.

- Transactions related to the property (expenses or income) appear on a partnership tax return.

- Title to the property is in the co-owners' names, but a partnership also exits between the co-owners.

- Co-owners of the property regularly engage in business activities commonly performed by a partnership. Especially if the business activities are related to the property being exchanged.

Even when one or more of these conditions do exist, there are ways to achieve a tax-free exchange, although one or more partners do not participate. The simplest way is if the other partners are able to buy out the partnership of the one that does not want to exchange. Then, the remaining partners are free to complete the exchange in the name of the partnership. Often the reason a partner chooses not to exchange property is because they want cash from the sale. Buying out their partnership often has the same effect, if the other partners have sufficient funds.

Another way is to fully dissolve the partnership and distribute the proportionate ownership into the names of the previous partners. The frequent problem with this is if the partnership owns several real estate properties and all must be distributed to dissolve the partnership. Additionally, the distribution of properties is likely to have income tax implications to the previous partners.

Another possible problem with dissolving the partnership and then quickly exchanging a co-owner's share of the property is that the IRS may determine that the property was not held long enough to qualify as an investment property. It may be determined that the co-owner has dealer status.

If the partnership is dissolved, be wary of jointly purchasing replacement property with a former partner. The IRS is likely to characterize the entire transaction as the exchange of one partnership for another.

Another option is for the partnership to exchange the property and distribute money or other compensation from the partnership to the partner that did not want to exchange the property. This can be a good option when the partnership owns several properties and does not want to dissolve the entire partnership.

There is no implicit reason that a partnership should not invest in real estate property and plan to use 1031 exchanges. However, it may be a good idea that the documents establishing and controlling the partnership contain explicit language about what occurs when not all partners agree to a 1031 exchange. Those that jointly own property without a partnership are wise to take steps avoiding a partnership-like appearance.

CHANGES TO A PROPERTY'S PURPOSE

There are times when it is beneficial to change the reason or purpose a property is held. Differences in tax codes affecting personal residences, vacation homes, and investment property occasionally may make it practical to convert these properties from one use to another. One drawback to successfully accomplishing these conversions is that the IRS has not established clear periods of time in which the property must be converted to qualify for tax-favorable treatment. Many experts recommend at least two years. The process of converting a property to a personal residence is clearly defined by the requirements of five-year ownership and living in the house for three of those five years.

Converting Investment Property to Personal Residence

At some point, a 1031 exchange may not be your preferred option when selling a rental property. Converting it to a personal residence and following the requirements discussed in Chapter 2 can qualify the sale for a $250,000 tax exemption ($500,000 for married couples filing jointly).

Converting Vacation Homes to Investment or Rental Property

Vacation properties or second homes do not automatically qualify as investment property or for 1031 exchanges. However, many people do purchase these properties as investments, and changing the use of the property may well be worth the effort. Using the property as a rental can qualify the property for a 1031 exchange — an attractive option, since capital gain on a vacation home cannot be eliminated in the same manner that it can for a principal residence.

Certain requirements exist to establish the property as a rental rather than a vacation home. Personal use of the home must be for less than 14 days a year or 10 percent of the time that it was rented to others. If it is rented 260 days, the allowable personal use grows to 26 days a year. The rent charged must be fair market value. Days spent repairing or maintaining the property generally are not considered personal use days. Another consideration is that you treat it as a rental property for tax purposes, accounting for rental income and expenses.

Converting Personal Residence to Rental

Those fortunate enough to have a problem with more than $250,000 ($500,000 for married couples filing jointly) capital gain on the sale of the primary residence might consider converting it to a rental property. This is similar to the vacation home to rental conversion strategy, except it only needs to occur if capital gain above these amounts needs to be deferred.

Again, the IRS does not have guidelines about how long the rental conversion must be in place to qualify. Many experts suggest two years of tax records which show the property as a rental investment is adequate.

PERSONAL PROPERTY EXCHANGES

Although not directly related to real estate investing, it is worth noting that the wealthy often take advantage of personal property exchanges. Personal property covers almost anything that can be manufactured, as well as some intangible things. Business equipment certainly falls into the category of personal property that can be exchanged. Intellectual rights, patents, and copyrights are among qualifying intangible personal property.

Consider using a 1031 exchange for appreciable business assets. Capitalized business assets are depreciated. Examples in previous chapters have shown that, with depreciation, the sale of an asset does not need to be for more than the purchase cost to cause a taxable sale. And there are business assets that do appreciate in value over time. Shipping vessels, truck fleets, and satellites are examples. As business needs change, a 1031 exchange is a tax-deferred method of selling unneeded equipment and acquiring the right equipment.

In August of 2004 the IRS changed classification systems for categorizing like-kind personal property. The Standard Industrial Classification (SIC) was replaced with the North American Industry Classification System (NAICS). The IRS is not as generous with like-kind classifications for personal property as it is for real estate. Just because it is like-class in the classification system does not ensure that it is like-kind. Although most computer equipment can be exchanged for other computer equipment, it may not be like-kind with other office equipment. Professional exchange guidance should be sought if the exchange may be questionable.

EXCHANGE CLUBS

Many commercial real estate companies organize speaking and presentation meetings that feature 1031 exchange experts. These clubs also offer real estate packaged for a 1031 exchange. Prepackaged real estate includes:

- Acreage
- Condominiums
- Apartments
- Operating businesses
- Lots to build on
- Time shares
- Personal property
- Cash, mortgages, bonds, and other paper to exchange or purchase property
- Mobile homes and mobile home parks
- Single and multiple family residential properties

Active exchangers are always seeking opportunities to exchange something they no longer need for something they want. With personal property, it becomes a barter system where putting deals together is an art. As an aid to the barter system, clubs may provide script that enables club members to exchange unwanted personal property for script and use the script to acquire a wanted item from another member. These are not always like-kind exchanges. A motor home may be traded for gems or artwork. Yachts are traded for timeshare condominiums. A variety of reasons motivate exchangers: Some people no longer want to make payments on a personal property, while others want to trade a luxury item for an income-producing property.

Many exchange club members work in the real estate profession. These clubs exist in every state but seldom are geographically limited. In addition to exchanging real estate and personal property, many exchange clubs share ideas about how to create or enhance wealth. Ideas include:

- Generating cash from a property that will not sell.

- Generating fast cash by selling a $100,000 property for $50,000 with an option to buy it back within one year for $60,000.

- The lender of a mortgage with a balloon payment about to be paid and who wants to defer the taxes exchanging with another mortgage-holder who makes regular installment payments and wants all the cash that the balloon payment offers.

Involving three, four, or five people in a transaction is not uncommon. Sometimes it is necessary to involve several people so that, in the end, everyone gets the property they want. This is called "a deal with legs" within exchange clubs. The owner of a $75,000 condominium at a ski resort in Colorado wants to acquire a timeshare in Hawaii, but the person with a timeshare in Hawaii is looking for a timeshare in Florida. To put the deal together, the owner of the Colorado condominium finds a third exchanger with a Florida timeshare that wants a Colorado ski resort property. The three put together a deal so that each trades into the property they want. Often cash, cars, and other personal property are involved to equalize the exchange because the properties have different values. These types of transactions would not happen without the existence of exchange clubs.

NOT TO EXCHANGE

There are times when it is better to sell for cash or installment payments rather than conduct a tax-deferral exchange. Passing up an exchange may be a good idea if:

- The selling price of the property will be less than your basis. Therefore, a capital gain will not occur to trigger taxes.

- You are in a very high tax bracket with little or no tax-deductible depreciation remaining in the property. Selling the property and paying the taxes can enable you to purchase a higher-value (leveraged) property with the needed tax-deductible depreciation.

- Other businesses losses offset the profit that will be realized on the property sale so that few or no taxes will be due.

- You simply need some of the cash that a regular sale will provide. Still, a partial exchange might be the better answer to defer at least part of the taxes.

SUMMARY

1031 exchanges are a powerful tool providing many opportunities and options to make almost any transaction possible. The reverse exchange resolves many issues by making it possible to purchase the replacement property before selling the relinquished property. One of the most common uses of the reverse exchange is to take advantage of a great real estate opportunity that will be lost if not acted upon immediately.

Reverse exchanges can relieve anxiety about the 45-day and 180-day time requirements when selling the relinquished property has a higher probability than finding the replacement property. Using the reverse exchange makes it possible to relocate a business from the relinquished property to the replacement property without first giving up the relinquished property. The construction exchange and combining reverse exchanges with construction exchanges also solves certain business problems. Building a new facility or performing a major renovation is possible within the 180-day time period when well planned.

The IRS continues to provide safe harbors for these types of 1031 exchanges. IRS revenue procedure 2002-37 and IRS bulletin 2004-33 are applicable to these exchange types.

Tenants in common allows up to 35 investors to pool funds for purchasing high-end real estate that not long ago was only available to institutional investors because of the high cost. The IRS has provided guidelines clarifying that these purchases are made by tenants in common rather than partnerships. Individuals can buy and sell undivided interests without co-owners being part of the exchange. Many tenants-in-common exchanges prefer to acquire triple net leases where the occupants are responsible for all management and expenses except for the structure itself.

Formal partnerships using 1031 exchanges must be aware of situations when a transaction could appear as an exchange of an individual's value in the partnership. This is most common when individual partners exchange property held in the name of the partnership. A partnership investing in real estate is wise to have an agreement describing how a resolution will be obtained when not all partners can come to an agreement as to how to use a 1031 exchange.

Creative use of 1031 exchanges can maximize profits on sales of second homes and the acquisition or sale of personal residences that exceed the $250,000 capital gain exclusion. Exchange clubs offer a variety of options for successful exchanges that otherwise would not be possible.

7

INSTALLMENTS WHEN THE TIME IS RIGHT

In October of 2006, the IRS released proposed regulation changes with REG–141901-05 that effectively ended the tax-deferral strategy known as a Private Annuity Trust. Until that time, a tax deferral had been obtained based on certain interpretations of several portions of the tax code. No specific code addressed Private Annuity Trusts, and the IRS put an end to them. Tax deferrals based on installment sales are codified in tax code section 453, and Charitable Remainder Trusts are codified in section 664. Both of these tax-favorable strategies were specifically excluded from the proposed regulation change in 2006.

The fact that the IRS specifically codifies installment sales emphasizes the importance of the safe harbor concept. The Private Annuity Trust is not an inherently abusive tax strategy and had a broad following within the estate planning and tax professions. Possibly, it will become codified if successfully challenged in tax court. Private Annuity Trusts have several traits in common with installment sales and Charitable Remainder trusts (discussed in the next chapter). Anyone previously considering a Private Annuity Trust should take a close look at installment sales and Charitable Remainder Trusts.

INSTALLMENT SALES CONTRACT

Installment sales come in many different forms and have several names:

- Contract for Deed

- Land Contract

- Agreement for Deed

- Real Estate Installment Agreement

Most often, these sale types have a key difference compared to a mortgage sale. These types of sales occur when the seller retains the title to the property until the final installment payment is made. When all terms of the contract are completed, the title is transferred into the name of the buyer. However, through the contract, the buyer should expect to have full ownership rights while making payments. In contrast, a mortgage pledges the property as security for repayment of the loan. The title is normally transferred to the buyer but pledged to the loan holder. A security note for the debt is signed, along with the mortgage, pledging the property as security.

The difference is of little concern unless a dishonest seller is involved. In dramatic instances, a dishonest seller might try selling the property to a third party without acknowledging the first buyer's claim to the deed. Also, what started out as a good title when the deal is made might have a lien or other encumbrance when it comes time to deliver the title. It is important to know the difference between contract sales and mortgage sales. Many people regularly refer to a mortgage when they really mean a contract sale. Many states use deeds of trust or similar laws rather than mortgages, including bank loans held as deeds of trust.

Installment sale contracts must deal with both desired and undesired possibilities that can occur over the length of the contract. Many unforeseeable events can occur with contracts running five, ten, fifteen, or more years. The contract goes beyond the sale agreement, and it is important that an experienced real estate attorney write it. If the other party to the sale has their attorney write the contract, you need to have an experienced attorney review and amend it.

If you have an outstanding mortgage on a property and intend to sell it on installments, it is important to verify there is not a "due on sale clause" in the existing mortgage. If there is, you may try negotiating with the lender to have it removed or modified to allow your installment sale to go forward. This is more likely to be acceptable to the lender if you have an adjustable-rate mortgage or if the old interest rate is higher than current interest rates. Calculate the value of deferred taxes when selling at a highly appreciated price. Determine if a slightly higher interest rate on the mortgage you owe makes sense. Depending on the circumstances, the installment sale may still be the best arrangement.

MORTGAGE RELIEF

In the event that a mortgage does exist on the property, the assumption of this mortgage by the buyer can be a taxable event for the seller. Sometimes called "phantom income," the debt relief is taxable in the year of the sale. The taxable amount is equal to the existing first mortgage that the buyer assumes. The seller prevents this from happening with a "wraparound mortgage,"

WRAPAROUND MORTGAGE

First Mortgage
+ Installment Contract
- Down Payment
= Buyer Carried Financing

which includes the value of the first mortgage plus all the financing that the seller carries back.

Phantom income or debt relief also occurs if the buyer takes out a new mortgage and uses the loan to pay off the first mortgage on behalf of the seller. When an investment property that is not free and clear is sold on installment, it is generally best to carry both the first mortgage and the installment contract.

CONTRACT TERMS AND CONDITIONS

Installment sale contracts are just one of the countless business contracts entered into every day in the United States. Determining how the contract and property title are held varies from state to state. In some states the title and the contract are held in escrow the entire time by an escrow company or an attorney. In other states, the contract must be registered with a government agency to notify interested parties that the buyer has rights to the property.

Defining the terms and conditions in the event of a default are critical components of the contract:

- Has the buyer defaulted when payments are in arrears two or three months?

- Is the seller obligated to resell the property and return any monies the buyer has paid?

- The money paid by the buyer becomes considered rent for the privilege of having had control of the property.

- Interest-only payments are more susceptible to default when the buyer has no equity in the property.

IMPORTANT INSTALLMENT SALE CONTRACT CONSIDERATIONS:

- Accurate legal description of the property
- Mineral, water, and air rights
- Existing or new easements
- Closing date of the sale
- Full sale price
- Down payment amount
- Full amortization schedule
- Due dates of installment payments
- Interest rate and calculation method
- Interest only payments to further defer capital gain tax

IMPORTANT INSTALLMENT SALE CONTRACT CONSIDERATIONS:

- Balloon payment at the end of a contract
- Late fees and penalties
- Prepayment clause
- Conditions and rights of buyer to resell the property
- Criteria allowing a future buyer to assume the installment sale
- Any contingencies
- Time allowed for due diligence
- Buyer's insurance obligations and the beneficiary of insurance
- Maintenance and repair requirements

PREVENTING EARLY PAYOFF

A contract favorable to the seller contains clauses that discourage or make early payoff difficult. This avoids triggering taxes to become due. Each state has regulations to protect the buyer from not being able to pay off a loan. Often, buyer protection is much stronger for a personal residence than it is for commercial and investment properties. An attorney practicing in the state the property exits is effective at structuring this clause of the contract.

Making the loan assumable by a future buyer discourages an early payout. The ability to negotiate a lower interest rate if rates decline also discourages the buyer from taking out a lower interest loan in the future.

BUSINESS RETIREMENT WITH AN INSTALLMENT SALE

For small business owners ready to retire, the installment sale is often the best and most lucrative option available. Not only are taxes deferred, but often a higher sales price can be obtained for the business than bank financing will approve. With seller financing, the final decision about the loan belongs to the property or business owner rather than with an institution that lacks the seller's motivation to complete the deal.

A competent businessperson can assess the same paperwork that a bank analyzes to arrive at a decision determining if a purchaser is an acceptable loan risk. The businessperson can seek additional analysis from their financial advisor. When evaluating an installment loan applicant, do not hesitate to ask the purchaser to provide information and proof regarding:

- Net worth
- Five or more years of income tax returns
- Related business experience
- Values of other assets, including their personal residence
- Credit history

A bank is not fully knowledgeable about the actual value of the business, property, and other assets. The seller has this knowledge and is able to determine if the risk assumed is acceptable, based on the security underlying the loan. Additionally, the seller is likely to be capable of stepping in and reviving the business should it become necessary to foreclose. The bank has only the value of the property and the remaining inventory as recourse if the business fails.

If a willing buyer has a questionable credit history but success in other areas indicating a probability they will succeed in your business, there are ways to hedge against the credit history, especially when a willing buyer has other assets. The buyer and seller negotiate the terms of the contract. A buyer with a troubled credit history may be willing to secure the loan with other assets in addition to the business, in effect securing the loan for more than 100 percent of its value. That is not to say that unwarranted risks should be taken with such a large transaction. Due diligence is always appropriate on the part of the seller, as much as on the part of the buyer.

A bank's decision might not be based on the buyer's credit history. Commonly, banks set a dollar limit on how much they will loan for certain business types or to individuals. Your high-dollar sale could fall through for no other reason than the bank's artificial loan ceiling. As the seller on an installment sale, you are not bound by these policy limits. A bank may be willing to loan the buyer $1 million but not the $1.5 million negotiated sale price. On an installment loan, you have the ability to grant the same person more credit. There might be a way to combine a partial bank loan and partial seller financed sale. Do not overlook that possibility either.

Often, a slightly lower interest rate is negotiated for an installment loan than a bank loan as an incentive to avoid early repayment. That same lower interest rate can also entice a higher selling price if the buyer has the prospect of paying for the business from future cash flow instead of a cash sale. The seller is always motivated, knowing that interest is being paid on deferred capital gains tax, a tax that will eventually be paid with inflated dollars.

A small business is often much more than just an investment. It can be the pride of a lifelong effort and the source of family income. An owner should consider what will happen to the business in the event of an untimely death or incapacitation. If the business will be sold to a known person, a prearranged buy-sell contract is a wise plan. Have a contract drawn up with the terms and conditions of the sale. A business partner or an adult child are likely candidates for a prearranged sale that will continue to provide an income for your spouse or family. Every year or two, the price in the contract should be updated to reflect changes in value.

GENERATE INCOME FROM UNDEVELOPED AND FARM LANDS

Undeveloped or raw land and farmlands are the most frequent candidates for installment sales. Part of the reason is because banks and other lenders are reluctant to lend against these types of properties, often considered speculative purchases. A good speculative purchase right in the path of rapid growth can turn into a highly profitable acquisition. But obtaining a bank loan will require 30 percent or more for a down payment. Often, only a seven-year mortgage for raw land can be obtained from a bank, which can lead to high mortgage payments for a property that does not provide income. Investors interested in this type of property should be prepared to do business with seller-carried financing. Likewise, an owner should be prepared to make an installment sale when the time comes to sell undeveloped land.

There are many reasons to invest in raw land. A few include the ability to:

- Plat into residential lots.
- Plat, add utilities, and sell to a developer.
- Develop and sell plots yourself.
- Obtain zoning changes that increase the value.
- Sell at an appreciated value to create an income stream.

There are drawbacks other than difficult bank financing. There are few, if any, tax advantages while you hold the property. Poor purchases of undeveloped land are more likely to result in a financial loss than other real estate investments.

When selling raw land, look at the following uses to market it:

- Recreational or resort development
- Industrial development
- Commercial and other business uses
- Residential development
- Farming or ranching

These common uses for raw land are all for development purposes, except for farming and ranching. A developer may be interested in seller financing during the development phase. An installment sale can have big rewards from rapid appreciation followed by interest on an installment sale that quickly pays off in full when the development is complete. Short-term seller financing for a developer is definitely worth considering when you are holding property that produces no income.

ENJOY FINANCIAL BENEFITS FROM DEFERRED TAX DOLLARS

Mr. Lee needs to determine the financial benefits that he will receive by selling his retail business on installments. An eager buyer offers $500,000 with the sale amortized over ten years at 6 percent. Mr. Lee wants to see how much the capital gains tax is in the first year. The first calculation

STEP 1	
Sales Price	$500,000
Expense of Sale	– $35,000
Gross Proceeds	$465,000

is subtracting the expense of the sale from the sale price to determine the gross proceeds, which will be $465,000.

In step two, he calculates the adjusted basis by subtracting $76,230 depreciation (seven years' worth) from the original purchase price. Mr. Lee made no capital improvements while he owned the property, or these would be added to the adjusted basis.

STEP 2	
Purchase Price	$300,000
Depreciation	– $76,230
Adjusted Basis	$223,770

Now that he knows the gross proceeds from the sale and his adjusted basis in the property, he can determine the gross profit. Step three of the calculation subtracts the adjusted basis from the gross proceeds to equal $241,230 in gross profit.

STEP 3	
Gross Proceeds	$465,000
Adjusted Basis	– $223,770
Gross Profit	$241,230

Once the gross profit is determined, the percentage of profit is determined in step four, using the sale price. The $241,230 gross profit is divided by the $500,000 sale price to equal a 48 percent profit. This is the percentage used to

STEP 4	
Gross Profit / Sales Price	$241,230 / $500,000
Payment Percentage Profit	48%
48% of Down Payment	$24,000
15% Capital Gain Tax	$3,600

calculate the amount of any payment that is profit and owes capital gains tax. The other 52 percent (100 percent - 48 percent) is the adjusted basis that does not owe any tax.

Mr. Lee did receive a 10 percent down payment of $50,000, shown in step four, and he will owe capital gains tax on that down payment. Using the 48 percent determines that capital gains tax is owed on $24,000 of the $50,000 down payment. Completing step four shows the tax rate is 15 percent of the $24,000 for a tax totaling $3,600 due in the tax year the down payment is made.

STEP 5: 1ST YEAR'S AMORTIZATION PAYMENTS @ 6%						
Month	Principal Paid	Interest Paid	Loan Balance	48% Capital Gain	15% Capital Gains Tax	25% Income Tax on Interest
Jan	$2,746	$2,250	$447,254	$1,318	$198	$563
Feb	$2,760	$2,236	$444,494	$1,325	$199	$559
March	$2,773	$2,222	$441,721	$1,331	$200	$556
Apr	$2,787	$2,209	$438,934	$1,338	$201	$552
May	$2,801	$2,195	$436,132	$1,345	$202	$549
June	$2,815	$2,181	$433,317	$1,351	$203	$545
July	$2,829	$2,167	$430,488	$1,358	$204	$542
Aug	$2,843	$2,152	$427,644	$1,365	$205	$538
Sept	$2,858	$2,138	$424,787	$1,372	$206	$535
Oct	$2,872	$2,124	$421,915	$1,379	$207	$531
Nov	$2,886	$2,110	$419,028	$1,385	$208	$527
Dec	$2,901	$2,095	$416,128	$1,392	$209	$524
Totals	$33,872	$26,079		$16,259	$2,439	$6,520

Although Mr. Lee will carry the contract for ten years, he is only interested in the first year of savings. In step five, he amortizes the $450,000 installment payments ($500,000 selling price - $50,000 down payment) over the full ten years. However, only one year of payments is shown here.

The amortization table allows the 48 percent of each principal payment to be calculated and the 15 percent capital gains tax to be applied to the capital gain. In January, $2,746 is paid toward the principal of the loan. Of that principal payment, 48 percent equals $1,318, which capital gains tax must be paid against. Of the entire January payment, a capital gains tax of $198 is owed. Calculating the capital gains tax for all 12 months shows a total capital gains tax of $2,439. Mr. Lee also has to pay taxes on the interest he earns. This is calculated as part of his normal income at 25 percent. Mr. Lee expects to pay $6,520 in taxes for the earned interest.

TAX SAVINGS FOR YEAR 1

Next, the total deferred capital gains tax is calculated. Referring back to step three, the gross profit of $223,770 is multiplied by 15 percent to determine that Mr. Lee would have owed $33,566

CAPITAL TAX DEFERRED	
Gross Profit × 15% tax rate	
$223,770 × 15%	$33,566

in capital gains tax if he had received the full sale price at closing.

The next two calculations determine the financial benefit that Mr. Lee receives in the first year of the installment sale. Mr. Lee acknowledges that he did not defer all the capital gains tax during the first year. It was determined that $33,566 would have been due from a normal sale and becomes the starting point to find the amount actually deferred. From this amount subtract the

YEAR 1 CAPITAL GAIN TAX DEFERRED	
Full Gain Tax	$33,566
Gain Tax on Down Payment	− $3,600
Installment Gain Tax	− $2,439
Tax Saving	$27,527

$3,600 capital gains tax paid against the $50,000 down payment (see step four). Next, subtract the $2,439 of capital gains tax paid on the first year of installment payments (see step five). Of course, the $27,527 is not the total of Mr. Lee's financial benefit from the installment sale.

The final calculation is made to determine the total earned from interest on the loan and the amount saved by deferring taxes into the future. The total interest paid to Mr. Lee is $26,079 (step five), but he paid $6,520 in income taxes, which is subtracted out to obtain the total interest earned of $19,559. The previous calculation established that $27,527 of capital gains tax was deferred. This is added to the interest earned to reach a total earned and saved of $47,086 in the first year of the installment sale.

TOTAL EARNED AND SAVED	
Interest Paid	$26,079
Interest Tax	− $6,520
Interest Earned	$19,559
Interest Earned	$19,559
Gain Tax Deferred	+ $27,527
Total Earned and Saved	$47,086

There are other calculations that can be made to emphasize the value of this money. Suffice it to say that $47,086 is 9.42 percent of the $500,000 sales price. Mr. Lee looks forward to enjoying the financial benefits this installment sale provides.

ORDERLY LIQUIDATION OF PROPERTY

The installment sale can be the right strategy for an orderly sell-off of multiple investment properties when retirement time arrives. You need to plan the exit strategy well in advance, eight or nine years, to maximize your profits. Begin keeping detailed records about the business or investment properties. Having lengthy and accurate records will convince potential buyers of the property's true profitability. Having the financial records audited each year adds greatly to reliability.

Multiple properties may take a longer time for maximum tax deferral. Installment sales of a few properties will provide a substantial income stream for many years but may not last long enough for the long life spans Americans are now enjoying. Multiple options may require multiple solutions. Along with an installment sale, for other properties consider:

- A 1031 exchange into a triple net lease property.
- Hiring a professional property manager.

- Exchanging for a property requiring less management.
- A collateralized installment sale with the start of distribution delayed.

These strategies enable you to significantly reduce your personal workload while enjoying the benefits of a lengthy income stream. Carefully selecting which properties to reduce the management effort on and which properties to sell on installment can control the taxes paid over time by remaining in the appropriate tax bracket. Once the contract for an earlier sold property expires, another one is available to continue the income stream uninterrupted.

Another advantage provided by long-term liquidation planning is the ability to pick a point in time when interest rates are high. This will, of course, increase the interest earnings generated by an installment sale.

Depending on your investment, its condition, and tenants, an installment income stream can be created by converting apartments into condominiums. With long-term tenants, you might offer very low down payments and seller-carried financing.

The conversion of real estate into an income stream has a positive effect on estate planning as well. Selling off enough property to get below the estate tax threshold can be a good strategy. Gifting some or all the cash flow can also help if the income is not needed.

The good news is, there are several exit strategies for the real estate investor to consider. Besides the installment sale, others to be considered are charitable remainder trusts, discussed later in the book, and collateralized installment sales, discussed next.

COLLATERALIZED INSTALLMENT SALES

The collateralized installment sale is based on IRS code 453, the same as installment sales. There are two big differences with the collateralized sale.

You are able to postpone the beginning of the payments to a future date, which in turn defers taxes coming due. Risk of default is eliminated to ensure a dependable income stream is available when you elect to begin it. You choose how the money is invested for future earnings. Another win-win situation happens when the buyer wants clear title to the property, and the seller desires installment payments. With a collateralized installment sale, both get what they want. Here is how it works.

First, the property is sold to a collateralized sales agent based on a contract instructing them to establish a collateralized installment sale account for your benefit. They sell the business or property for the full asking price. The end buyer does have to deliver the full asking price at the time of closing, using loans, personal funds, or other financing.

You do not take possession of the sale proceeds because that would be a taxable event. Instead, the collateralized sales agent opens a collateral account with a third party that is legally pledged to you. The account is invested according to the instructions you provide. You choose the third party where the account is established, based on your own level of confidence and that of your financial advisor.

You may not access the funds or the investment, except via the installment payments. However, you can direct the account custodian to sell one asset and acquire another asset of your choosing.

Taxes are fully deferred until you begin receiving installment payments in the amount originally determined by yourself. The collateral and proceeds remain safe from any creditors during the entire contract. This creates a highly secure installment sale structure that cannot be obtained from traditional installment sale contracts.

COLLATERALIZED SALES IN 1031 EXCHANGES

The collateralized sale works well with certain circumstances encountered in 1031 exchanges. The diagram illustrates a partial 1031 exchange combined with a collateralized installment sale. The result is full deferral of capital gains tax until you elect to begin installment payments, even though it is only a partial 1031 exchange.

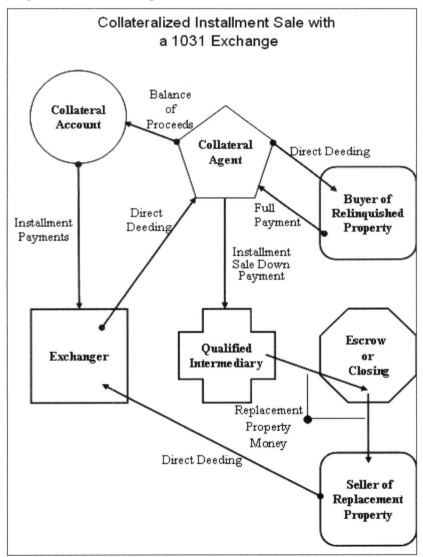

The collateralization agent steps in to purchase the relinquished property on an installment payment and then sells it to the end buyer for the full price.

The proceeds (less the down payment) are used to establish the collateral account with a third party for your benefit. The qualified intermediary continues the normal 1031 exchange to purchase the replacement property with the down payment and other funds that you provide from financing if necessary. Proceeds (including deferred taxes) from the collateralized installment sale continue to earn a return on investment, as directed by you, until payments begin.

In another scenario, the collateralization agent steps in to buy the exchange agreement from the qualified intermediary if you are unable to identify a replacement property within 45 days. The entire sale of the relinquished property becomes boot. However, it is in the form of a collateralized installment sale with tax-deferred status until payments are made.

CASE STUDY #5: COLLATERALIZED INSTALLMENT SALE

It's Not Your Father's Installment Sale:
Turning Illiquid Assets into Financial Assets,
and Deferring the Tax on Doing So by Stanley D. Crow, J.D.

We all know what an installment sale is, right? It's a sale of an asset pursuant to a contract pursuant to which:

• The purchase price is paid in more than one calendar year;

• The seller retains a lien on the asset sold, as security for the unpaid balance;

• The seller retains the risk of having to foreclose or repossess, if the buyer doesn't pay as agreed;

• The buyer doesn't get free and clear title to the asset until the purchase price is fully paid; and

• If the seller and buyer put up with all of that, the seller enjoys the right to defer tax on the gain on sale under §453 of the *Internal Revenue Code* until such time as the seller actually receives the principal of the purchase price.

That was the installment sale your father knew, and because of those limitations which he just *knew* had to be present, installment sales have remained the unwanted and comparatively seldom-used backwater of business and real estate transactions.

CASE STUDY #5: COLLATERALIZED INSTALLMENT SALE

But that's not what an installment sale *must* be. All that an installment sale *must* be is this:

• The purchase price is paid in more than one calendar year; and

• The seller enjoys the right to defer tax on the gain on sale under §453 of the *Internal Revenue Code* until such time as the seller actually receives the principal of the purchase price.

Nothing in §453 requires that the seller retain a lien on the asset sold. Nothing in §453 requires that the seller retain the risk of having to foreclose or repossess. Nothing in §453 prevents the buyer from obtaining free and clear title to the asset immediately.

So how can the seller enjoy the income stream and tax deferral from an installment sale, without also retaining credit and foreclosure risk? And how can the buyer obtain clear title to the asset without encumbering that asset or something else?

The Installment Accommodator

When the objectives of seller and buyer conflict, the answer often lies in bringing a third party into the deal to resolve the conflict and allow both seller and buyer to get what they want. For the seller in an installment sale, that's an attractive return on investment, a secure cash flow, no risk because of the buyer's credit, and no further required involvement with the asset that is being sold. For the buyer, that's clear title to the asset, complete control of the asset, and the freedom to encumber or improve the asset without concern about the seller's wishes or requirements.

An installment accommodator enables both seller and buyer to get what they want, by the accommodator's becoming the intermediate buyer and reseller of the asset, much as a qualified intermediary becomes the intermediate purchaser and reseller of a business or investment property which an exchanger is relinquishing in a tax-deferred exchange under §1031 of the Internal Revenue Code. The installment accommodator enters into a contract to purchase the asset from the seller and to pay for the asset over any number of years that may be specified in the contract. The installment accommodator proceeds (usually immediately) to resell the asset to the ultimate buyer for cash, which the installment accommodator places in the hands of an independent third party in the installment accommodator's name, as collateral which is legally pledged to the seller as security for the installment accommodator's obligation to pay the unpaid balance of the purchase price.

CASE STUDY #5: COLLATERALIZED INSTALLMENT SALE

Financial Assets in the Hands of a Third Party: A "Collateralized" Installment Sale

The independent third party manages, invests, or otherwise obligates itself to make the installment payments to the seller on behalf of the installment accommodator, pursuant to the installment contract.

Voila! The seller enjoys a secure income stream from the invested cash collateral, the seller enjoys deferral of the tax on the gain on sale, the seller retains no credit or foreclosure risk, and the buyer has a free and clear asset with which to do as the buyer may want.

All of this becomes possible through the installment accommodator's role, which decouples the security from the asset that is being sold and enables the seller to turn an illiquid asset into financial assets, without having to pay the tax on the gain first. Therefore, the seller's investment return is based on the entire sale proceeds rather than on only the net after taxes.

The most descriptive term for an installment sale which takes this form is that it is a "collateralized" installment sale; *i.e.*, the security for the unpaid principal comes from the side, from a "collateral" direction rather than from within the transferred asset.

Comparison with 1031 Exchanges

A collateralized installment sale has many advantages as compared with a tax-deferred exchange under §1031 of the *Internal Revenue Code*.

To begin, collateralized installment sales under §453 are not limited to business or investment property, or to like-kind properties. There's no 45-day limit in which to identify property for reinvestment purposes, and there's no 180-day limit in which to complete that reinvestment. The tax on excess cash in the deal can be deferred, unlike "boot" in a 1031 exchange. Upon reinvestment, a new basis is available for depreciation, instead of the old carryover basis as in a 1031 exchange.

Maybe most important of all, a collateralized installment sale does not put the seller under pressure to act quickly, to buy *something*, as in the case of a 1031 exchange.

It is demonstrably the case that 1031 exchanges increase, on average, the cost of acquiring replacement properties. That price premium is hidden, but it is real, it can be substantial, and it reduces the return on investment from the replacement property. In contrast, in a collateralized installment sale the seller retains complete freedom of action with regard to selling and buying, at the right time, the right property, at the right price.

Enhance an Installment Sale with a Debt Accommodation

A very important reason why a collateralized installment sale is not your father's

CASE STUDY #5: COLLATERALIZED INSTALLMENT SALE

installment sale is how today's installment sale can work in tandem with a debt accommodation to increase substantially the transaction's capacity for tax deferral.

The sale of encumbered property ordinarily produces capital gains tax for the seller, on the amount of the debt of which the seller is relieved at the closing. Whether the seller either leveraged the seller's purchase of the property in the first place or borrowed money out of the property for other purposes, the sale of the property is usually the day of reckoning, when the payment of the debt will be treated as if it were cash paid at closing to the seller. Between the leverage and depreciation deductions that were taken during the seller's holding period, zero-basis situations upon sale are very common — and that can mean that the seller will be cash out-of-pocket upon the sale; by the time the tax is paid, the seller will have less cash in hand after the sale than before it.

A debt accommodator can provide the solution to that part of the seller's tax problem, by refinancing the existing debt in such a way that the seller does not have a relief-of-debt situation. Moreover, the installment payments to the seller can provide the money with which to service the refinanced debt at very little net cost to the seller.

That way, the tax on that part of the gain that is represented by the debt will not be due until the refinanced debt is paid, and that may be years away. In the meantime, the seller may enjoy unrestricted use of the borrowed money.

The $5 Million Provision of §453A

Your father's installment sale didn't have to cope with *Internal Revenue Code* §453A, which requires the payment of interest to the IRS for that part of the tax that is deferred because of contracts entered into in any one year by the taxpayer for more than $5 million in deferred installments.

Besides splitting transactions into more than one year and having the ownership of the asset being sold be divided among multiple taxpayers, the key to obtaining installment reporting of the gain on the largest transactions is through combining a collateralized installment sale through an installment accommodator with a properly structured debt accommodation through a debt accommodator. Done right, the deferral on the large-dollar component of the deal is through avoiding relief of debt, while the installment contract remains in an amount which does not trigger §453A.

A Powerful Installment Sale for Today's Transaction Needs

These techniques are taking installment sales out of the backwater where they have resided and are making them a disposition method of choice for sophisticated transactions, with tax advantages combined with optimal investment and a secure income stream.

ADVANCED STRATEGIES FOR INSTALLMENT SALES COMBINED WITH 1031 EXCHANGES

Often, you are going to need sound financial advice and the help of other knowledgeable experts with some of these advanced techniques.

Do a partial 1031 exchange by taking a substantial down payment from an installment sale to use for a down payment on the replacement property. Keeping the installment payments for income is taxable boot. However, taxes on the boot are deferred the same as installment payments are on any other seller-financed sale. If the replacement property generates enough income to make any loan payments owed, you will have an income stream from the installment sale of the relinquished property and another property for continued investment.

The capital gain portion of the payment can be quite high on this type of transaction. The basis from the relinquished property is carried forward into the replacement property. Recall that the installment loan is composed of basis, capital gain, and interest. The basis is the only potion of a loan payment that is not taxable. If all the basis moves into the replacement property, the only remaining portions of the installment payments are taxed, as interest and capital gain.

Another option is having the qualified intermediary make the seller-carried financing from the relinquished property payable to the seller of the replacement property as part of the purchase. In this scenario, you help the buyer of the relinquished property finance the deal and gain the benefit of earning interest. Or the installment note can be sold on the secondary market by the intermediary and the proceeds contributed to the purchase of the replacement property.

An exchanger may get creative assisting the buyer of the relinquished property. Rather than making a direct installment sale of the property inside the exchange, the seller of the relinquished property can consider making a loan to the buyer of the relinquished property outside the exchange and secured by another property or asset the buyer owns. The buyer uses the loan to complete the purchase of the relinquished property without installment payments secured by the property. The exchanger can now buy the replacement property without taxable installment payments or having to sell the installment contract at a discount on a secondary market.

INSTALLMENT SALES BY RELATED PEOPLE

It is often a bad idea to make an installment sale to a related person if the related person will sell the property (or otherwise dispose of it) before completing the purchase from the related person. The first owner will lose the tax-deferred status. Taxes become due for the year the second sale occurred.

This is another situation where the definition of related people goes well beyond bloodlines. Ownership or control of business corporations, trusts, partnerships, and other entities is included in the definition of related people.

SUMMARY

The installment sale has long had many uses in creating an income stream and deferring taxes. In October 2006 it took on a bigger role in the overall strategy to preserve and increase wealth when the IRS announced proposed regulation changes ending the use of private annuity trusts but specifically stating that section 453 installment sales and section 664 charitable remainder trusts were unaffected.

An installment sale is heavily based on the underlying contract. The United States has a Uniform Commercial Code intended to simplify business transactions across state borders. However, many of these codes are primarily intended for the exchange of goods and merchandize. Real estate is unique because it does not move across state borders. Individual states continue to have separate processes for recording real estate ownership, transferring ownership, zoning codes, foreclosure processes, and other differences. Real estate attorneys knowledgeable about the state in which you are conducting business need to be involved in writing the terms and conditions of the contract.

Some contract elements are common to most installment sale contracts. Down payment amounts, amortization schedules, mineral rights, prepayment clauses, and many other issues should be carefully addressed in the installment contract.

The financial benefits are twofold with the installment sale. First is not having to pay the capital gains tax in the year of the sale; rather it is deferred and paid over time with inflated dollars as payments are made. Second is the opportunity to earn interest income from the deferred tax dollars on top of the appreciated value you acquired from the investment. six-step calculation was presented to aid in determining the actual financial benefit achievable.

Examined were some of the most common uses of installment sales, including the retirement sale of a small business to generate an income stream, and the sale of raw land providing little or no income unless successfully speculated for appreciation. Banks do not easily provide desired lending for this type of investment, leaving it to the investor's creative abilities, which can be handsomely rewarded.

The orderly liquidation of investment property lessens the management responsibility, while providing a needed retirement income. With adequate planning, the financial benefits of a real estate investment career include deferred taxes and an income stream that continues for many years.

Finally, creative and effective uses of the installment sale were explored with the collateralized installment sale and advanced strategies of combining installments with a 1031 exchange. In the uncountable scenarios that encompass real estate investing, the installment sale has a definite role in creating and preserving wealth.

8

CHARITABLE REMAINDER TRUSTS HAVE BIG TAX ADVANTAGES

The Tax Reform Act of 1969 made the Charitable Remainder Trust (CRT) possible.

A CRT provides an income stream for either a predetermined length of time or a lifetime in exchange for the irrevocable trust. At the end of that time, the remainder of the trust is donated to the charity. You realize a tax deduction in the tax year the CRT is funded or the property title is transferred. Several factors influence the amount of tax deduction received. The calculation is the present value of the amount the trust will leave to charity at a future date. The life expectancy of the beneficiary receiving the payments (usually the grantor of the trust) heavily influences the tax deduction if it is a lifetime trust. Life expectancy is based on age, not on health. If all the tax deduction cannot be used in one year, it can be carried for up to an additional five years. Capital gains tax is avoided when the property is sold by the CRT, once again using deferred taxes to enhance an income stream.

IRS DEFINITION OF CHARITABLE REMAINDER TRUST

Charitable Remainder Trust

In a charitable remainder trust, the donor transfers assets to an annuity trust or unitrust. The trust pays the donor or another beneficiary a certain amount each year for a specified period. In an annuity trust, the payment is a specified dollar amount. In a unitrust, the payment is a percentage of the value of the trust, as valued each year. The term of the trust is limited to 20 years or the life of the designated recipients. At the end of the term of the trust, the remaining trust assets must be distributed to a charitable organization. Contributions to the charitable remainder trust can qualify for a charitable deduction. This charitable contribution deduction is limited to the present value of the charitable organization's remainder interest. Revenue Procedures 89-20, 89-21, 90-30, and 90-31 provide sample trust forms that the Service will recognize as meeting charitable remainder trust requirements.

Like so many things in the business world, you are able to design a CRT to suit your needs. This should be done carefully because of the long-term implications and irrevocability of the trust. There are several different trust types to choose from, and the manner in which payments are made is highly flexible when first established. Set payments for the duration of the trust, a set percentage, and deferred payments are all options. Additionally, you do not have to be the beneficiary of the trust. You may decide on an heir or other person as the beneficiary. Under certain circumstances, this can be used to eliminate the high estate tax rates. Ultimately, there is ample flexibility setting up a charitable remainder trust.

CRT TAXES

Capital gains tax is deferred until the beneficiary receives payments from the CRT and the taxes are slowly paid with inflated dollars. Because the CRT continues to invest and generate earnings, the tax components in the CRT payment stream can be complex. The CRT can be expected to earn a combination of tax-exempt income and taxable income. The CRT does not pay taxes itself; you, the beneficiary, pay them. The components of the payments you can expect are:

- Ordinary income
- Capital gains tax
- Tax-exempt income
- Return of principal (or basis)

The proportion in each year's payments will vary because of changing returns of investment in each category from year to year.

Important requirements of CRTs are:

- The minimum annual payout rate is 5 percent.

- The maximum annual payment is 50 percent.

- The present value of the remainder interest passing to charity must equal at least 10 percent of the value of the trust.

- File IRS form 5227 annually whether or not the CRT had unrelated business taxable income (UBTI).

- A copy of the trust document must be sent to the IRS the first year form 5227 is filed.

- A federal employer identification number must be established for the CRT.

TYPES OF CHARITIES THE IRS RECOGNIZES DEDUCTIONS FOR

Only the five following types of organizations are qualified non-profit organizations:

1. A community chest, corporation, trust, fund, or foundation organized or created in or under the laws of the United States, any state, the District of Columbia, or any possession of the United States (including Puerto Rico). It must be organized and operated only for one or more of the following purposes:

    - Religious
    - Charitable
    - Educational
    - Scientific
    - Literary
    - The prevention of cruelty to children or animals
    - Certain organizations that foster national or international amateur sports competition also qualify

2. War veterans' organizations, including posts, auxiliaries, trusts, or foundations, organized in the United States or any of its possessions.

3. Domestic fraternal societies, orders, and associations operating under the lodge system.

4. Certain nonprofit cemetery companies or corporations.

5. The United States or any state, the District of Columbia, a U.S. possession (including Puerto Rico), a political subdivision of a state or U.S. possession, or an Indian tribal government or any of its subdivisions that perform substantial government functions.

The first four are straightforward, but number five is better understood with a short example. You contribute cash to your city's police department to be used in a reward program for information about a crime. The city police department is a qualified government organization, and your contribution is for a public purpose. You can deduct your contribution.

The ability to carry the deduction forward for five years is important because there are limits to how much can be deducted each year. Your deduction for charitable contributions is limited to 50 percent of your adjusted gross income, but often 20 and 30 percent limits may apply. In addition, the total of your charitable contributions deduction combined with certain other itemized deductions may be limited. The 50 percent limit rule applies to charities. The 30 percent limit rule applies to veterans' organizations, fraternal societies, nonprofit cemeteries, and certain private non-operating foundations.

There are limited situations in which the IRS will deny the deduction. These include:

• Conditional donating when there is a substantial possibility the condition will not be met.

• An heir is likely to legally challenge the donation.

- The charitable donation is made to an organization practicing some form of discrimination.

Benefits of charitable remainder trusts include:

- The trust incurs no capital gains tax, enabling more money to be invested to fund your income.

- Income tax deduction that ranges from 30 to 70 percent of the gift amount, depending on the beneficiary's age and the rate of the payout.

- Lifetime payments can be substantially more than the current rate of return the asset pays, often two to three times for property when only rent can be depended on for income because the capital gains tax on appreciated value is too high for a sale to occur.

- Property or other assets are removed from the donor's estate, unless the beneficiary is not the donor or spouse.

- Eliminates property tax payments.

MR. AND MRS. OMEGA'S CRT

Mr. and Mrs. Omega are ready to dispose of the $4 million office building they have owned for 25 years, having purchased it for $300,000. Remaining depreciation no longer adequately shields income, and the building will likely need major repairs in the years to come. They do not want to take a chance on having to repossess it in an installment sale. The capital gains tax will exceed $500,000 in an outright sale. They begin considering a charitable remainder trust that will provide a lifetime of payments. Mr. Omega is 72, and Mrs. Omega is 69 years old.

After paying $68,063 in depreciation recapture tax and $550,838 in capital gains tax, the Omegas are left with $3,381,099

INVESTED AT 6%	
Sale Price	$4,000,000
Depreciation Recovered	$68,063
Capital Gain Tax	$550,838
Available to Invest	$3,381,099
Annual Return at 6%	$202,866

to invest at 6 percent. Calculations of a 6 percent return show an annual income of $202,866 from an outright sale.

With the charitable remainder annuity trust (CRAT), which provides a fixed payment, the depreciation recapture tax of $68,063 will be repaid and leaves over $3,931,937 invested in the trust. They choose a payout rate of 7 percent per year. The result is an annual income of $275,236 and a tax deduction of $1,233,449, further reducing taxes over the next several years.

CRT	
Sale Price	$4,000,000
Depreciation	$68,063
Capital Gain	$0
Available to Invest	$3,931,937
Annual Payment	$275,236
Tax Deduction	$1,233,449

Take it one step farther to see the repeatable effect when 50 percent of the income from the CRT is not taxed but all income from the 6 percent investment is taxed. This assumes 50 percent of the CRT earnings have UBTI. Without a CRT there is a smaller return on their investment at $202,866, but the Omegas would pay tax on the entire amount because they did not have a good tax strategy.

INCOME TAX AFFECT				
Investment	Annual Payment	Tax Free Portion	Tax Payable @ 35%	Spendable Income
6% Return	$202,866	100%	$71,003	$131,863
CRT	$275,236	50%	$48,166	$227,070

The tax amounts to $71,003 and drops the annual spendable income to only $131,863. On the other hand, the CRT income is only partially taxed and leaves $227,070 of spendable income, a clear indication that this tax strategy has big advantages. A 50 percent UBTI rate is very high. It is used to simplify the example, while still accounting for multiple possible variations in taxes owed. A likely variation is that the Omegas would owe some tax on the deferred capital gain that would effectively be cancelled by the deduction from the charitable donation being carried forward for several years.

MANAGEMENT OF CRTS

Although the combined benefits of charitable remainder trusts are rewarding, they can be complicated to manage. The IRS estimates almost 100 hours are needed just to complete and submit Form 5227. Many CRTs also require Form 1040 to be submitted annually. Most major charitable organizations offer trustee services in appreciation of your donation, without charging any administration fees. The institutions often retain outside financial services that provide much more than just preparing the tax forms.

IRS TIME ESTIMATE TO COMPLETE FORM 5227
The time needed to complete and file this form will vary depending on individual circumstances. The estimated average time is:
Recordkeeping . . . . .65 hr., 17 min.
Learning about the law or the form . . . . 11 hr., 24 min.
Preparing the form . . . . 19 hr., 24 min.
Copying, assembling, and sending the form to IRS . . . . 1 hr., 52 min.

Common trustee services include:

- Establishing a portfolio of investments.

- Managing assets if you choose to self-advise the account.

- Conducting due diligence on investments.

- Providing accounting services and financial reports on donor accounts.

- Providing investment strategies and reviews.

- Managing deposits, transfers, and distribution of funds.

- Providing performance reports.

- Preparing federal annual tax returns.

- Preparing state tax returns.

- Monitoring tax code changes at the federal and state levels.

Any of these tasks can be challenging. The combination is often overwhelming, especially if more than one donation or account is established. Not all charitable foundations are able to offer or perform these tasks. Another generous and helpful offering from the larger institutions is to manage donations you make to them, as well as donations made to other institutions.

Generous and financially capable donors may elect to establish a charitable foundation of their own. Professional charitable service companies are available to establish and manage personal foundations for a fee.

DECIDING BETWEEN CRUT AND CRAT

The charitable remainder unitrust (CRUT) and charitable remainder annuity trust (CRAT) are the two most commonly used, although several others exist. The primary difference between the two account types is that the CRAT pays a set and dependable amount of income monthly, quarterly, semi-quarterly, or annually. The CRUT pays at the same frequencies but as a percentage of the trust balance. The payment received will vary from payment period to payment period depending on the income the trust earns. Additionally, there are four variations to the CRUT. The CRAT does not have variations other than initially selecting the amount the trust will pay out annually (between 5 and 50 percent).

Both the CRAT and CRUT must leave a minimum of 10 percent of the amount transferred into the trust to the charity (present value at the time of transfer). Either type of trust can be established to provide a lifetime income stream or be established for a set amount of time, which cannot exceed 20 years. Trusts established for a set number of years will pay a higher amount than a lifetime income. The reason is that the lifetime trust must have a 5 percent or less probability of becoming exhausted before the end of the beneficiary's life, as established by IRS life expectancy tables. Your age, or the time length of the trust combined with the annual payout percentage, affects the tax deduction received.

In the following comparison chart, all the variables used to determine annual income and the tax deduction are held constant except the tax deduction and the time length of the trust. A $2 million property is placed in the trust with 7 percent annual payments, which generates $140,000 income paid quarterly. The ages of the two beneficiaries are held constant for each calculation at 72 and 70. The IRS provides a discount rate used to determine the allowable tax deduction based on expected income the trust will earn. The result is a CRUT with a term of ten years obtaining a tax deduction of $994,282 at the high end and a CRAT held for 20 years, providing a tax deduction of $358,566 at the low end.

COMPARISON OF CRAT AND CRUT TAX DEDUCTIONS — SIX VARIATIONS						
Variable	CRAT Lifetime	CRAT 20 Years	CRAT 10 Years	CRUT Lifetime	CRUT 20 Years	CRUT 10 Years
Tax Deduction	$547,024	$358,566	$946,711	$659,460	$494,340	$994,282
Constants						
Annual Income	$140,000	$140,000	$140,000	$140,000	$140,000	$140,000
Number of Beneficiaries	2	2	2	2	2	2
Age of 1st Beneficiary	72	72	72	72	72	72
Age of 2nd Beneficiary	70	70	70	70	70	70
Property Value	$2M	$2M	$2M	$2M	$2M	$2M
Payment Frequency	Quarterly	Quarterly	Quarterly	Quarterly	Quarterly	Quarterly
Annuity Rate	7%	7%	7%	7%	7%	7%
IRS Discount Rate	6%	6%	6%	6%	6%	6%

One uncontrollable variable is inherent to the CRUT calculations. Because the CRUT annual payment is a percentage of the fund, it varies the amount of income provided over the years depending on how much the trust earns. There is no way to accurately predict future CRUT earnings.

The annuity rate (annual payout percentage) paid to the beneficiary has the most effect on the income received for a CRAT. The annual payout percentage plus the income of the trust affect the income received from a CRAT. The 10 percent remainder to the charity and 5 percent probability that the trust will become exhausted also affect how much is paid to the beneficiary each year. The following comparison chart uses the same constants as the previous chart, with the exception of maximizing the income paid each year, thereby using the maximum allowable annuity payout rate. Theoretically, the payout rate could be as high as 50 percent; however, the 10 percent remainder and 5 percent exhaustion probability effectively limit the payout to the rates shown.

The result is a significant variation to the income and tax deduction. In each scenario, the tax deduction is close to the required 10 percent charitable remainder, except for the lifetime CRAT that leaves over 24 percent to charity. The income varies from a CRAT lifetime lowest payout of $145,945 annually to the highest of $426, 540 for the ten-year CRUT. In all cases, except the ten-year CRAT, the CRUT pays a better income. Also notice that the lifetime CRUT pays more than the 20-year CRUT. The ten-year CRUT does pay a substantially higher annual income, but when the trust ends, the oldest beneficiary will be only age 82 and might need the income to continue. Other scenarios can be considered, such as a 15-year CRUT. Remember, the CRUT can provide a higher or lower amount of income depending on the trust's annual earnings. However, the CRUT is the most commonly selected charitable remainder trust for people wanting to maximize income.

COMPARISON OF CRAT AND CRUT TAX INCOME — SIX VARIATIONS						
Variable	CRAT Lifetime	CRAT 20 Years	CRAT 10 Years	CRUT Lifetime	CRUT 20 Years	CRUT 10 Years
Annual Income	$145,945	$153,400	$239,250	$315,800	$225,556	$426,540

Tax Deduction	$485,329	$201,457	$200,001	$200,020	$200,000	$200,012
Maximum Annuity Rate	7.29%	7.67%	11.96%	15.79%	11.27%	21.32%
Constants						
Number of Beneficiaries	2	2	2	2	2	2
Age of 1st Beneficiary	72	72	72	72	72	72
Age of 2nd Beneficiary	70	70	70	70	70	70
Property Value	$2M	$2M	$2M	$2M	$2M	$2M
Payment Frequency	Quarterly	Quarterly	Quarterly	Quarterly	Quarterly	Quarterly
IRS Discount Rate	6%	6%	6%	6%	6%	6%

The lifetime payment or predetermined time length CRAT are the only two versions. The CRUT, on the other hand, has four other variations to consider.

CRUT VARIATIONS

The standard CRUT was used for the comparisons in the previous charts. This version pays an income as a percentage of the fund every year. In years that the fund does not have earnings or has losses, the trust will use capital to pay the minimum percentage owed. Most, if not all, years will have earnings. In years with earnings, less or no capital will be needed to provide the beneficiary's income. Years with earnings that exceed the payout will actually grow the value of the trust. Beneficiaries electing a small payout in the early years often see payout amounts grow in later years, keeping pace with or exceeding inflation.

The net income CRUT does not use the trust principal to make payments to the beneficiary. In years the trust has lower earnings than required to make income payments, income is reduced. A payout is made to the point of exhausting all the earnings. A year without earnings results in no income from the trust.

The net income with makeup CRUT compensates if the trust fails to make a full annual income payment. In good years, the trust makes up for any amounts not paid in previous years. The trust principal remains untouched, but if earnings exceed the required payout, payouts missed in previous years will be made up.

The flip CRUT begins as a net income CRUT and "flips" into a standard CRUT when a pre-determined date or event occurs. The event can be almost anything: the death of a spouse, when the trust reaches a certain earnings level, or when a specified high value asset is sold. The flip CRUT protects the trust's principal until either a certain date or event occurs. After the flip, the trust begins paying out of the principal, if necessary, to make income payments.

MECHANICS OF ESTABLISHING A CRT

Once the type of CRT and benefiting charity are selected, the process of establishing a CRT is relatively simple for the donor. The trustee prepares the CRT documentation for review by the donor, financial advisor, and legal advisor. Property or other assets are transferred to the trustee to be managed or sold so that the funds can be reinvested.

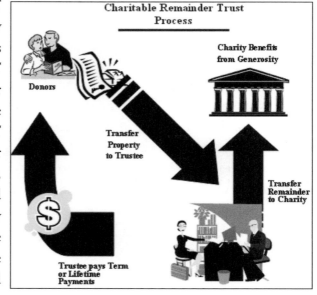

In accordance with the CRT agreement, income payments are made to the beneficiary. The trustee continues to manage the trust for the duration it is established. At the conclusion of the trust, the remainder of the assets are delivered to the charity, enabling it to continue its mission.

When establishing the trust, the donor has control of:

- Designating the beneficiaries.

- Choosing the trustee.

- Designating the benefiting charity.

- Determining the rate income is paid, within established limits.

- Selecting how long the trust is established.

As with most IRS-regulated activities, there are prohibited transactions. Examples include:

- Disqualified people may not sell assets to the trust.

- Disqualified people may not buy assets from the trust.

- Disqualified people may not do business with the trust.

Disqualified people include the donors, beneficiaries, trustee, lineal descendants, ascendants, and business entities that have a substantial relationship the donor or trust. Specific relationships are further defined in the IRS code.

THE WEALTH REPLACEMENT TRUST

There is recourse for those who establish a trust but still want heirs to benefit from their good fortune. Depending on age and health, a life insurance policy payable to heirs is the most likely answer. The life insurance policy may not need to be as high in value as the property used to establish the CRT. First, the highly appreciated assets would have paid a substantial tax that could not be passed to heirs. Second, any estate tax would further reduce the property's value that did pass to heirs. Third, it may be possible to establish another trust that receives the proceeds from the life insurance policy so that proceeds pass to heirs outside the estate through an irrevocable life insurance policy. Not only does the insurance pay outside the estate, but the proceeds do not pay income tax. A policy worth much less than the donated property can actually be worth more to heirs. CRTs combined with an insurance policy in a wealth replacement trust can definitely be a win-win solution for all involved.

A good source of funds to purchase the life insurance policy is the savings obtained with the tax deduction from establishing the CRT. The improved income from the CRT can be another source for funding the insurance policy. If you have only one heir, it may be possible to purchase a life insurance policy outside your estate without establishing another trust. A responsible heir can purchase the policy on their own. You can gift the premium cost to them each year. Naturally, it is important to obtain the advice of a tax consultant first.

OTHER TAX-FAVORABLE CHARITABLE GIVING

In addition to the CRAT and CRUT, there are other tax-favorable ways to donate to charities and nonprofit organizations. These include:

- Charitable Lead Trust
- Pooled Income Fund
- Retained Life Estate Benefits
- Charitable Gift Annuity

IRS DEFINITIONS OF CHARITABLE LEAD TRUST

- **Charitable Lead Trust**

  A charitable lead trust pays an annuity or unitrust interest to a designated charity for a specified term of years (the "charitable term"), with the remainder ultimately distributed to non-charitable beneficiaries. There is no specified limit for the charitable term. The donor receives a charitable deduction for the value of the interest received by the charity. The value of the non-charitable beneficiary's remainder interest is a taxable gift by the grantor.

- **Charitable Lead Annuity Trust**

  A charitable lead annuity trust is a charitable lead trust paying a fixed percentage of the initial value of the trust assets to the charity for the charitable term.

- **Charitable Lead Unitrust**

  A charitable lead unitrust is a charitable lead trust paying a percentage of the value of its assets, determined annually, to a charity for the charitable term.

CHARITABLE LEAD TRUST

The charitable lead trust (CLT) has the ability to pass wealth to future generations but is susceptible to the IRS discount rate that changes monthly. The month a CLT is established or the proceeding two months determine the discount rate affecting the CLT.

CLTs are available both as an annuity and as a unitrust. Both trust types are set up to pay a percentage of the trust's earnings to the charity. Any earnings not paid to the charity may be taxable. Two options when establishing a CLT are grantor or nongrantor. If you choose a grantor trust, you will receive a tax deduction the year the trust is established. You remain the owner of the trust, and all

COMPARISON OF LEAD ANNUITY AND UNITRUST		
Variables	Nongrantor Annuity 20 Years	Nongrantor Unitrust 20 Years
Tax or Estate Deduction	$604,920	$628,667
Subject to Gift or Estate Tax	$395,080	$371,333
Constants		
Annual Income to Charity	$50,000	$50,000
Property Value	$1,000,000	$1,000,000
Annuity Rate	5%	5%
IRS Discount Rate	5.6%	5.6%

income earned (including that donated to charity) will be included and taxed as your income. At the end of the trust term, the balance remaining in the trust is returned to you. This type of CLT is frequently used to gain a large tax deduction in the year the trust is established.

A nongrantor CLT gives up ownership of the trust. At the end of the trust term, the balance remaining in the trust is delivered to your designated beneficiary. Because they do not own the trust, they are not eligible to take the tax deduction when it is established. For gift and estate tax purposes, the value of the trust (property) is reduced by the amount of the tax deduction you could not take. This type of CLT is used to reduce gift and estate taxes.

The chart shows an example of both a CLT annuity and a unitrust with a

20-year term. With the $1 million trust paying a 5 percent annuity rate to the charity each year, the charity receives $50,000. In exchange for this, the annuity trust is entitled to a $604,920 tax deduction that reduces the heirs' taxable amount to $395,080. The numbers for the unitrust are slightly better with the remaining taxable portion at $371,333. Depending on many variables, including changes in the estate tax exclusion limits, this could enable an estate to avoid paying any taxes.

The IRS discount rate can change on a monthly basis and has a significant effect on the estate tax deduction. Closely consider the discount rate that will be applied when the trust is established. Ages of the donors also have a significant effect. The example shows the differences for a range of rates on a charitable lead unitrust. This scenario assumes the trust is established for the life duration of a married couple rather than for a set number of years. Two sets of ages are compared. A $1 million trust pays a 5 percent annuity to the charity. The results show a lower IRS discount rate improves the tax deduction. It improves further when the donors are younger because the charity benefits longer from the trust before it is passed to the donors' heirs.

IRS DISCOUNT RATE AFFECT ON CHARITABLE LEAD UNITRUST				
	Ages 72 and 70		Ages 65 and 63	
IRS Discount Rate	Subject to Estate Tax	Estate Deduction	Subject to Estate Tax	Estate Deduction
3%	$433,500	$566,500	$334,010	$665,990
5%	$437,640	$562,360	$338,200	$661,800
7%	$441,700	$558,300	$342,300	$657,700
9%	$445,660	$554,340	$346,330	$653,670
11%	$449,540	$550,460	$350,280	$649,720

RETAINED LIFE ESTATE

The retained life estate is offered by some but not all charities. This charity gifting method allows you to obtain the charitable tax deduction during your lifetime and spend the rest of your years in the home. Ownership of the home is transferred to the charity in exchange for the tax deduction.

Most personal residences qualify, including:

- Primary residence
- Condominium
- Farms with or without a house
- Vacation home
- Stock in a cooperative housing corporation

The retained use of the home can be either for the rest of a person's life or for a set number of years. Perhaps a donor has a vacation home they expect to use for another 10 years before they wish to donate it. Maybe plans are in place to leave the primary residence for other living arrangements in a few years. These are the types of situations when it makes sense to obtain a tax donation and relinquish the home after a set number of years.

RETAINED LIFE ESTATE	
Tax Deduction	$579,910
Term of Retained Use	10 years
FMV of Property	$1,000,000
Value of Improvements	$900,000
Life of Improvements	40 years
IRS Discount Rate	5.60%

Many personal factors go into determining the tax deduction obtained and the amount taken each year. Competent financial advice is needed. The example assumes a $1 million property. The value of the house or structures is $900,000 and has a useful life of 40 years, after which the appreciated value will be approximately the same as the current value. This scenario could provide a $579,910 tax deduction while the donor remains in the house for another ten years. A similar home retained for life by a married couple, ages 72 and 70, might obtain a tax deduction of $413,550.

CHARITABLE GIFT ANNUITY

A charitable gift annuity provides the donor with an income stream and tax deduction in exchange for a donation of appreciated stocks, cash, real estate, or other assets. Rather than a trust, this is a contract between the annuitant and charity. The income stream is backed by the total assets of the charity, not just the value contributed by the annuitant. Some states regulate charitable gift annuities.

Generally, the American Council on Gift Annuities establishes the rate of return. Rates of return increase as the age of the annuitant increases. The payments are not income to the annuitant; they are a partially tax-free return of the annuitant's gift. If funded with appreciated real estate, likely tax components of the payments include ordinary income, capital gain, and partially tax-free earnings.

The charitable gift annuity can be set up for a single life, two lives, or two lives with right of survivorship. The person receiving the payments does not have to be the donor. Common versions of the charitable gift annuity are:

- Immediate Charitable Gift Annuity

- Deferred Charitable Gift Annuity

- Flexible Charitable Gift Annuity (start date is determined after the contribution is made)

- College Tuition Charitable Gift Annuity

POOLED INCOME FUND

The pooled income fund is another lifetime income stream coupled with tax-favorable treatment. The pooled income fund comes under section 642 of the IRS code rather than section 664 as the CRT does. Contributions to pooled income funds are treated favorably for income tax, gift tax, and estate tax.

IRS DEFINITION OF POOLED INCOME TRUST

Pooled Income Fund Trust

A pooled income fund is an unincorporated fund set up by a public charity to which a person transfers property, reserving an income interest in, and giving the charity the remainder interest in, that property. The code and regulations under Section 642 establish trust requirements. These funds file Form 1041.

Your charitable donation is commingled with that of other donors in exchange for a proportionate annual payment based on the fund's investment earnings. At the end of the donor's life, the remaining value of their portion is removed from the fund and given to charity.

The income is normally for the benefit of the donor but does not have to be. The income may be paid to the donor during his or her lifetime concurrent with another individual with the right of survivorship for the second person. All the income, or a portion of the income, can also be allotted to another individual for the lifetime of the benefiting individual. Almost any combination of beneficiaries is permitted.

Tax benefits and consequences for contributing to a pooled income fund include:

- No IRS recognition of capital gain on donated property.

- Property with debt owed realizes a capital gain to the donor in the form of debt forgiven.

- Deductible for income, gift, and estate purposes based on value at the time of donation.

- For estate taxes the donor's value of the fund is first included in the estate and then excluded based on the donation to charity, effectively removing it from the estate.

POOLED FUND TAX DEDUCTION VALUES BASED ON AGE AND RATE OF RETURN DONATION OF $1M				
	Age 60	Age 65	Age 70	Age 75
Rate of Return	5%	5%	5%	5%
Annual Income	$50,000	$50,000	$50,000	$50,000
Tax Deduction	$406,240	$472,550	$543,250	$615,100
Rate of Return	7.5%	7.5%	7.5%	7.5%
Annual Income	$75,000	$75,000	$75,000	$75,000
Tax Deduction	$285,560	$350,650	$424,260	$503,160
Rate of Return	10%	10%	10%	10%
Annual Income	$100,000	$100,000	$100,000	$100,000
Tax Deduction	$211,960	$271,400	$342,040	$421,230

Rate of return determines the annual income. The age of the donor and the payout rate determine the value of the tax deduction. As the rate of return increases, the tax deduction decreases. As age increases, the allowable tax deduction increases.

Pooled income funds can be an excellent way to convert low cash flow, highly appreciated properties into a dependable lifelong income stream and obtain significant tax deductions.

Summary of benefits of a pooled income fund:

- Dependable source of income.

- Potential for substantially better income in exchange for low rate of return property.

- You and another can be named beneficiary with survival benefits.

- Allowed to add to the gift and increase income at a later time.

- Immediate income tax deduction for a deferred charitable gift.

- Reduce or eliminate estate tax.

- Does not incur capital gains tax upon transfer of the property.

- Satisfaction of charitable giving.

SUMMARY

Charitable remainder trusts and other charitable vehicles can be very beneficial to eliminating or reducing taxes, as well as providing the gratifying accomplishment of helping others. Wealth replacement trusts using a life insurance policy are a great strategy for providing an inheritance in addition to the charitable donation. The charitable lead trust provides an income to the charity, reduces your taxes, and still provides for your heirs. The retained life estate is another win-win for the taxpayer and the charity. You can obtain major tax deductions during your lifetime, while continuing to live in your home or use vacation property. The charitable gift annuity and pooled income fund provide income streams along with tax deductions. Use the following summary chart for a quick reference of your opportunity for philanthropy combined with highly regarded tax reductions. It is a great opportunity for you to share your good fortune and wealth with others.

CHARITABLE OPTIONS COMPARISON			
Charitable Option	Objective	Action Needed	General Benefits
Charitable Remainder Annuity Trust	A fixed and potentially increased income	Establish a charitable trust with property or other assets	Immediate income tax deduction and fixed income for life
Charitable Remainder Unitrust	Protect principal with varying income stream	Establish a trust that pays a percentage of the trusts's assets; income varies	Immediate income tax deduction; annual income for life with potential to increases
Wealth Replacement Trust	Provide inheritance	Use increased income or tax deduction to fund life insurance policy	Heirs receive life insurance payout instead of property
Charitable Lead Trust	Reduce gift and estate taxes on assets planned for heirs	Create a trust that pays a fixed or variable income to charity for a set term and then passes to heirs	Reduced size of taxable estate; retains property in the family, often with reduced gift taxes
Retained Life Estate	Gift personal residence or farm with lifetime right of your use	Transfer title for home to charity, but retain occupancy	Current income tax deduction with charity obtaining residence upon death
Charitable Gift Annuity	Income with fixed annual payments from a contract rather than a trust	Gift to charity in exchange for contractual payments	Immediate and future savings on income taxes; fixed payments for life
Pooled Income Fund	Improved income from low rate of return property	Commingle property or other assets with other donors	Current income tax deduction; possible income improvement

9

WEALTH GOALS AND STRATEGIES

———

Whether you are investing in multimillion-dollar real estate or buying your first residential property, goals and strategies are key to staying on track to a wealthy life style. An important strategy is to maximize your return on the income produced by the property and the appreciated value. With these as cornerstones, add the advantage of a tax-favorable transaction strategy to meet your goals of acquiring and preserving wealth.

Overall, residential real estate in the United States can be expected to appreciate at a rate of 11 percent a year, much higher than the rate of inflation. Although that provides a good rate of return, your goal should be higher. A well-crafted real estate investment should have a cash flow before taxes of 10 to 12 percent, after expenses and finance payments. Add the cash flow to appreciation, and your investment is producing more than a 21 percent return on investment. With a solid investment strategy that includes few or no taxes, the rate of return goes much higher.

One tax consequence from real estate investing is the ability to write off any losses that may occur. If a loss does occur, you want to be able to take advantage of it to reduce taxes on other investments and possibly reduce income tax paid on a salary or other sources. There are IRS constraints regarding passive income typically derived from real estate investing.

PASSIVE INCOME VERSUS ACTIVE INCOME

The IRS categorizes rental income as passive income, but interest (such as installment sales) is non-passive income. Therefore, losses from passive business activities do not reduce taxes on other income, such as the interest from an installment sale. However, rental income for real estate professionals is non-passive income (this is an exception to the passive rental income rule). These differences of income categorization become important if business losses occur — especially if the individual has multiple income streams. Anyone holding multiple properties will likely have multiple income streams, and the number of income streams can vary from one tax year to the next. The concept and definitions of passive and non-passive income came from Congress's attempt to eliminate certain excessive tax schemes.

Prior to these changes, people were able to use real estate depreciation to reduce the taxes owed on large incomes derived from another profession. People with large incomes would purchase rental properties that provided high depreciation write-offs but would create a business loss when rental income was significantly less than the depreciation. The depreciation loss would then be used to reduce taxes on a large income (preferably to lower a high tax bracket) from a different profession. The tax code changes may have ended an abusive tax scheme but also have consequences for legitimate business activities that generate passive income. As a result, it is important for real estate investors to understand the difference and tax consequences between passive and non-passive income (and losses).

PASSIVE INCOME

Rental income is treated as passive income even if you materially participated in rental activity, unless you are a real estate professional. A real estate professional must meet two conditions:

1. More than half of all personal services you provided during the year (include all businesses and trades you engaged in) were in the real

estate profession, and you materially participated. Personal services only count if you owned at least 5 percent of the business.

2. You performed 750 or more hours of service by materially participating in a real estate trade or business.

You cannot count your spouse's activities toward determining if you meet the requirements.

Material participation requires passing any one of these seven tests:

1. Does the taxpayer and/or spouse work more than 500 hours a year in the business?

2. Does the taxpayer do most of the work? If taxpayer does not meet the 500-hour test, but his participation is the only activity in the business, he materially participates; i.e., a sole proprietor with no employees.

3. Does the taxpayer work more than 100 hours and no one (including non-owners or employees) works more hours? Example: If the owner puts in 175 hours a year and an employee works 190 hours a year, taxpayer would not meet material participation test.

4. Does the taxpayer have several passive activities in which he participates between 100–500 hours each, and the total time is more than 500 hours? The following activities should not be included in the above test: rental activities, activities involving portfolio or investment income, and activities in which the taxpayer does most of the work.

5. Did the taxpayer materially participate in the activity for any five out of ten preceding years (need not be consecutive)? Example: A taxpayer retired, and his children now run the business, but he stills owns part of the partnership.

6. Did the taxpayer materially participate in a personal service activity

for any three prior years (need not be consecutive)? Personal service activity includes fields of health, law, engineering, architecture, accounting, actuarial science, performing arts, and consulting.

7. Do the facts and circumstances indicate taxpayer is materially participating? Test does not apply unless taxpayer worked more than 100 hours a year. Furthermore, it does not apply if:

   a. Any person, other than the taxpayer, received compensation for managing the activity.

   b. If any person spent more hours than the taxpayer managing the activity.

You can count your spouse's activities in determining material participation.

The first four tests refer to the number of hours of participation in the tax year, tests five and six cover material participation in prior tax years, and the final test applies to the facts and circumstances, but is highly restrictive.

Real estate trades and business include:

- Brokers
- Managers or operators of real estate properties
- Renting and leasing properties
- Construction and development companies
- Otherwise converts property uses

If you are a real estate professional, rental income is not considered passive income and can be used to offset active or earned income.

AT RISK LIMIT

Although passive losses cannot be used to offset active income, all passive income and losses are accumulative. Losses from one passive income stream are used to offset positive income from a different income stream.

However, there is a limitation known as the At Risk Limit. Total losses from one investment cannot exceed the total amount invested and at risk in that particular investment.

Real estate partnerships are a good example of the at risk limit. Mr. Williams buys into a 20 percent share of a limited real estate partnership for $25,000; this is one of several real estate investments that he owns. Because he is a limited partner, he does not share in the overall risk to the partnership. His risk is limited to the $25,000 invested. The partnership has a $175,000 loss. Mr. Williams's 20 percent share of the loss is $35,000. His investment that is at risk is only $25,000, and therefore his tax write-off against other passive income is limited to only $25,000. Additionally, he cannot carry over the remaining $10,000 to other tax years. An exception does exist to the rule not allowing a carryover to exceed the amount at risk. If Mr. Williams was to invest another $10,000 into the partnership, the additional investment would be at risk, and he could then use the carried-over $10,000 loss as a write-off against any passive income. Mr. Williams would also be able to use the carryover loss to offset a profit if he sold the share of the partnership for more than the original $25,000.

There are many exceptions and variations to the at risk limit rules. For instance, non-recourse loans used to purchase property are not considered at risk funds because only the property used as security is at risk. The investor's loss is limited to the risk, the original investment, and any portion of the loan that has been paid off. Also, any insurance coverage for a loss lowers the amount that an investor has at risk. The less there is at risk, the less that can be used to reduce taxes owed on other passive income.

SPECIAL $25,000 ALLOWANCE

There is a silver lining in the dark cloud of having rental loses that cannot be written off against non-passive income. In the unwanted event of a bad rental scenario, there is an allowance to write the loss off against non-passive income if you meet certain conditions.

If you or your spouse actively participated in a passive rental real estate activity, you can deduct up to $25,000 of loss from your non-passive income. This special allowance is an exception to the general rule disallowing passive losses from reducing non-passive income. Losses from passive activities can be applied against the tax on non-passive income up to $25,000 after taking into account any losses on passive income.

If you are married, file a separate return, and live apart from your spouse for the entire tax year, your special allowance cannot be more than $12,500. If you lived with your spouse at any time during the year and are filing a separate return, you cannot use the special allowance to reduce your non-passive income or tax on non-passive income.

The maximum special allowance is reduced if your modified adjusted gross income exceeds certain amounts. A modified adjusted gross income (MAGI) phase-out rule does reduce or eliminate some of a landlord's ability to use this special allowance. In 2005, the phase-out began for those with a MAGI above $100,000. For every dollar above the threshold, the allowance is lowered by half a dollar. The phase-out is complete, and no allowance is given for MAGI above $150,000. Phase-out limits and tax code are subject to change, so check current code if you think this situation might apply to you.

A brief example of how this allowance works: Ms. Chant is a married taxpayer with an $85,000 salary (non-passive), $10,000 income from a limited liability company she invested in (passive), and a $16,000 loss from a rental real estate she owns (passive). Her modified adjusted gross income is less than $100,000. Ms. Chant uses $10,000 of the rental loss to offset the $10,000 in passive income from the LLC. Because she actively participated in the rental activities and met the other requirements, she can use the remaining $6,000 loss to offset her non-passive $85,000 salary.

Before you try to determine what is passive and what is non-passive income, you will need a plan for acquiring the income. Becoming wealthy seldom happens by happenstance. Planning and strategies are the surest way to make it happen.

GETTING STARTED STRATEGIES

Start at the beginning. Sit down with paper and pencil. List all your assets and all your liabilities. Determine how much capital you have to invest. Look into the future at major expenses, college tuitions, a growing family, prospects of having to relocate, and so on. Take these into account when developing your plan. Will you need to sell a property in 15 years to finance a college education? Make sure you have planned to sell that property and have the correct one to sell when the time comes.

Decide early what you want to specialize in to maximize returns. Learn everything there is to know about the specialty. Plan ahead if you want to add another specialty or change specialties in the future. Management specialties to consider are:

- Maximizing cash flow from rentals.
- Maximizing appreciation.
- Equity build-up by paying off mortgages.
- Acquiring and managing multiple properties.
- Leveraging into one or two large properties.
- Capital improvements.
- Constructing new properties.
- Purchasing languishing businesses for improvement and resale.
- Sweat equity.
- Renovation and resale.

You will need a general knowledge of all the management specialties and likely will employ several over your career. However, there is little need to become overly knowledgeable about construction if you intend to be a landlord. Whether you are a landlord, performing sweat equity, or making renovations for resale, the specialist will need to know quite a bit about maintenance and repair. If you have skills, fine. If do not have the skills, include a plan to acquire them before making the first real estate purchase. Your investment will quickly turn into a loss if you have to hire a plumber every time a faucet leaks.

Every property owner will need basic accounting skills to determine cash flows, evaluate financing terms, perform due diligence, and keep accurate accounting books. As you build wealth, you will likely hire an accountant to help with much of this, but you still need to be able to read and comprehend the statements and analyses the experts provide.

Make these decisions early and put a plan together with specific timelines to follow. Track the plan and know when you are ready to invest in property with the skills necessary to succeed. Besides management specialization, there needs to be a strategy and plan for the types of property for investment.

Property types:

- Strip mall
- Apartments
- Residential house
- Business
- Office building
- Duplex or multiplex
- Foreclosures

Specialized investment in property types creates several advantages. Business owners that lease part of your strip mall have very different needs and expectations than residential tenants. A business owner will become very concerned about lost revenue if a problem with the property inconveniences business operations or even causes it to close. A residential tenant expects the appliances to operate correctly but does not face a loss of revenue when the heating element in the stove quits working.

The quality of the property and its location have to be decided and planned for. Will a property located 50 miles away from you be acceptable if you plan to make periodic repairs and maintenance? Ownership at a crime-ridden location is going to have its own set of problems to deal with. Residential houses have more stable tenants than many apartments but fewer units to be rented. Often the cash flow rate for a house is less than for an apartment complex. More units involves screening new tenants more frequently.

Business ownership requires knowledge about the business or hiring a competent manager. The right business may provide a better return on investment but may also include hiring and managing employees. A strategy of acquiring multiple businesses or selling and purchasing businesses to step up the value is going to be more complex than rental real estate. These are just of few of the reasons that deciding on a strategy and building a plan to obtain the goal are important.

RISK PHILOSOPHY

Risk is both age and money sensitive. A young real estate investor is likely to take a larger risk because they have less to lose and plenty of time to recover from a mistake. Conversely, the older investor does not have the luxury of time to recover. Still, if an older investor has accumulated several million dollars, the difference in a big or small mistake is not the same as for a beginning investor with less than $100,000 at risk. Consequences to the two would be very different from a $100,000 error.

With the accumulation of wealth comes experience and knowledge. An experienced investor will recognize a misrepresented property or exaggerated rental profits. The experienced investor likely has a feel for business cycles and is better suited to optimize the buy and sell timing.

Every individual has a different tolerance for risk. The key is not taking risks that you cannot afford. Consider:

- How much of your money and how much of other people's money is being put at risk?

- Why is the property for sale?

- How easy will it be to resell the property?

- Do current and future local economic conditions look favorable?

- What are the risks of tenants damaging the property?

- What is the current and future vacancy rate?

- Does a lender have recourse to other assets you own?

- Are there any known or probable physical defects with the property?

- Is it an investment with highly predictable income or speculation that it will appreciate?

- Is future cash flow predictable and sustainable?

Each property will have unique risks associated with it. This list of things to consider is certainly not exhaustive. The smart investor studies the risks and understands their risk tolerance.

MEET THE EXPERTS

- Real estate tax accountants
- 1031 exchange professionals
- Due diligence professionals
- Inspectors and engineers
- Local zoning and planning departments
- Investment and financial advisors
- Real estate attorneys
- Appraisers
- Real estate brokers
- Tradesmen

You are not going to hire all these experts and keep them working for you all the time. However, you should know who to contact when they are needed. Interviewing them ahead of time can create a readily available list. Experts often become very specialized, and some may not be suited to your goals and strategies. If foreclosures or fixer-uppers are your real estate strategy, the most important experts on your list may be inspectors, contractors, and roofers. Those using complex financial arrangements for large acquisitions will need more assistance from accountants, financial advisors, and attorneys. Investors intending to exchange into new properties regularly will need the services of due diligence professionals more often.

Telephone them and talk with them. Create a short script that quickly and clearly gets to the point of the call. Explain your ambitions and goals; they might give you 15 or 20 minutes of free time. Ask penetrating questions if a subject comes up that you are not clear about. It may be a subject that furthers your project or stands squarely in the way of completing it. Continue calling experts until you are comfortable that you have found one that supports your goals and strategies.

Go to the local zoning and planning meetings and be aware of future developments. Spend time reviewing zoning maps. There is a plethora of information to be learned from aerial photos and zoning maps. Often, satellite photos are immediately available on the Internet. You never know what you might learn from an aerial photo. You would want to know that a new sewer plant is being planned or built a few blocks from a property you are considering. You would also want to know that the local planning department intends to acquire a right of way for a street-widening project that goes through the parking lot of an apartment complex. The same with zoning — never assume a second- or third-hand document has the correct zoning information about a property. Zoning can be one of the most important pieces of information about an investment property. It is best to know exactly what the zoning is and what that particular code entails.

SET MEASURABLE GOALS

Goals should be measurable. A goal to purchase and renovate two residential houses in the first year followed by four the second year can be measured and tracked. Decisions can be made from measurable goals. If the first year comes up a little short because it took three months to find the second house after the first one was sold, maybe you will decide to begin looking for replacement property shortly after beginning work on the current property. Measurable goals tell you when you are on track or when changes are needed to get back on track.

Measurements have different periods. Acquiring rental property might only occur every five years or more, but keeping track of cash flow needs to happen monthly, if not weekly. Track your efforts to stay current on the real estate market. Did you attend only four planning department meetings when you had intended to go to six? Are you staying current with real estate trends? Have values appreciated in the manner you expected over the last six months? What is the trend with rents and local employment? Measure and track your attention to the details that affect your investments.

THE BUSINESS PLAN

A business plan should not be something that you only consider and intend to get around to one day. It should be mandatory before you make any real estate investment. Begin with one for your overall investment business and create additional plans for each investment property.

The overall and individual property plans have many uses. Well conceived and articulated, the plan creates a road map for your investments. Whether presented to lenders, investors, partners, or advisors, it clearly states your intentions and understanding of real estate investing.

A good business plan goes into detail. The overall investment business plan should be between 25 and 50 pages. It should be so detailed that you have to censor some information from potential competitors because it contains proprietary information. Major sections in the business plan are:

- Executive summary
- Company description
  — Overview
  — Mission, goals, objectives

— Services and strategies

- Market analysis and plan

  — Industry

  — Target investment market (property type, size, cost, etc.)

  — Analysis of investment strengths, weaknesses

  — Analysis of competitors' threats

  — Analysis of investment opportunities

- Target market

  — Market size

  — Customer specifics

- Competition

  — Statistics

  — Characteristics

- Competitive strategy

  — Proposals

  — Unique qualifications

- Management team

  — Advisors

- Startup and growth plan

- Technology plan

- Financial plan or forecast — 5 or more years

  — Income statement

  — Cash flow

  — Balance sheet

- Measurements of progress

- Appendix

Having a business plan in place is essential to achieving your goals. If you want to make professional money, you need to run your real estate business like a professional, with a plan to which you can hold yourself and others accountable. A well-crafted, well-thought-out business plan that is referred to often will make this happen. The plan needs to be updated for changes to goals, strategies, competition, or market conditions.

The initial business plan for each investment is a natural outcome of the due diligence process and should be accomplished before the property is purchased. Presenting an overall business plan and a property-specific business plan to a lender or investor establishes credibility faster than any sales pitch.

DETAILED PROJECT PLAN

Starting any business venture requires enormous planning if it is to be successful. Real estate investing is no different. A detailed project plan brings all the requirements into one picture. In addition, a master project plan creates a big picture to ensure that each element is planned in relation to others. Inevitable changes to one part of the plan can be reviewed against impacts to other portions of the plan. Important and difficult decisions become easier when the consequences can be seen in the big picture.

The following diagram is the beginning of a real estate investor's startup plan. Each investor has unique requirements for beginning an investment business. Research about the local real estate market and competition is universal. But individuals have unique needs in learning how to manage a business. This is a long-term plan for acquiring wealth. Certainly, such an important undertaking deserves substantial planning and attention to detail. The sample project plan shows approximately eight months from beginning research until beginning acquisition of the first property. This will vary greatly between investors, depending on existing business knowledge and experience.

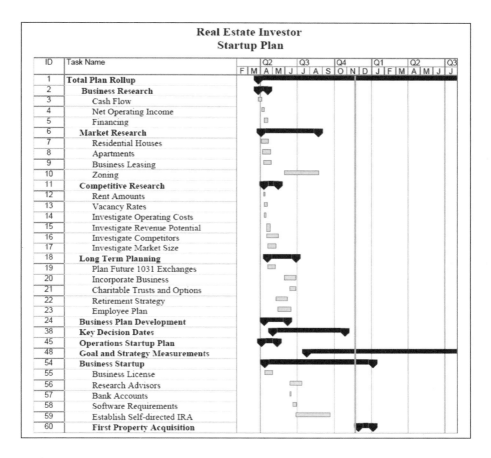

ID	Task Name	Q2			Q3			Q4			Q1			Q2			Q3
		F	M	A	M	J	J	A	S	O	N	D	J	F	M	A	M	J	J
1	**Total Plan Rollup**																		
2	**Business Research**																		
3	Cash Flow																		
4	Net Operating Income																		
5	Financing																		
6	**Market Research**																		
7	Residential Houses																		
8	Apartments																		
9	Business Leasing																		
10	Zoning																		
11	**Competitive Research**																		
12	Rent Amounts																		
13	Vacancy Rates																		
14	Investigate Operating Costs																		
15	Investigate Revenue Potential																		
16	Investigate Competitors																		
17	Investigate Market Size																		
18	**Long Term Planning**																		
19	Plan Future 1031 Exchanges																		
20	Incorporate Business																		
21	Charitable Trusts and Options																		
22	Retirement Strategy																		
23	Employee Plan																		
24	**Business Plan Development**																		
38	**Key Decision Dates**																		
45	**Operations Startup Plan**																		
48	**Goal and Strategy Measurements**																		
54	**Business Startup**																		
55	Business License																		
56	Research Advisors																		
57	Bank Accounts																		
58	Software Requirements																		
59	Establish Self-directed IRA																		
60	**First Property Acquisition**																		

Real Estate Investor
Startup Plan

THE FIRST PURCHASE

Real estate is one of the few purchases that require negotiations. Businesspeople may have experience negotiating business contracts and will be well served by those skills. Others need to hone their skills before venturing into the real estate market.

Information is vital to negotiation. Gather all that you can before making an offer. Knowing the reason the property is being sold is probably the best information you can have access to, but often the seller will not reveal the reason. If negotiating for a residential property, a conversation with the neighbors may prove worthwhile. The same can be true of apartment tenants or business property lessees. You are going to want to know something about these people anyway, so use the conversation time constructively.

Attitude is the other major factor in real estate negotiations. Remain unemotional at all times. Always be prepared to walk away from a property if it becomes obvious that you will never get close to an acceptable price. Having conducted a net operating income study, you know exactly what you can afford to pay for the property and what an acceptable return on your investment is. Nothing else matters unless terms and conditions are in place for an acceptable return on the investment.

An adversarial approach is seldom useful; a cooperative attitude is much more effective. Clearly state what it is that you want from the deal and back it up with facts. Listen carefully to what the seller is telling you. Listening is often the most underused negotiation skill. From listening comes new and useful information. Once you determine what is important to the seller, go through the standard investigation process by asking:

- Who
- Where
- When
- How

The object of negotiations is to find a win-win solution satisfying the buyer and the seller. Granted, this can be difficult when price is the main haggling issue. Win-win is not about compromising. In a compromise, everyone gets less than they want. A compromising negotiator often loses the deal before it begins, by starting with overly lofty requirements and expecting to give in on some. The other side might just walk away because the starting point is unreasonable.

Getting to a win-win solution means keeping priorities aligned with requests. Rather than compromise, offer alternatives that align with the seller's priorities while backing up your priorities with facts. Realistic alternatives are particularly effective if early in the process it appears an issue is not negotiable by one of the sides.

Another effective technique is setting aside a difficult issue for a future discussion and focusing on easier to solve areas of the purchase agreement or contract. Often, time and partial success on other issues leads to solutions of the difficult ones.

Twelve effective negotiating tips:

- The value of trust in negotiations cannot be overstated. You may use powerful strategies when negotiating, but failing to do so in good faith quickly kills a deal.

- If you want something specific from the deal, ask for it and do not be hesitant when doing so. Make it clear that it is an important part of the negotiation.

- Prioritize the order in which you want to negotiate issues. Often, knowing the outcome of one issue either creates more flexibility or less flexibility for another.

- Reserving an important issue as the final issue can be effective if the other side is enthusiastic about the overall deal. Or it can be a deal-breaker if the other side is already reluctant about the deal.

- Do not broadcast your real estate expertise. The seller may become reluctant to accede to price and terms if they think an expert has the advantage.

- Remember that until the deal is signed, everything is negotiable. A newly arisen difficulty might best be solved by going back and renegotiating a previously settled issue to reach an equitable solution.

- Do not go backwards too often; frequently renegotiating closed issues will not be viewed favorably by the other side.

- Do not put an offer on the table thinking that you can improve it later. Once a proposal is made, the other side will not favor another version that is less beneficial to them.

- If needed, explain the benefits the other party will receive from a creative counteroffer. The benefits are not always intuitive.

- Interpersonal skills are critical to negotiation.

- Body language can speak much more than the spoken word during negotiating, for the buyer and seller. A good strategy is to guard your own body language while learning to read the seller's. Body language is not universal. One person may tap fingers on a table from habit and another from nerves.

- Acknowledge when a breakthrough occurs. Do not just passively move on to the next point. Take the opportunity to set a positive momentum going forward with a comment like, "That was a tough one to accomplish; now I feel good about settling the other issues."

Failing to successfully complete a negotiation is disheartening. However, if the deal just will not work, you have to walk away from it. What you take away is information and experience useful for the next offer.

SUMMARY

Business basics are the same whether you are a highly experienced or less experienced investor. Establishing goals, strategies, and plans dramatically increases the potential to successfully accumulate and preserve wealth.

Taxes always play a part in business, ranging from tax-favorable transactions to understanding passive income. The U.S. Congress closed abusive tax loopholes that allowed depreciation to reduce reportable salary income for people not actively participating in real estate. Still, real estate professionals meeting rigid requirements can treat rental income as regular income for the purpose of writing off business losses. Also, all investors can write off passive losses against other passive gains, within the limits of the At Risk Limit. Another exception to the passive income rule is the special $25,000 allowance that active participants use to write off passive losses against non-passive income if their income is below a modified adjusted gross income.

Strategies to begin real estate investing require research and decision-making long before the first property is purchased. Will you specialize in maximizing profits from rental income or focus on leveraging your way into multiple properties and then refocus to maximize rental profits? Trying to do too many things at once leads to a less than stellar performance. You need an understanding of many of the concepts involved in real estate investing, but mastering one before moving on to the next will accomplish goals more quickly.

The same is applicable to selecting the type of property for investment. Many first-time investors choose residential houses because they have experience purchasing and maintaining their own home. What is important to remember is that different investment properties require different sets of skills. Apartment tenants have different needs and expectations than retail businesses.

Interviewing advisors that you will rely on needs to be done in advance. Not all experts have the same experience or will have an investing philosophy that is compatible with yours. While it is not desirable to have all your advisors think the same as you, if you are a risk taker it is not much help to get advice from an ultraconservative advisor who avoids risk rather than analyzes it.

The next step is establishing meaningful and measurable goals. These should be financial and strategy related. Track the measurements on a regular basis to understand if the strategies are producing the intended financial results. If the two are not synchronized, make adjustments, preferably to the strategies rather than the goals. Do not expect success without a well-thought-out, detailed business plan. You need a master business plan for the long-term and individual business plans for each investment property. The umbrella covering all these activities is the project plan that provides the big picture and shows if activities sequentially support each other.

After all the research, decision-making, goal-setting, and planning, the opportunity comes to make the first real estate purchase. Here is the most realistic test of the business plan and strategies. When properly followed, you will be confident that you have all the necessary information and skills to successfully negotiate into the perfect first property on your road to future wealth.

10

BUSINESS STRUCTURES TO PROTECT ASSETS

The use of shelters to protect personal and business assets is a prudent business reality. It is not intended to deceive legitimate creditors or hide assets from someone that has a justifiable claim against your business or personal property. Frivolous lawsuits, lawsuits targeting deep pockets rather than the truly responsible offender, and identity theft are realities in today's business world.

The sole proprietor business structure remains the most common business type for many reasons, mostly due to the simplicity. Unfortunately, almost all the sole proprietor's business and personal assets are vulnerable to creditors if there is a business error with the potential of a lawsuit. Imagine the successful real estate investor operating as a sole proprietor who hires a part-time handyman to perform maintenance and light repairs for his properties. Driving to a triplex rental to shampoo the carpets of a vacant unit, the handyman strikes a pedestrian. The employer (the real estate owner) could quite possibly be found liable for the handyman's action. As a sole proprietor, not only are all his business properties subject to litigation, but his personal home, vacation home, vehicles, and everything else he owns is vulnerable to the lawsuit. Fortunately, there are ways to segregate the property to reduce the investor's financial exposure.

SEGREGATE BUSINESS ASSETS

Through IRAs, limited liability companies, traditional incorporated companies, S corporations, and other arrangements, the investor's assets can be segregated for protection from creditors, lawsuits, and other methods of obtaining possession of the assets.

The correct business entity separates the owner's business assets from his personal assets. This generally leaves only the business assets available for judgment from a lost lawsuit, bankruptcy, or to creditors. Assets can be further segregated by forming a separate business entity for each investment property. The real estate investor that owns two apartment buildings and a strip mall should consider establishing a different business entity for each property, thereby reducing the ability of business activities at one property to affect another. Under the right business structure, if for some unfortunate reason the strip mall was forced into bankruptcy, creditors would have a difficult time gaining a judgment that liquidates the apartments in payment of the strip mall's obligations.

SOLE PROPRIETORSHIPS

Sole proprietorships are the most commonly established business types, especially when working from a home office, working part-time, or beginning a small business. Fortunately, it is also the simplest business to register and establish. Normally the legal requirement is no more than filing for a local business license, which requires a nominal fee. Depending on your location, registration may be required with a city or town, state, or both. When one agency is contacted, they will inform you if registration is also required with another agency. Sole proprietorships are often known as mom-and-pop businesses, although they have the ability to grow into much more complex operations.

The legal requirement for a sole proprietorship is that only one person owns the business. There are no partners or shareholders. You may have as many employees as required and conduct all types of business, such as service, retailing, wholesale, and manufacturing. The key feature is that you own the entire business as an individual.

Being the single owner has some advantages over other business types. You have complete control of the business, making all policy decisions, deciding what properties to acquire, how quickly to grow the company, and how to finance investments. There is no need to gain agreement from partners or a board of directors. There are no articles of incorporation to be filed with the state, no bylaws to create or partnership agreements to be reviewed and filed with attorneys.

Being the only owner also entitles you to reap all the profits and claim all the expenses from the business. These are accounted for on your personal income tax return, although some local business taxes might apply; you will be informed of these when the company is registered. No formal accounting is required beyond what you deem necessary to run the business and comply with income tax requirements. Another financial advantage is the ability to establish tax-exempt retirement accounts. When you make the decision to retire or end the business, it can be sold as an ongoing operation, inventory liquidated, or service accounts may be sellable. If those options are not preferred, the business just ceases to exist.

The disadvantage of sole proprietorships is the unlimited personal liability. You are the company, and just as you gain all the profits, the liabilities belong to you as an individual. This means that personal assets beyond those of the company can be sought by creditors or as a legal judgment. Many beginning investors find it difficult to raise the necessary capital to fund a fledgling business. A non-financial reality that some people think is a disadvantage is not having a partner or knowledgeable individual available to help make difficult decisions. Similarly, it is a one-person show, and you need to take care of all the business activities, providing services, ordering supplies, tracking expenses, and making sales. These concerns can be overcome by hiring employees as the business grows. Finally, when you retire as the owner, the entity ceases to exist. Although it can be passed to a family member or sold to anyone, the new owner becomes the new business entity.

SOLE PROPRIETOR BUSINESS INSURANCE

Business insurance provides some protection to the sole proprietor. Certainly, fire and damage insurance should be carried for each property owned. After that, the selection of which types of insurance to carry will vary with individual needs:

- A business owner's policy protects the business property from fire and damage. It often includes liability if an employee is injured at work and may include insurance against business being interrupted. Levels of coverage vary considerably and need to be reviewed closely to meet your needs.

- Umbrella insurance includes business liability insurance and pays after the limit is reached on the primary insurance.

- Personal property insurance for office equipment, computer, and telephones.

- Business income and extra expense insurance replaces income lost because of a disaster. Extra expenses are paid for such things as renting a temporary office while the permanent office is repaired from a disaster.

- Commercial automobile insurance.

- Professional liability insurance (often called errors and omissions insurance).

- Product liability insurance.

- Special equipment insurance.

The business owner's policy can be purchased prepackaged or customized to meet your specific needs. Insurance costs can be managed by accepting higher deductibles and using a risk-management process.

THE TRADITIONAL CORPORATION

Creating a corporation is the same as creating an artificial person for doing business. This artificial person becomes liable for the debts and actions of the company. One or more people purchase shares to gain a percentage of ownership of the business, and an individual's liability is limited to their percentage of ownership. Liability is limited to the business assets and does not include the owner's personal assets. A corporation enjoys tax advantages, such as the ability to defer many taxes, not being taxed on the cost of insurance, not being taxed on the cost of travel, and deductions for funding retirement plans. However, the existence of an artificial person also creates a tax disadvantage. Corporation income is taxed separately from the owner's income, and the owner again pays taxes on any profits that become personal income, usually distributed as dividends. This is commonly referred to as double taxation.

Incorporation must follow state statutes that vary, although most states follow the federal Model Business Corporation Act. Creating articles of incorporation begins the process. These vary depending on state requirements but follow guidelines. The corporate name must be included, along with the nature and purpose of the business, which can be fairly broad. The capital structure must be explained, including the number of shares that can be issued. The management structure is normally part of the articles of incorporation but can be included in the bylaws that are adopted after incorporation. The bylaws define the roles of directors, officers, and shareholders. Bylaws can also establish how dividends are paid, how often directors must meet, and procedures for shareholder meetings.

One reason people choose to incorporate is because it is easier to raise startup money. Often, it can be done without investing your own funds. The financial risk is spread among more people when shares are sold to raise funds. Loans can be obtained by issuing bonds. When combined with significant tax savings, the corporation structure can be the right way to go. For companies with few shareholders, there are less complex ways to incorporate the business.

One seldom considered liability risk does exist with corporations. It is the opposite of a business activity making personal assets vulnerable. Owning corporation shares can leave the corporation vulnerable to personal actions. Consider a property investment corporation owned by three sisters. Alice owns 60 percent of the stock shares, while Julie and Sheryl each own 20 percent. Alice hires a worker to perform repairs on her personal swimming pool, and he is injured. Alice's homeowner's insurance specifically excludes coverage for hired labor. The worker successfully sues, and part of the settlement requires Alice to turn over her 60 percent of the corporation stock shares. The worker gains the controlling interest in the business. If Alice had held ownership of the stock shares in the name of another company, she may have avoided losing ownership.

CLOSE CORPORATION

A close corporation can be established when ownership of the company is held by a single person, family members, or relatively few people. Frequently the people are owners and employees of the corporation. Depending on the state, ownership is limited to between 30 and 50 individuals. Shares are seldom sold outside the close group. If more shares are offered to raise money, the shares normally have to be offered to existing owners before being available to outsiders. This prevents existing owners from having their percentage of ownership reduced. Another advantage is the ability to incorporate the business in the least complex manner. If all shareholders agree in writing, the corporation can operate without directors, bylaws, annual meetings, stock certificates, or formal documentation of shareholder decisions. The close corporation is run more like a partnership but can enjoy the benefits of a corporation. Many states recognize the similarity to partnerships and allow much more flexibility in how they can operate.

Articles of incorporation have to be created for a close corporation, but they may be different than a traditional corporation. Transferring ownership outside the close ownership group is usually controlled by the articles or another formal agreement. Consider if three brothers owned a small chain of retail stores, and one brother decided to sell his portion of the ownership to a person the other brothers did not know or did not want to be in business with. The new owner could insist on changing the way the business is managed. A formal agreement should exist to control how ownership is transferred. The agreement could allow the other brothers to buy the shares before they are offered to an outsider. On the other hand, the one brother could receive a lower percentage of the profits while not actively working in the business. The intention of a close corporation is flexibility without the rules of a traditional corporation. An advantage is the ability to include only selected policies important to the business. However, formal shareholder agreements need to be made for important events that occur, such as the death of an owner.

Another consideration is that each owner has the ability to make business commitments independent of other owners. Unless it is agreed that only one person will make commitments, the resources of the business can be overcommitted, debt can be assumed without the agreement of all involved, or other agreements binding on the business can be made.

Close corporations have the disadvantage of being taxed on corporate profits and on personal income tax when the profits are distributed.

S CORPORATION

An S corporation is a variation of the close corporation with the benefit of avoiding double taxation. Many entrepreneurs choose this business type because it includes many of the characteristics of sole proprietorship, partnership, and incorporation but has an added tax advantage. The double taxation typical of corporations is eliminated for businesses qualifying as an S corporation. The S corporation chooses whether to pay income tax at the corporate level or to pass profits on to owners, where they are paid only as personal income. If the corporation wants to use the profits for growth, it can retain the profits, pay corporate income tax, and plow them back into the business. In this case, the owners do not report profits as personal income. If profits are paid to the owners, they are taxed as personal income. Taxes are paid at either the corporate or personal level, but not at both. The profits cannot be paid to owners as dividends because a traditional corporation would have already paid income tax before the dividends were paid. As a result, the IRS tax rate on dividends is less than most personal income tax rates. Therefore, the S corporation profits must be taxed as ordinary income on the owner's tax return.

The tax advantage eliminates the need for an owner-employee to draw an excessive salary that lowers corporate profits and allows more of the income to be taxed only as personal income. Without the S corporation, the IRS might question this practice. In truth, there is an advantage for the employee-owner to receiving a smaller salary. The business and employee must each pay half of the 15.3 percent FICA (Federal Insurance Contribution Act) taxes based on the employee wages. FICA is the combination of social security and Medicare taxes. This tax does not apply to profits distributed to employee-owners. The temptation becomes to pay a lower salary to avoid this tax while being compensated from profits. The IRS is aware of this, and a reasonable wage prevails in the end.

If the business has financial losses, the losses can be used by individual owners to offset other income. Even if the business income is not paid to the owners, the business pays income tax at the owner's personal level rather than the higher corporate level. This becomes attractive when the business wants to keep the money for other opportunities. An S corporation can also offer employee benefits and deferred compensation plans.

When the company does not pay the income to owners or invest it in other business opportunities, the owners must report the income on their personal income tax and pay taxes on the income. For that reason, many businesses create an agreement that they will pay at least enough to cover the personal income tax the business transfers to each owner.

The requirements to qualify as an S corporation are mostly a result of federal income tax law. The tax law was changed in 1996 to increase the number of shareholders that can own an S corporation from 35 to 75. All owners of an S corporation are required to be citizens or residents of the United States. Nonresident aliens cannot be owners. No more than 25 percent of an S corporation's income can come from passive sources, such as interest-bearing bank accounts or ownership in other companies' stock shares. It must be a domestic corporation, meaning that it does business in the same state in which it is incorporated, although it can also do business in other states. It must have only one classification of stock, but shareholders can have different voting rights. There are specific circumstances in which an S corporation is required to pay income taxes even when these conditions are met. Tax attorneys, accountants, or the IRS can provide specific information.

Establishing an S corporation first requires that a traditional or close corporation be formed in your state. Next, the shareholders must decide to apply to the IRS for S corporation treatment and record the agreement in meeting minutes or by some other formal method. The last step is completing and filing Form 2553 with the IRS. Information required on Form 2553 includes names and signatures of all owners and the number of shares owned or the percentage of the business owned. Each owner's Social Security number must also be included. The name and contact information for an officer of the company is necessary if the IRS needs more information. The beginning date of the financial year the business operates is also required. The company's financial year must be the same as the calendar year unless a good business reason is provided to the IRS.

S corporations are more complex to establish than sole proprietorships but offer the limited personal liability that comes with incorporation. The ability to pay taxes at the personal rate is another benefit worth strong consideration. In some cases the S corporation is the best way to structure a business.

Shareholders of either a C or S corporation transferring appreciated properties out of the corporation to themselves must pay capital gains taxes, although the property was not actually sold to a third party.

PARTNERSHIPS

Partnerships are another common business type. A partnership is an agreement between two or more people to join funds, other assets, labor, and skills in a common business. There is an understanding that profits or losses will be shared. Sharing the profits or losses does not have to be equal among partners. It could be based on each person contributing different amounts of assets or skills and deserving to receive different percentages of the rewards. There can also be managing partners and silent partners that contribute different levels of effort to the daily management of the business. Any difference in how the profits or liabilities will be shared should be recorded in a formal agreement. A partnership is similar to a sole proprietorship in many ways, as the partners are treated as individuals, but it also has some things in common with the independent entity of a corporation.

Some states recognize the partnership as a separate entity that can sue or be sued separately from the individual owners. Property can at times be held in the name of the partnership rather than as individuals. Federal laws frequently permit partnerships to be treated as an entity in federal courts, bankruptcy proceedings, and to file federal informational tax returns.

A partnership is not a separate entity that pays federal income tax the way a traditional corporation does. The partnership passes profits on to the individuals much the same way an S corporation does, and each partner reports their share of profits on personal tax returns.

A partnership agreement known as articles of partnership is created and filed with the state. Almost any terms and conditions the partners wish can be included. Typically, the rights of the partners are included in these articles. Management of the business, percent of ownership, compensation, property rights, and the right to inspect accounting books are usually included. If the length of time the partnership will exist is not specifically included, any partner can dissolve the partnership at any time. When it is not documented how profits will be shared among partners, a court will share them equally.

Defining how profits will be divided is important. Suppose Alice contributes $75,000 in funds, and Bill contributes $25,000 to start a partnership renovating houses. Both work equally hard, and the partnership becomes a great success. After a year, there is $100,000 in profit to be divided, but nothing in the agreement says how it will be shared. Alice wants $75,000 of the profit based on a 75 percent contribution to the startup. Bill wants to share the profits equally and receive $50,000 based on doing an equal amount of work toward the success. Without an agreement, a court would split the profits 50 percent for each partner.

There are duties, powers, and liabilities when considering a partnership. There is a financial duty that all partners act in the utmost good faith for the benefit of the partnership. This prevents a partner from independently competing with the partnership. Each partner has agency power for the business and can enter into any business transaction on behalf of the partnership, as long as it is allowed by the partnership agreement. This could be something like giving a warranty on a product or service that is sold. There can be joint liability of the partners. If one partner is sued, he can insist that the other partners be part of the lawsuit. If the sued partner does not insist on the other partners being part of the suit, the partnership assets cannot be used to settle any judgment that might go against the individual partner.

Most of the sole proprietorship advantages apply to partnerships, especially the ability to report profits as personal income. The ability to form a partnership is almost as easy, although time spent to create an agreement is time well spent. The ability to raise funds increases when two or more people contribute and share loan repayment risks. Often, partners have skills that complement each other, creating a better-balanced business. Their combined efforts at times land contracts that none of the partners could win alone. If the company hires employees, it can often attract top candidates when the possibility to become a future partner is an incentive.

Unique disadvantages exist. In some situations, the actions of one partner create liability for all the partners. Because more than one person is involved with the management of the company, disagreements can happen. Profits of the business must be shared with others. A partnership may abruptly end if a partner withdraws or dies.

All the business entities have some disadvantages. The uniqueness of your business is a big consideration in determining which set of advantages can best be leveraged and which disadvantages present the least risk

LIMITED LIABILITY COMPANY

From the perspective of asset protection and separating personal liability from business liability, the limited liability company (LLC) is likely the best business entity for most real estate investors. The LLC is a blend of the best characteristics of a sole proprietorship, partnership, and corporation, while leaving out the less desirable elements of the other business structures.

Limited liability companies are controlled by state statutes and require articles of incorporation. Although federal guidelines have been established, only about one-fourth of the states have adopted them. Therefore, requirements, advantages, and disadvantages can vary from state to state. The information needed for the articles of incorporation is often the same as for a traditional corporation: name of business, address, names of owners, and information about how the limited liability company will be managed.

Advantages of a limited liability company:

- Personal liability protection for members.

- Can choose to be taxed either as a corporation or at the personal income tax level.

- No need to meet the requirements and formalities of a corporation to maintain the business status.

- Can contribute and distribute appreciated property tax free between individuals and LLC.

- Business losses can be deducted on individual tax returns.

- Members can draw up their own contract, allowing for flexibility in management and responsibilities.

- Greater flexibility in allocating income to members than a corporation — for example, an LLC can have various classes of stocks while an S corporation can issue only one type of stock.

- Adding the term LLC to a business name can be perceived as more credible than a sole proprietor.

Disadvantages of a limited liability company:

- Many, but not all, states require more than one member before an LLC can be established. There is a trend toward more states allowing single owners of an LLC.

- Some traditional corporation-type documentation is involved with the LLC that sole proprietors do not have. It is important to draft the operating agreement to meet both state and federal requirements in order to preserve the LLC status and not have it classified as a corporation.

- The LLC does not live forever the way a corporation does. The operating agreement establishes how the LLC is dissolved and is an area that the IRS looks at for designating it as a corporation for tax purposes.

- The traditional corporate structure should be used if it is anticipated that a company will one day go public.

- Variations in state regulations can affect liability and tax standing when doing business in another state.

LIMITED LIABILITY PARTNERSHIP

The limited liability partnership is similar to the limited liability company, except it is designed for professionals normally doing business as partners. The main advantage is limiting the personal liability of the partners from the negligent actions of another partner(s). Again, state statutes vary and can affect how liability laws are applied when doing business in a different state. Often, a supervising partner remains liable for the actions of a junior partner.

The limited partnership is another variation. A limited partnership has at least one general partner and one or more limited partners. The general partner is the managing partner and has full personal responsibility for the partnership and all debts. The limited partners contribute assets to the business, and their liability is limited to their contributed asset value. Creation of a limited partnership is more complex than for a general partnership. A certificate of limited partnership, which resembles a corporate charter, is often required.

IRAS

Your IRA offers protection from creditors in certain states. Some states defer to federal bankruptcy law or allow a bankrupt individual to choose federal law over state law. Chapter 11 of federal bankruptcy law prevents awarding some assets to creditors. IRAs generally fall into the category of a payment plan based on age, since a qualified distribution does not occur until age 59 1/2. This applies to several of the retirement accounts discussed in Chapter 3. The United States Supreme Court unanimously upheld this interpretation of the code as recently as April 2005.

EXCERPT FROM U.S. FEDERAL BANKRUPTCY CODE 11 U.S.C. § 522

The debtor's right to receive —

... a payment under a stock bonus, pension, profit sharing, annuity, or similar plan or contract on account of illness, disability, death, age, or length of service, to the extent reasonably necessary for the support of the debtor and any dependent of the debtor ...

How this applies to Roth IRAs remains a gray area. Recall that income tax has been paid on Roth IRA contributions, and these contributions can be withdrawn at any time. Also, there is no age requirement to begin Roth withdrawals. For these reasons, Roth IRAs do not have the same bankruptcy protection as other retirement accounts. Courts have made different rulings on whether the Roth IRA is excluded from bankruptcy creditors, and the issue may not be resolved for some time.

IRA LIMITED LIABILITY COMPANY

An IRA establishing an LLC is relatively straightforward. The LLC adds another level of protection from creditors and lawsuits while, as owner of the LLC, your IRA provides the tax advantages. The LLC enjoys the asset protection of a corporation while being taxed like a partnership. The income passes through to the owner for tax purposes. Of course, the IRA, as owner, does not pay taxes. The steps to accomplish this are:

1. Open the self-directed IRA account.

2. Transfer existing IRA assets to the self-directed IRA account.

3. Establish an LLC with the secretary of state.

4. Obtain LLC's employer identification number (EIN) from the IRS.

5. Set up a bank account for the LLC.

6. Instruct the custodian to place the IRA assets into the bank account of the LLC.

7. The LLC makes investments as instructed by you through the IRA account.

8. The LLC returns all earnings from investments to the IRA for tax-free treatment.

Other self-directed retirement accounts may invest through the LLC as well. The IRA could be run through other business entities also. However, the LLC almost always makes the most sense for simplicity and tax reasons.

An advantage and potential downfall is the ability of the IRA owner to conduct investment transactions without going through the self-directed IRA custodian. Using the LLC checkbook to make investments has earned these types of accounts the name "checkbook-controlled IRA." This can save time and custodial charges; however, the downside is the lack of custodial oversight to avoid prohibited transactions. One prohibited transaction and the entire IRA can be declared disqualified by the IRS, resulting in the IRA being distributed and taxes being required along with penalties. The IRS has issued recent publications regarding prohibited transactions between IRAs, LLCs, and IRA owners. As with most individual scenarios, it is best to obtain competent legal and tax advice.

PIERCING THE CORPORATE VEIL

Piercing the corporate veil is the terminology used to describe a court action taken to make an individual personally and financially responsible for a corporation's actions. It assumes that the primary reason the corporation exists is intentionally to pass personal responsibility off to the corporation.

Typical factors considered by the court:

- Lack of adequate business capital indicates fraud was intended.

- Lack of corporate assets.

- Failure to observe corporate formalities, shareholder meetings, meeting minutes, and board of director meetings.

- Commingling business and personal assets.

- Clear personal use of corporate assets.

- Failure to pay dividends.

- Embezzlement or disguised deduction of corporate funds by a key shareholder.

- Concealment or misrepresentation of shareholders.

- The corporation being used as a front for personal deals.

- Manipulation of assets or liabilities for personal benefit.

- Other factors the court finds relevant.

Once the corporate veil is pierced, it is as if the corporation never existed. The shareholders become financially liable for all the corporation debts, rather than only to the limit of their investment.

SUMMARY

The successful real estate investor learns about the importance of protecting business assets early. With multiple real estate holdings, it is important that business troubles from a single holding do not spill over onto profitable holdings. Each holding may use the same business structure, or each may be better suited for a different business structure.

The sole proprietorship is the most common business structure in the United States and is the least suitable to protect business and personal assets from creditors or lawsuits. It does provide the benefit of being extremely simple to establish and does not suffer from double taxation the way a traditional corporation does. However, newer business structures are proving more effective at providing asset protection without double taxation. The S corporation can be structured to avoid double taxation, while still providing a great deal of flexibility in the way it is managed. The S corporation limits shareholder liability to the amount invested without making the shareholder personally liable for the business's debts. Proper incorporation language can eliminate the need for much of the formal documentation required of traditional corporations. Using the wrong incorporation language could result in the corporate veil being pierced and fully exposing shareholders as if they were sole proprietors. Therefore, it is important that competent legal counsel be involved when establishing an S corporation.

The limited liability company is another preferred business structure that should be closely examined. Only recently available in all 50 states, it is not yet standardized in all states. Because not all states allow LLCs to be owned by a single individual, it may not be available to some real estate investors. However, the appeal of the LLC is such that those investors that are able to can combine an LLC with a self-directed IRA account for added protection and even more flexibility managing the IRA. Again, competent legal advice is needed to review your specific situation and provide the best guidance.

A comparison chart of the major business types is provided below.

COMPARISON OF MAJOR BUSINESS TYPES

Attribute	Sole Proprietorship	Partnership	Corporation	S Corporation
Method of Creation	Created at the will of the owner	Created by agreement of parties	Charter issued by state — statutory authorization and compliance	Close Corporation Chartered by state and IRS Form 2553
Legal Position	Not a separate entity; owner is the business	Not a separate entity in many states	Always a legal entity separate from owners — a legal existence for the purpose of owning property, being a party to litigation, etc.	Same as corporation — always a separate legal entity
Liability	Unlimited liability	Unlimited liability	Limited liability of shareholders— shareholders are not liable for the debts of the corporation	Limited liability of shareholders — shareholders are not liable for the debts of the corporation
Duration	Determined by owner; automatically dissolved on owner's death	Terminated by agreement of the partners, by death of one or more partners, by withdrawal of a partner, by bankruptcy, and so on	Can have perpetual existence	Can have perpetual existence
Management	Completely at owner's discretion	Each general partner has a direct and equal voice in management unless defined otherwise in the partnership agreement	Shareholders elect directors, who set policy and appoint officers	Can elect directors or appoint officers, or each individual can have voice defined by agreement

COMPARISON OF MAJOR BUSINESS TYPES

Transfer of Interest	Interest can be transferred but individual's proprietorship then ends	Although partnership can be assigned, assignee does not have full rights of a partner	Shares of stock can be transferred	Shares of stock can be transferred, number of owners can not exceed 75 individuals; often ownership transfer requires agreement by all owners or existing owners have right to purchase all available shares
Taxation	Owner pays personal taxes on business income	Each partner pays pro rata share of income taxes on net profits, whether or not they are distributed	Double taxation — corporation pays income tax on net profits, with no deduction for dividends, and shareholders pay income tax on disbursed dividends they receive	Each owner pays prorate share of income taxes on net profits, whether or not they are distributed
Fees, Organizational, Licenses, Annual Reports	None	None	All Required	Fees required, but shareholders can elect to operate without directors, bylaws, annual meetings, stock certificates, or formal documentation of shareholder decisions
Transaction of Business in Other States	No limitation	Often no limitation; a few states have enacted statutes that must be complied with	Normally must qualify to do business and obtain certificate of authority	Normally must qualify to do business and obtain certificate of authority

11

ESTATE PLANNING

Taxes are not the only reason that the successful wish to avoid having a will probated by a court of law; lack of privacy is another reason. The deceased's financial affairs become a public record, along with anyone named in the will. Unscrupulous salespersons and promoters use the opportunity to separate your beneficiaries from the inheritance when they are emotionally vulnerable.

Probated wills also take considerable time to distribute the inheritance to allow creditors time to file claims and interested people an opportunity to contest the will. And for these inconveniencies the court charges the estate a probate fee. Depending on the state, these fees can vary from a few hundred dollars up to several thousand. Additionally, the executor of the estate will likely need the assistance of an attorney to navigate the legal requirements of a complicated will. The revocable living trust is becoming a popular alternative to the will.

REVOCABLE LIVING TRUST

A revocable living trust avoids the probate process because you collect your assets and transfer the titles to them to the trustee but continue to benefit from the assets for the remainder of your life. If you fail to do this, you will not avoid probate. No taxes are paid at the time the living trust is established. You will most likely establish yourself as the trustee and effectively retain full control of your assets, and you are able to buy and sell through the trust just as you would if property or other assets were titled in your name.

Because it is a revocable trust, it can be cancelled or changed at any time. Successor trustees are named in the event that you become incapacitated or upon your death. Naming more than one successor trustee is a good idea in the event one of them becomes incapacitated. Also, two or more trustees can double check the activities of each other.

Ownership title must actually transfer to the trust. Property that is typically transferred to a trust includes:

- Securities
- Real estate
- Certificate of deposits
- Bonds

- Home
- Bank accounts
- Stocks
- Life insurance

There is a direct tax benefit from establishing a revocable living trust. While no taxes are due when it is established, the grantor will pay income tax on any income earned by the trust. Gift and estate taxes will be owed when the trust is distributed to beneficiaries.

A will is used to transfer any assets not in the trust at the time of death. This is sometimes called a "pour over will" because it pours the remaining assets into the trust. At death, most revocable trusts switch to an irrevocable trust. The instructions in the trust agreement are used to distribute the assets to beneficiaries, without being probated by the court.

If young children are the beneficiaries of the trust, the successor trustee can continue managing the assets in the trust until the children reach an age at which they can do it themselves. It is almost impossible to contest a living trust. When a will is contested, the assets are frozen, and they cannot be distributed until the claim is resolved. Assets in a living trust are not frozen until the legal challenge is resolved. Anyone wishing to contest the trust must file suit against each of the beneficiaries; in the meantime, the assets in the trust can be distributed. Due to the added privacy, those outside the family have no way of knowing what the trust contains.

SECOND-TO-DIE LIFE INSURANCE

A second-to-die life insurance policy is another consideration for estate planning. Also known as a survivorship life insurance policy, it is often used to pay any estate taxes due upon the death of a surviving spouse. This can enable real estate holdings to be passed directly to heirs without having to sell some to pay estate taxes.

Because the policy spans two lives, these policies have a reduced cost compared to standard life insurance policies. Another benefit may be that an otherwise uninsurable person may be insurable when the policy spans two lives. The policy should be purchased by an irrevocable life insurance trust to prevent the insurance proceeds from becoming part of your estate.

Second-to-die insurance can be purchased with discounted dollars. A $1 million policy might cost $10,000 per year to fund but pay 100 percent at death. Living another 30 years involves paying $300,000 in premiums to receive a $1 million pay out. Recall from Chapter 8 that these types of policies are often funded from the tax relief or the improved income obtained from a charitable remainder trust.

LIFE INSURANCE

Make sure that any life insurance policy is kept separate from your estate. The policy should not be in your own name, or it will be considered part of your estate and could be taxed heavily. While the beneficiary of a life insurance policy does not pay taxes on the proceeds, the estate of the deceased does if the policy is not correctly structured. It is best is to create and fund an irrevocable life insurance trust that is never part of your estate. Have the trust purchase the policy so that it has never been part of your estate. Name any beneficiary or multiple beneficiaries, and they will receive the proceeds tax-free outside the estate.

If you already have a policy that is susceptible to estate taxes, transfer the policy into an irrevocable trust as soon as possible. The IRS requires that the trust own it for at least three years before your death to exclude it from your estate. Additionally, if the current value of the policy (the value before your death) is more than the current annual gift allowance ($12,000), there could be a consequence to your unified credit. Consider naming several beneficiaries to take advantage of the ability to make an unlimited number of $12,000 annual gifts.

TRANSFERRING THE BUSINESS

Transferring a flourishing real estate business to descendants can be accomplished without destroying the business through taxes if children or others want to assume ownership. This can be done to provide the parents with a retirement income and the satisfaction of knowing their hard work continues with the next generation. Often, this involves selling the business to the children, gifting the business to them, or a combination of both.

FAMILY LIMITED PARTNERSHIP

A family limited partnership should be created when plenty of time remains to annually gift a portion of the company to the children. The parents can remain the general partners and bear responsibility for the management of the business. A partnership agreement defines the roles of both the general partner and limited partners. Each year the maximum allowable gift allowance is used to transfer interest in the partnership to the children. The partnership agreement can be worded to prevent the limited partners (children) from selling their interest in the partnership or pledging it as security for a loan. Once majority interest in the business is transferred to the children, the partnership agreement can be amended to make the new owners general partners.

EMPLOYEE STOCK OWNERSHIP PLAN

The employee stock ownership plan (ESOP) can be used to sell the business to multiple employees as an exit strategy for the owner. The ESOP is a qualified employee benefit plan that has tax benefits. The ESOP can borrow money to purchase stocks in the company. These stocks are typically purchased from the business owner, giving the owner a retirement income. The owner establishes the ESOP and borrows money to purchase the stock. The stock is given to employees as part of their annual compensation. The business repays the loan used to purchase the stock and receives a tax deduction for both the interest and principal paid on the loan. Reasonable dividends paid on the stock are also a tax deduction for the business.

Because there is not likely a secondary market for this stock and the owner-employees want to maintain full control, the business is required to purchase the stock back from departing employees within five years.

TRANSFERRING THE FAMILY HOUSE

A qualified personal residence trust (QPRT) can offer several tax advantages. Established in 1990 by Congress to prevent the family home from being sold to pay estate taxes, this can be an important estate planning tool. Congress made two exceptions to two important tax rules when this was established. If a person makes a gift but retains an interest in the property, it is not considered to be for estate planning purposes. It is often valued at the full market value, although the person receiving the gift does not obtain full benefit of its use. Not so in this situation.

The parent titles the house to an irrevocable trust that names a beneficiary who will receive the house at the end of a set number of years. The length of time the trust runs is important. The home reverts to the parent's estate if the trust is still in effect when the parent dies. There are tax consequences to the heir if the parent decides to repurchase the house at the end of the trust's term. The common solution is for the parent to rent the house once the trust expires, and the heir takes the title. The parent can continue to live in the family home for the remainder of their life and still benefit from tax-favorable treatment by passing the house to heirs.

In 2003, the IRS issued procedure 2003-42 with recommended language for a QPRT, essentially providing a safe harbor for establishing a QPRT. The bulletin is a lengthy document; only a brief excerpt is provided in Exhibit 12.1. With a QPRT, the donor is often also the trustee. This is convenient because the donor (transferor) remains responsible for payment of associated expenses, along with retaining the right to live in the house. The donor may enjoy all the benefits and advantages of the home without outside involvement for the duration of the trust.

EXHIBIT 12.1 EXCERPT FROM IRS PROCEDURE 2003-42

Administration of Trust

(1) *Use and Management of Residence.* The Trustee shall hold and maintain the Residence as a personal residence of the Transferor during the period beginning on the date of creation of the trust and continuing through the date of termination of the trust (hereinafter "the term of the QPRT"). During the term of the QPRT, the Transferor shall have the exclusive rent free use, possession, and enjoyment of the Residence.

(2) *Payment of Expenses.* The Transferor shall be responsible for the payment of all costs associated with the Residence, including but not limited to mortgage payments, property taxes, utilities, repairs, maintenance, and insurance. The Trustee's responsibility for the maintenance of the Residence and for other costs associated with the Residence is limited to the extent of any trust income and additions of cash for that purpose received by the Trustee in accordance with this Article II. If the Trustee has insufficient funds to pay these costs and expenses, the Trustee shall notify the Transferor, who shall be responsible for the unpaid balance of these costs and expenses. In addition, the Trustee from time to time may make improvements to the Residence, but the Trustee's authority and responsibility to do so is limited to the extent of any trust income, insurance proceeds, and additions of cash for that purpose received by the Trustee in accordance with this Article II.

The tax-favorable treatment is difficult to quantify because many variables are involved, such as the parent's age, the time the trust runs, the IRS discount rate in effect when the trust is established, and the value of the house when entered into the trust. A short example would be a 50-year-old father placing a $1 million home into a trust when the IRS discount rate is 5.6 percent. The trust is established to run only ten years to improve the probability that the father will outlive the trust. IRS actuarial tables establish the value of the house at the end of ten years as $537,000, substantially less than the $1 million value. For gift tax planning, the value of the house remains at $537,000 and forever locked at the time the trust is established. This is below the estate's unified credit and allows the house to pass tax-free to the children.

WILLING RETIREMENT ACCOUNTS TO CHARITY

Qualified retirement accounts can be particularly taxing when they are distributed to an estate upon death. The wealthy that need estate planning to avoid the heavy estate taxation will want to consider the double taxation that can be imposed on retirement accounts. Except for the Roth accounts, retirement accounts did not pay income tax when originally placed into an IRA, 401(k), SEP-IRA, or other qualified account, nor has income tax been paid on the earnings from these accounts. All along, the plan has been to distribute these funds at a reduced income tax rate after retirement. Upon death, the entire amount must generally be included for estate tax purposes. The IRS requires that this money, and any other that represents unpaid income tax, be accounted for as income in respect of a decedent (IRD).

Philanthropists often donate to charities and pass other assets on to heirs. As a donation, the income and estate tax are fully avoided on these accounts. This is a particularly effective strategy, as it also accomplishes the goal of bringing the estate below the estate tax exclusion limit. Careful choice of what is donated can eliminate the estate tax, reduce income tax, benefit a charity, and have little or no impact on heirs.

A good example is Mr. Frank's several million dollars in assets. Some of it remains in a SEP-IRA, some is in the form of easy to manage real estate, and some is in shareholder stock. Mr. Frank intends to donate an amount to charity that brings the estate below the estate tax exclusion limit. He chooses to donate that amount from accounts that have never paid income tax. Heirs will receive highly appreciated stocks and real estate that passes to them tax-free. The highly appreciated stocks and real estate also pass to the heirs with the basis stepped up to fair market value at the time they are received.

A spouse has full survivorship rights to most retirement accounts. This tax strategy likely requires that a spousal consent form be signed. Additionally, spousal consent requirements vary from state to state. A new spousal consent may be required if state residence changes. Of course, competent tax advice is necessary to accomplish this strategy. One tax consideration is to ensure the estate never takes distribution of the retirement funds; they must pass directly to the chosen charity.

There are other methods that enable charitable remainder trusts to be established with retirement funds and allow an heir to benefit from an income stream and the remainder to be donated to charity. These can provide additional tax deductions for the estate when the charitable remainder trust is established.

CONVERTING TO A ROTH IRA

As always, depending on individual circumstances, converting a traditional IRA to a Roth IRA can be a good estate planning move. Because taxes have already been paid on a Roth IRA, there is no minimum age when withdrawals must begin. If you do not need or want the funds from your IRA, consider converting it to a Roth IRA before it passes to an heir. The heir will never pay taxes on withdrawals either.

When you make the conversion, deferred taxes become due on the traditional IRA. Possibly this can be included in a strategy to lower the estate below the estate tax exclusion limit while maximizing the benefit to the heir.

This is a method of creating an inexpensive annuity for a child or other heir. A husband at age 69 converts a traditional IRA to a Roth and avoids having to begin mandatory withdraws at age 70 ½. Upon his death, the Roth IRA becomes the property of his surviving wife. She is allowed to change the title of the Roth IRA into her own name and may not receive any payments during her lifetime. She passes away after the Roth IRA has continued to grow tax-free earnings for another 20 years. The couple's daughter takes ownership of the Roth IRA after her mother passes away. The daughter is required to begin taking withdrawals from the IRA shortly after her mother's death, but the withdrawals are tax-free. The one drawback to this strategy for the wealthy is the Roth IRA is only available to those with an adjusted gross income below $160,000 (in 2006) for married couples and $110,000 for single taxpayers.

DYNASTY TRUSTS

The dynasty trust was a valuable estate planning tool for the wealthy prior to changes the U.S. Congress made in 1986. Still, there are many people that can benefit from the reduced effectiveness of the trust. The biggest change made was limiting the size of the trust to $2 million for married couples or $1 million for single people (in 2006). Often, it is funded by using a portion of the estate tax exclusion limit, which was $4 million for a married couple in 2006. The tax benefit is realized by future generations, not the current estate.

A dynasty trust is established to last 21 years beyond the life of the last beneficiary living when the trust is established. A newborn grandchild that lives to be 90 years old enables a dynasty trust to exist for 111 years (90 + 21).

A well-managed trust allowed to grow for many years can accumulate substantial earnings. Everything paid out of the trust is federal tax free to the beneficiaries, including what is paid out at the conclusion of the trust.

A $2 million trust making a modest 6 percent per year would compound to $11.5 million in 30 years. Averaging 8 percent per year would compound the same $2 million into over $20 million in 30 years. At 8 percent it becomes over $200 million if allowed to compound for 70 years. While not providing immediate benefit to the family, dynasty trusts have the ability to create great family wealth long term.

A variety of trusts exist to help with estate planning. Many have several similar elements but might go by a different name. Others incorporate different tax-favorable facets that may be more in line with your circumstances and needs. Some variations rely on the tax-free earnings of Roth accounts, and others fund the trusts tax-free by starting early and using the annual tax-free gift limit to fund the trust. A variation exists to meet most anyone's needs.

OTHER ESTATE CONCERNS

Estate planning does go beyond the preservation and transfer of wealth. Although outside the scope of this book, keep these other concerns in mind when discussing your estate needs with an advisor:

- Who will care for minor children?

- How much wealth will the children need?

- At what age should the children receive access to the wealth?

- Do I have enough resources available today to take care of them?

- What should I do to fill any shortfall in resources?

- If my spouse remarries, how do I ensure my wealth is passed on to my children?

- How do I ensure a partner I am not married to will be taken care of?

- Do I need a third party to manage my estate after I am gone?

- Do I need a durable power of attorney?

- Should I have a health care proxy?

- How should wealth be distributed to children of multiple marriages (his, hers, and ours)?

- How do estate and gift tax laws affect marriages when one or both spouses are not United States citizens?

Death is a terribly sad and emotional event, likely even more difficult if the loss is a family patriarch or matriarch. Going through probate or the process of distributing the living trust is a constant reminder of the loss. You can simplify and speed up the process by having all the necessary information gathered where it is accessible to the right person or people. This may be with an attorney for safekeeping or a safe deposit box. Items that need to be available are:

- Birth certificate

- Last will and testament

- Formal address information

- Citizenship paperwork if not a U.S. citizen

- Social Security number

- Copy of marriage license

- Copy of any previous divorce decree

- Spouse's name, citizenship, address, and other personal information

- Children's names, addresses, and personal information

- Parents' names, addresses, and personal information

- Grandchildren's names, addresses, and personal information

- Any guardianship-related paperwork

- Prearranged funeral and burial plot information
- List of personal belongings and who they should go to
- Any prenuptial agreements or community property agreements
- List of all assets and where title or important papers are located
- List of passwords, combinations, keys, or instructions to access needed paperwork
- List of business associates or others, such as attorneys, accoun-tants, financial advisors, and brokers that need to be notified
- List of bank accounts
- Insurance policies
- List of any death benefits due from Social Security, unions, and fraternal organizations
- Certificates of deposit
- Stocks and bonds
- IRAs or other retirement plans
- Trust documents
- Pension plans
- Copies of recent income tax returns
- List of outstanding creditors and accounts payable
- Copies of mortgages, real estate titles, dates of purchase, where titles are recorded, co-owners, property insurance information, names of tenants
- Partnership agreements
- Incorporation documents, current contracts, and other important business papers

- List of charitable donations to be made upon death
- Automobile and other vehicle titles
- Estimate of estate value, liabilities, and inheritance taxes owed
- Copies of power of attorney
- List of personal friends that should be notified
- Notation of the last time this information was updated

The list is not complete but should help you think about items belonging on the list. This will be a difficult time for the family, but even in death, you will have made a final effort to bring some comfort to them.

SUMMARY

Your estate is everything you have accumulated during your lifetime, and it is primarily up to you to make decisions about how it is finally distributed. It includes personal property, real estate, investments, residences, retirement plans, trusts, life insurance policies, and many other things to which your family attaches value. You owe them a properly planned distribution or continuation of your estate.

A good place to begin is with a detailed list of everything you believe to be of value. Next is a need to determine your priorities with each major asset. Is the goal to minimize taxes on that asset or donate it to charity in exchange for a tax deduction? Other assets will be kept in the family; how will they be managed? Will certain properties be given to specific children? Or will a family trust best accomplish the wealth preservation you have in mind? A picture will begin to develop as the properties are segregated by priority. With substantial wealth, it is common for most of the available strategies to be used but applied to different assets. Once the list is in order, the next step is to either discuss your preferences with the beneficiaries and those affected or, if you prefer, obtain the services of a competent and trusted estate planner to make the necessary arrangements. An estate plan needs to be reviewed regularly. The wise investor understands the value of establishing the estate plan early in life. At the same time, property is exchanged frequently to obtain a better return, and wealth accumulation is the goal. The frequent turnover of assets requires regularly scheduled updates to the estate plan. With acquired wealth, the older investor makes fewer changes and needs to update the estate plan less often.

12

BRINGING IT ALL TOGETHER

O ffshore secret bank accounts attract scared businesspeople that need to hide their wealth from the IRS, court judgments, and creditors. Many of these people eventually either flee the country or end up in more legal trouble. That type of behavior is attributable to greed rather than legitimate work and savvy business practices.

This book stays away from questionable business practices. The opening chapter introduced much of the IRS code relied on for perceptive and legitimate real estate investing. Next, it built an understanding of how these business practices are applied in the real world and used understandable examples. A general timeline was followed, showing how these strategies might be applied throughout a lifetime, up through estate planning. This final chapter uses a fictitious married couple to work through a lifetime of real estate investing that begins with nothing but accumulates substantial wealth during a life of diligent and earnest investment.

PLANNING A WEALTHY FUTURE

No Direction	The Right Decision	Planning Phase
Age 20	Age 21	Age 21–22 and ongoing

Nancy and Perry Barron are typical young Americans embarking on life with hopes of fulfilling the American dream, including a healthy, prosperous family. Meeting and marrying while attending courses at the local community college, both decided corporate careers were not their interest. With limited accounting and business skills, they knew that family members and friends had been successful at real estate investing. Coming up with the capital was the first problem they thought was stopping them from taking this path.

Enjoying a family Thanksgiving dinner, Perry initiated a discussion about raising capital with his uncle, who owned several business properties and apartment buildings. His uncle suggested Perry did not need much capital to get started but should seriously consider avoiding a few mistakes that he had made as a young investor. The conversation spotlighted the need for a solid plan that included specific points in time that Nancy and Perry would take major steps to increase their holdings. The uncle agreed that a full college education was not needed to successfully invest in real estate, but strongly urged the young couple to learn about the local real estate market and favorable tax laws that could help them. He spoke about how it took him too many years to figure out that bigger real estate profits came with a long-term vision and good tax planning.

Nancy and Perry discussed it further before deciding the uncle's advice was sound. Perry had taken a few business courses and was aware that, without a good business plan, they were likely to flounder. The young couple agreed they would embark on a real estate investment career, and the first step was learning more before building a detailed plan.

They continued living in the same modest apartment from their college days. They took simple jobs to pay the bills and began building a small savings that would serve them well when the time came for the first purchase. Perry began by reading a few real estate investment books and watching the local real estate listings. Soon he figured out that he needed to attend the zoning and planning meetings, as well as study local maps. With sincere interest, he began driving around town just to better understand the different neighborhoods and prospect what properties had the most potential to quickly appreciate in value.

Nancy knew she had a role in this plan and read the same real estate books. She and Perry agreed Nancy was better suited to accounting and bookkeeping skills. She found time to learn more about the tax codes, which pleased Perry because she could now do the annual income tax return.

Being energetic, diligent, and anxious, they were ready for the next step after six months of research. They began talking about what should be included in the business plan, keeping good notes, especially when a decision was made. Soon they decided that a residential house with a large detached garage convertible into a mother-in-law apartment made the most sense for their first purchase. It would be relatively low cost, provide them with a house, provide the opportunity for capital improvement through sweat equity, and result in a rental unit. It was time to put the plan together.

THE BUSINESS PLAN

The business plan was another shared task. Perry was primarily responsible for describing how the business would be run, formalizing the market analysis that he had been conducting, and deciding on the business structure. Nancy worked on the details of the first few years of financial forecasts and investigated sources for the first loan.

A decision was made to invest in a neighborhood where the competition was aggressive. This made sense because property values appreciate faster when more people are interested in the property. Nancy and Perry were convinced that, with their new knowledge and a good plan, they could buy the right property, at a good location, and know exactly what price was acceptable.

The plan was to live in the first property for between two and three years. Summers spent doing remodeling and repair work for his uncle gave Perry confidence that he could convert the garage into a good rental unit in less than eight months, even if he worked only in the evenings and on weekends. The plan was to collect rent for about two years and seek professional advice about investing the profit. Overall, they believed this to be a low-risk plan for their first venture. They were relying on small but steady incomes during this time; a failure or setback in completing the garage would result in no additional income, but they would still have a house instead of their current apartment. All these considerations were documented in the business plan. The first three years of the plan looked reasonable and manageable. A concern about financing the remodel work remained to be solved.

Perry drew some rough construction plans based on a typical detached garage on the west side of town. During this process it occurred to him that the garage would provide a better income if there were two smaller apartments instead of one large one. He was not sure if this would be allowed, so another trip to the planning department concluded this could be done if the lot was a particular size and fully separate entrances existed for both rental residences. Off-street parking and acceptable septic or sewer service were needed also. Perry concluded this was doable if the right property was found. Both apartments would be one bedroom and would likely rent to young singles. This meant that only two additional parking spots were needed. The neighborhood of interest was connected to the city sewer. A discussion with the planning department indicated Perry's concept would be approved. A further benefit was that fewer materials would be needed for the first apartment, at a lower cost. Nancy's financial projections indicated they could swing it by saving about two months longer than originally planned and using rental income from the first apartment to buy materials for the second. They might have to discount the rent while Perry worked on the second apartment.

All this was time consuming and slowed progress on the long-term business plan. It took several months to complete the near-term plan and the project plan, but it was finally finished and every detail imaginable was included. The couple was confident they would succeed.

Naturally, both had learned about 1031 exchanges and knew that had to be part of the future plan. Long term, they decided to stay in the residential rental business but increase the number of units they owned. Because they would be living in the main house of the first purchase, the second would include a partial exchange for the value of the apartment and personal residence exclusion for their residence. With the combination of capital improvements, appreciated value, deferring taxes, and a successful venture under their belt, they believed the second purchase would be a ten-unit apartment building. Ideally, it would have a separate residence for the owners, but that might be asking for too much. However, by age 25 they thought they could own ten apartment units.

The bank manager was very impressed with the detailed and well-thought-out business plan. He was completely amazed that Perry already had rough working blueprints for the apartments. Not only were they pre-approved at the level they asked for, but the bank agreed to a future construction loan for the first apartment if the purchased property looked promising.

THE FIRST INVESTMENT

Business Entity	Property Research	Due Diligence	Remodeling	Retirement Account
Age 22–23				Age 24

It was finally time for some big changes in the lives of Nancy and Perry Barron. With the full backing of the local bank, their efforts shifted from evenings and weekends researching and building a business plan to looking for the perfect property. The competition for the first purchase was likely to be either first-time homebuyers or another rental investor. With a superior plan, they had a confident command over the financial numbers. The plan to remodel a garage into apartments enabled them to pay a higher price for the house and still make a better profit than a less sophisticated investor could. From a business point of view, the most important component of the purchase would be the location and the right house on a property sized to meet the planning requirements.

There was one item of business that needed attention before making a purchase offer. They had concluded that, for this first purchase, a sole proprietorship business structure would be sufficient. A small business insurance policy would be purchased about the time remodeling began on the garage. Since only an individual can own a sole proprietorship, Perry registered it in his name, but doing business as Nancy and Perry Investments. It took only a few minutes to complete the online forms and submit a $25 fee, officially establishing the business entity.

With a working knowledge of the west side of town, no energy was wasted looking at every house in town with a detached garage. Using a map, they were quickly able to determine if a new listing met the first criteria about location. Weeks went by, and they became very excited about moving out of the apartment but persevered according to the plan. They did venture out to look at houses having a single-car garage detached from the house, but these just did not meet the plan. Nancy would regularly swing through the neighborhood on her way home from work in the afternoons. One day this paid off. A house that appeared to match their needs was for sale by owner. She was prepared with a few critical questions and stopped to see if the owner could answer them. Being a businesswoman, she had to restrain herself as the owner gave the right answer to each question. Yes, the lot size was a little more than 32,000 square feet, and yes, when his children were in high school they often parked five cars completely off the street. The house had been connected to the city sewer years ago when it became mandatory. Nancy left it at that, not wanting to ask questions about the garage that would allow the owner to conclude what their plans were. That was their proprietary business secret, and Perry could quickly determine if the garage met their requirements with an inspection and a tape measure. She left the owner with an agreement to return with her husband in a couple of hours to take a closer look.

Perry and Nancy could not stand wondering if they had finally found their first investment property. They were back in less than an hour. The owner was a little perplexed when they took more interest in the large garage than they did in the house itself. However, they took a close look at the house and knew it was soundly built and would be much more comfortable than the apartment. Two days later, they made an offer contingent on performing a due diligence on financial numbers and a complete inspection of the structure. They assured the owner they had the bank's pre-approval but declined to show the paperwork because he would become aware of the approved dollar level. The owner was quite surprised at how close the offer was to the exact value of the house that he had researched before putting it on the market, especially coming from such a young couple. Nonetheless, the next day he counter-offered, saying that he would accept their offer and allow up to a month for them to perform due diligence and two months for the deal to close. However, he reserved the right to continue marketing the house until the due diligence was complete and could accept a second offer up until Nancy and Perry removed the due diligence clause from the offer. By the end of the day, they had a signed purchase agreement.

Over the next two weeks the Barrons spent all their spare time fine tuning each element of the project plan based on having solid numbers to work with. The owner provided the property tax statements, insurance statements, utility bills, and other necessary paperwork for Nancy to update the financial statements. She also researched comparable sales in the neighborhood by going back almost ten years. Just as the broader neighborhood search had revealed, there was a strong trend of continued real estate appreciation in this specific neighborhood.

Perry updated the remodeling plans to agree with this specific garage. He obtained estimates for the necessary materials. Perry considered another trip to the zoning and planning departments, but was able to obtain tentative confirmation over the telephone that everything would be accepted. Seems the staff in these departments remembered Perry's attention to detail from his previous visits. An engineering inspection was completed of the house, the garage, and an old oil tank buried near the property line. Everything passed the due diligence, and the clause was accepted but replaced by another clause that could kill the deal should something else not actively investigated become apparent before closing. Both parties were ready for closing long before the two-month requirement. Within six weeks, Nancy and Perry were the very proud owners of their first real estate property at the age of 23.

Flush with success from following a detailed plan, it was not long before Perry was well into the remodeling project. Another reason for selecting this neighborhood was that it was on a direct bus route to the local college. Perry used his summer vacation to hustle the completion of the first apartment in time for the beginning of the fall school quarter. They had eight rental applicants to choose from the first week it was advertised. Naturally, Nancy had researched the best way to select a preferred tenant, and they became landlords about the time Perry turned 24.

As soon as Perry finished the second apartment, it would be time to slow down a little and enjoy life. What a life — going from directionless 20-year-olds living in a modest apartment to homeownership and being landlords in less than 4 years. With confidence, they began a family while they continued following their long-term plan. Before their first daughter arrived, the Barron family researched retirement accounts and chose to establish a traditional IRA at this point in their life. Life was right on schedule, and they had talked to a couple of financial advisors. The financial advice they received was to make sure the IRA was fully funded each year, and soon it would be capable of making real estate purchases on behalf of their eventual retirement. They knew it would soon be time to relinquish this first investment and use a 1031 exchange to move up to a better investment. They planned to move up in quantity of rental units this time and diversify into multiple holdings the next time. With good planning, that should happen about the time their oldest child started school. They hoped to have a personal residence in a good neighborhood by that time.

EXCHANGING UP

Preparing to Exchange	LLC	2 Properties	A Longer Holding Period
Age 25			Age 32

They required a year lease on the apartments to ensure rent during the summer months when students moved home, took internships in other cities, or moved out of the apartments for other reasons. They only missed two monthly rent payments when the students graduated and new tenants moved in. Nancy's financial projections were incredibly accurate at the end of three years. It was time for another big financial move that would be a little riskier this time. They wanted to exchange into at least a better property with more units that provided more income.

Being forward-looking people, they had begun working with a financial advisor who specialized in real estate and was knowledgeable about 1031 exchanges. A good six months before they planned to enter an exchange, Nancy and Perry started their detailed research. After learning about reverse exchanges, they thought possibly they had found their answer to reducing the risks associated with the 45-day identification period and the 180 days allowed for closing on the replacement property after closing on the relinquished property. Further pondering and consideration helped them arrive at the conclusion that using their limited resources to obtain the replacement property first could not provide the amount of leverage they needed. The decision came back 180 degrees to a delayed 1031 exchange where the fully deferred capital gains tax, as well as depreciation recapture tax, joined with their appreciated house value to maximize the leverage. The financial advisor had been helpful with spreadsheets, demonstrating how to best leverage into a better property. Nancy performed some calculations, becoming convinced they could probably do better than the business plan had previously forecast.

With solid knowledge about the exchange, they honed their knowledge of the real estate market conditions. This was a different transaction than the purchase of a residential house. Nancy and Perry would have up to ten rental units and be landlords to families rather than college students. There were several issues to consider, not the least of which was the condition of the building, competitors' rental rates, and stability of the tenants. This time it would be more than Nancy and Perry could do themselves. A commercial real estate agent was engaged, the financial advisor suggested a qualified intermediary to conduct the exchange, and an attorney was retained to review documents provided by the current apartment building owners. They still were not sure if they would use a professional due diligence business or attempt conducting that themselves. Since no specific property had been found, they left that decision for later.

Perry realized that, although they were only 25 years old, they were beginning to acquire some significant personal wealth and real estate. The sole proprietorship business structure was no longer adequate protection for the growing business. He had the attorney begin the process of establishing a limited liability company before the 1031 exchange occurred. Having the real estate properly titled to the LLC made good business sense, but the house and apartments were currently titled in their personal names. The attorney and intermediary were sure they could work it out to meet IRS requirements.

In the meantime, Nancy took the updated business plan to the bank, along with preliminary financial projections for a ten-unit apartment building. The bank agreed to finance based on an owner-occupied down payment if she and Perry lived in one of the units and carried additional insurance. Nancy knew they were not going to have any trouble moving up to a higher profit-producing property. She also knew that the right place would provide the depreciation write-off they needed to shield profits from their income taxes. The banker may have been pleased with the success of the business plan, but Nancy was ecstatic about its success.

The commercial real estate agent understood the criteria established by Nancy and Perry. This being a college town, there were quite a few apartment buildings meeting the ten-unit criteria, although none were currently on the market. The Barrons' criteria did not specify whether the apartment building had to be family-oriented or student-oriented. However, purchasing an apartment building in a college town was no coincidence. That had been part of the original research on how to focus their expertise. The decision remained a good match with the local real estate market.

The two entrepreneurial investors were nervous about marketing the house and garage apartments without any replacement property meeting their criteria on the market. The agent showed them a couple of places two towns away, but the Barrons resisted the temptation because they had very little knowledge of those markets. The good news was that the agent kept them informed that no competition appeared to be waiting for a similar property to come on the market. She could not be positive of this, but years of experience made her relatively confident.

It became a waiting game to find the right time to place their property, which they were sure would sell quickly, on the market. After several months, and looking at properties that just were not quite right, the right one came on the market. Nancy and Perry reacted quickly by placing their own property on the market and making an offer for the replacement property contingent on closing a sale on the house/apartments within 60 days. Having studied the finances, Nancy suggested they discount the relinquished property 3 percent to motivate a buyer.

The seller of the ten-unit complex was not thrilled with the 60-day contingency plus another 60 days for due diligence, but he believed in amicable negotiations and made a reasonable counteroffer. The Barrons agreed to begin incurring the expense of the due diligence without being sure of a sale on their property. Being confident of a quick sale, this seemed a win-win solution. They also identified two other properties that really did not meet their criteria but were the most acceptable backup properties available. The relinquished property sold after they explained to the buyer that they would not have any additional expense by entering into a 1031 exchange. The replacement property easily closed within the 180-day requirement. The Barrons had successfully completed their first 1031 exchange and were the owners of an apartment complex at age 25.

EXCHANGING OUTWARD

A Home	Two Investment Properties	A Great Opportunity
Age 28	Age 32	Age 35

The apartment investment turned out to be a good move for Nancy and Perry. Both continued working full-time, which was difficult with children and the rental units to manage. The rental income was good, and Perry minimized the maintenance and repair expenses by doing most of it himself. They lived in the largest unit, and nine rental units kept Perry busy while Nancy kept track of rentals, expenses, screening perspective tenants, and other administrative tasks. They were anxious to have a house for their personal residence but thought the best move was to stay in the apartment for at least seven years. By that time, the second child would be in school, and they definitely wanted to be living in their own home.

After two years, Nancy and Perry knew that selling the apartment complex would afford them a large, prestigious house, but that was not part of the plan at this time. The profits from the rentals fully funded the IRA each year, and the remainder was invested with a watchful eye toward purchasing a home. Both earned respectable salaries from their day jobs, but the cost of raising a family required most of that. Living in one of the apartments was a positive and a negative. It helped considerably with their personal housing expenses and did enable saving a small part of their paychecks. On the other hand, they were not earning any profit from the unit they occupied. It took three years, but between rental profits and salary savings, they put together a down payment for a home that became reality at age 28. They could have afforded more, but the decision was for a modest house in a middle-class neighborhood.

Both entrepreneurs closely monitored the local apartment complex market. The next planned 1031 exchange had been to leverage the ten-unit complex into two apartment complexes, preferably 8-unit and 15-unit complexes. Being more confident based on past success, they would be more flexible this time. Perry was a little concerned about being responsible for 23 separate rental units and trying to keep up with the maintenance.

The local economy was doing well, and new retail outlets had been opening in several parts of town. Most had succeeded in remaining open beyond the first year, which tested if a store could endure. Nancy and Perry joined a 1031 exchange club to learn more about the retail rental market and about creative financing methods. When they were 32, the ten-unit apartment complex was exchanged for a fifteen-unit complex and a small strip mall that had six retail shops that had been in business for at least five years. In their early thirties, the Barrons had leveraged other people's money to control $1.5 million of property that paid for itself and provided what was becoming a good supplemental income.

The IRA continued to compound and grow each year with the help of a financial advisor specializing in corporate stocks. However, the plan had always been to roll it over into a self-directed IRA for real estate investment. They considered joining the IRA with borrowed money, but the numbers just did not quite work out when considering the tax owed on unrelated business tax income (UBTI). Fortunately, there were strong indications a buyers' market was developing for residential housing. It was a rental investor's delight. After a few years of a prosperous economy, a downturn was occurring. House sales were declining and people wanting a family home were choosing to rent during these uncertain times. Once convinced this was a great opportunity, Nancy rolled the IRA into a self-directed account. Perry negotiated an outstanding price on a relatively new house where the owner was overextended, and it closed two months later with financing making up the difference between the IRA value and the purchase price. A month later, renters were making the payments on another investment property owned by the Barrons. This profit margin was slim because of the loan and UBTI. The loan term was for ten years, and the profit margin would increase each year as the loan balance decreased. Having monitored the local economy and real estate market, the Barrons were able to add a bargain-priced house to their real estate portfolio at age 35.

TAKING THE COLLATERALIZED INSTALLMENT OPTION

Upscale Home	Installment Sale	Early Retirement	Dream Vacation
Age 37	Age 38	Age 39	Age 40

Although life had been good for Nancy and Perry until now, it started to become very good around age 35. Their day careers were flourishing, and they had more than the equivalent of a third income from the rental profits. The rental profits were more than ample to invest and save toward the down payment for the upscale home they had always wanted but postponed.

When the Barrons were 37, the modest family home was converted into another rental, and the family moved into a five-bedroom home with acreage outside town. Perry rarely performed much maintenance on the investment properties anymore. Over the last several years, he had come to depend more and more on local tradesmen. Nancy oversaw the accounting books but had a local accounting firm perform most of the routine accounting entries. Both drove new cars, and the children were growing up the way Nancy and Perry had envisioned. All in all, life was good.

Investment and savings accounts were in great shape, and retirement accounts were healthier than anything they could foresee needing in later years. After years of hard work, they were ready to reap the rewards. Knowing that the prosperity would continue and the real estate investment holdings would keep growing through future 1031 exchanges and other astute business practices, the Barrons concluded that two full-time careers were no longer necessary. The decision was made that Nancy would quit her day career and take over daily management of the rental properties. She was fully invested in her company's retirement plan, and Perry's health insurance would cover the entire family for a higher premium. Having started with little, they had never desired a lavish life style, just a comfortable one. The one financial shortcoming about Nancy quitting her day job was making the mortgage payment on the new family home.

They concluded that a partial 1031 exchange combined with an installment sale would cover the home mortgage without seriously impeding the cash flow from their investments. The options to determine which property to exchange were carefully examined. The retail property was seriously considered because it had the smallest return on investment. The downside was that any hiccup in the installment income stream or an early payout triggering the deferred capital gains tax would have to be made up somehow. The answer became using a collateralized installment sale in which the buyer paid the full purchase price to a third party that invested the amounted intended for installments. A portion would be used as a down payment for the replacement property. The collateralized installment sale would earn interest on the deferred capital gains tax, which would slowly be paid as installments where received. An early payout was easily avoided since they would have indirect control over the collateral. It looked like dependable risk management for a deal where the numbers just barely worked. At age 38, they exchanged the retail property for a small six-unit apartment and set up collateralized installment payments that would cover some of the mortgage on the family home. A year later, at age 39, Nancy gave notice to her employer and stayed home to manage the real estate investments full-time. Because of the reduced expense of relying on others for management services and Nancy's keen eye to limit expenses the overall profit margin on the investment increased nicely. Nancy and Perry took a well-deserved dream vacation at age 40.

DOING GOOD WITH WEALTH

CRUT	Life Insurance	CRAT
Age 53	Age 54	Age 60

The Barrons had seen the future clearly. Over the years, the investments continued to grow through appreciation, rental profits, and 1031 exchanges. As Perry pondered retirement, it appeared they had created a perpetual money machine. They gave generously to charities each year, receiving an income tax deduction in return. Each child received the maximum annual gift the IRS code allowed. Two of the children invested it wisely and one not so wisely.

The parents had a concern for their youngest, that he might not have quite the motivation for planning and follow-through when long hours and perseverance were needed. With over $7 million in assets at age 53, Nancy and Perry decided it was time to be more giving. They established a $1.5 million charitable remainder unitrust with a favorite and well-established charitable organization. Selecting the net income with makeup version ensured the principal remained intact. Rather than establishing themselves as beneficiaries, their adult son was named as beneficiary. They received a substantial income tax deduction that year, for which they really had no need.

At a young 54 years of age and in good health, the Barrons used the income tax savings to purchase a second-to-die life insurance policy that would pay their two daughters $1 million each at some future time. As earnings from their investments continued to accumulate, the Barrons continued to make generous charity donations. When they were 59 1/2, their IRA income stream became available. For a few months they pondered postponing distributions from the IRA. Deciding to continue deferring taxable distributions from the IRA until age 70 1/2, they elected to fund a charitable remainder annuity trust for ten years that would benefit them with an income stream and charity. They would postpone the IRA until it became mandatory to begin distributions. The Barrons truly believed their tax-deferred earnings helped others more through prudent charitable management than wasteful government spending. A CRAT income stream made better sense than taxable distributions from the IRA. Following this belief, the money was put where it would work the hardest, as they had always done.

TAKING CARE OF THE FAMILY

As is obvious by now, Nancy and Perry were organized and planned the important events in their lives. A living trust had been in place for many years, but at age 65 they decided to make a few final decisions, mostly regarding the actual transfer of the more profitable investments to the children. A dynasty trust was fully funded at $2 million with most of the remaining assets. Earnings and growth of the dynasty trust were anticipated to be substantial if distributions did not begin for 20 years. It would be available to help their grandchildren get started toward a wealthy and comfortable life.

From age 65 until well into their 80s, both Nancy and Perry were able to vacation and enjoy many recreations without any financial concerns. Not only had their success given them a good life, but many others benefited as well.

INDEX